D0058320

American
HOOKUP

LISA WADE

American
HOOKUP

*The New Culture of
Sex on Campus*

W. W. NORTON & COMPANY

Independent Publishers Since 1923

New York / London

For information about permission to reproduce selections from this book,
write to Permissions, W. W. Norton & Company, Inc.,
500 Fifth Avenue, New York, NY 10110

For information about special discounts for bulk purchases, please contact
W. W. Norton Special Sales at specialsales@wwnorton.com or 800-233-4830

Manufacturing by Quad Graphics, Fairfield
Book design by Ellen Cipriano
Production manager: Louise Mattarelliano

ISBN 978-0-393-28509-3

W. W. Norton & Company, Inc.
500 Fifth Avenue, New York, N.Y. 10110
www.wwnorton.com

W. W. Norton & Company Ltd.
15 Carlisle Street, London W1D 3BS

1 2 3 4 5 6 7 8 9 0

*To the students
who shared their stories,
with gratitude for their insight,
alacrity, and candor.*

Contents

Author's Note

None of the students referred to in this work appears here under his or her real name. Students' physical features and potentially identifying characteristics have also been changed in many instances, as have the names of places such as residence halls and bars. In rare cases, an individual student appears under different pseudonyms in different sections of the work.

American
HOOKUP

The New Culture of Sex

"I love it here," Owen said happily, a freshman in college just back from winter break. "Last semester," he told me, "was one of the most interesting, exciting, and strangest times of my life."

Owen had grown up in a farming town in central California, graduating from a high school of about sixty students. Such a small group of peers made puberty awkward. "Everyone knew everything about everyone else," he said, so sexual experimentation was rare and, when indulged in, secretive. He'd had one clandestine affair, which he remembered fondly, but despite his good looks—lean and tallish with a broad, lopsided smile and tousled dark hair—Owen's sexual activities in high school were limited.

College promised to be a whole new world. His campus offered what felt like an endless supply of potential partners and more anonymity than he'd ever dreamed of. In his first semester, he sought casual sexual encounters with what he called "gusto," and he had his fair share of good luck. "I'm shy and nerdy," he admitted, "but I clean up pretty well." It was everything he'd hoped it would be.

"I'm basically in a paradise full of girls I'm attracted to," he said, exhilarated, "everyone is fucking each other."

As his second semester progressed, though, his excitement started to waver. "A lot of the social life I've experienced," he observed wryly, "is some twisted sort of self-perpetuating vicious cycle of unrealistic expectations, boundless enthusiasm, and copious amounts of alcohol." He complained about mind games, soured friendships, and women who liked him only for his looks. "I can't expect any of the girls I'll meet on a Friday night to care about my personality or my favorite books," he grumbled. "That's just unrealistic." Some only talked to him when they wanted to share his weed. It was discouraging.

He partly blamed himself. "Oftentimes I just flat-out lack grace," he conceded. Other times he wasn't as openhearted as he wanted to be, acting distant or dismissive toward women to avoid being rejected himself. But he also felt like there was something particularly difficult about negotiating casual sex on campus. "I find it especially hard to try to smooth out a relationship with a girl whom I barely know beyond what color underwear she wears," he said, with a characteristic degree of self-deprecation.

As Owen's second semester progressed, he sounded increasingly uncertain, even morbid. "When I think about my sex life," he confessed, "it feels like my insides tie themselves tight together before they boil and rot." He hated the gossip that often followed an encounter. He began doubting himself. Things got dark and he started obsessing. "Worrying about it saps a lot of time and energy from my life," he said in frustration. By the end of the year, despite his initial interest, he had sworn off casual sexual encounters entirely: "I can't handle another negative sexual relationship in my life. My heart might break."

❖   ❖   ❖

On campuses across America, students are sounding an alarm. They are telling us that they are depressed, anxious, and overwhelmed. Half of first-year students express concern that they are not emotionally healthy, and one in ten say that they frequently feel depressed. The transition from teenager to young adult is rarely easy, but this is more than just youthful angst. Students are less happy and healthy than in previous generations, less so even than just ten or twenty years ago.

As Owen's transformation suggests, the sexual environment on college campuses is part of why. He anticipated an erotic and carefree life and, at first, that's what college seemed to offer. But, over the course of his first year, he became increasingly disillusioned. The reasons why are related to his specific encounters and are complicated by his personal story, but there is nothing unique about his disappointment.

One in three students say that their intimate relationships have been "traumatic" or "very difficult to handle," and 10 percent say that they've been sexually coerced or assaulted in the past year. In addition, there is a persistent malaise: a deep, indefinable disappointment. Students find that their sexual experiences are distressing or boring. They worry that they're feeling too much or too little. They are frustrated and feel regret, but they're not sure why. They consider the possibility that they're inadequate, unsexy, and unlovable. And it goes far beyond the usual suspects. Owen, for example, is not the kind of student who usually attracts concern. He's a handsome, heterosexual white guy with a healthy sex drive. He should have thrived. He didn't.

Thus far, the culprit seems to be the hookup. Sociologist Kathleen Bogle sparked the conversation in 2008 with *Hooking Up: Sex, Dating, and Relationships on Campus*. She described a new norm on campus that favored casual sexual contact and argued that this was especially harmful to women. Michael Kimmel, the well-known sociologist of masculinity, agreed. Hooking up is "guys' sex," he explained in *Guyland* that year; "guys run the scene." More recently, journalist Jon Birger added math, concluding that a shortage of men in college gives them the power to dictate sexual terms, making campuses a "sexual nirvana for heterosexual men." These thinkers, and many more, argue that hooking up is just a new way for men to get what they want from women.

Journalists Hanna Rosin and Kate Taylor have countered the idea that hooking up only benefits men. At the *Atlantic* and in the *New York Times*, they've suggested that casual sex allows women to put their careers and education before men. In their view, it's a way of giving the middle finger to the "Mrs. Degree," that now outdated but once quite real reason why women sought higher education. Rosin goes so far as to say that future feminist progress "depends on" hooking up, with serious relationships a "danger to be avoided at all costs." Their anecdotal evidence is backed up by social scientists like Elizabeth Armstrong and Laura Hamilton, who show in *Paying for the Party* that women with economically stable families and ambitious career plans are more likely than other women to be successful at hookup-heavy party schools.

Meanwhile, at *Rolling Stone* and *New York* magazine, the whole scene is portrayed as a poly, queer, bacchanalian utopia with lots of skin and a little light BDSM. Not only is it not sexist, it's nonbinary. Maybe this is what the future looks like. At *Elle*, columnist Karley Sciortino seems to think so. She defends hooking up, but only because she thinks that worrying about it amounts to little more than old-fashioned fuddy-duddery. All this talk about young people and their sexual choices, she insists, is just "moral panic" and "reactionary hysteria." What's really harmful, she argues, is suggesting that women might not enjoy casual sex. She's not alone in expressing annoyance at the "kids these days" fretting. It can seem like a lot of hand-wringing to students, many of whom wish everyone would just mind their own business.

Hookups have been damned, praised, and dismissed in the popular and academic presses, feeding a debate about whether we should applaud or condemn the "hookup generation," and drawing out prescriptions for students' sex lives from both the right and the left. But, as is so often the case, the very premise of the debate is wrong.

The idea that college students are having a lot of sex is certainly an enthralling myth. Even students believe it. In Bogle's landmark study, students guessed that their peers were doing it fifty times a year. That's twenty-five times what the numbers actually show. In Kimmel's *Guyland*, young men figured that 80 percent of college guys were having sex any given weekend; they would have been closer to the truth if they were guessing the percent of men who had *ever* had sex. Students overestimate how much sex their peers are having, and by quite a lot.

In fact, today's students boast no more sexual partners than their parents did at their age. Scholars using the University of Chicago's General Social Survey have shown that they actually report slightly fewer sexual partners than Gen-Xers did. Millennials look more similar to the baby boomer generation than they do to the wild sexual cohort that they are frequently imagined to be.

There are students on campus with active sex lives, of course, but there are plenty with none at all and some with sexual escapades that are, at best, only "slightly less nonexistent" than they were in high school. The average graduating senior reports hooking up just eight times in four years. That amounts to one hookup per semester. Studies looking specifically at the sexual cultures at Duke, Yale, and East Carolina universities, the universities of Georgia and Tennessee, the State University of New York at Geneseo, and UC Berkeley report similar numbers. Not all students are hooking up, and those that do aren't necessarily doing so very often. Neither are students always hopping out of one bed and into another; half of those eight hookups are with someone the student has hooked up with before. Almost a third of students will graduate without hooking up a single time.

Despite the rumors, then, there is no epidemic of casual sexual encounters on college campuses. So, hookups can't be blamed. There just aren't enough of them to account for the malaise. Neither does two sexual encounters every twelve months, possibly with the same person, look like either female empowerment or male domination; if so, it's quite a tepid expression of power. There certainly is no bacchanalian utopia, poly, queer, or otherwise. Students are too busy not having sex to be enacting the next revolution. The cause of students' unhappiness, then, can't be the hookup. But it *is* about hooking up. It's hookup *culture*.

◆   ◆   ◆

Hookup culture has descended upon college campuses like a fog. It's thickest on Greek row, where students hope to find wild parties, hot bodies, and easy sex. It's dense, too, in the large off-campus houses known for dirty bathrooms and high-octane drinks. It gathers and dissipates in student dorms, filling the halls as students pre-party and primp on weekend nights and emptying out as it follows them to nearby bars and clubs that flaunt laws against serving minors.

The fog of hookup culture isn't confined, though, to where students live and party. It creeps through the quad and reaches into the classrooms and study halls where academics are supposed to prevail. On mornings after big parties and games, it hovers over the bright non-sexy dining halls, where students nurse hangovers over brunch and tell their stories from the previous night. By afternoon, it has occupied life online, too. Students take pictures and hookup culture blankets social media.

Hookup culture is an occupying force, coercive and omnipresent. For those who love it, it's all sunshine, but it isn't for everyone else. Deep in the fog, students often feel dreary, confused, helpless. Many behave in ways they don't like, hurt other people unwillingly, and consent to sexual activity they don't desire.

Campuses of all kinds are in this fog. No matter the size of the college, how heavy a Greek or athletic presence it boasts, its exclusivity, its religious affiliation, or whether it's public or private, hookup culture is there. We find it in all regions of the country, from the Sunshine State of Florida to the sunny state of California. Students all over say so. Hookups are "part of our collegiate culture," writes a representative of the American South in the University of Florida's *Alligator*. If you don't hook up, warns a woman at the University of Georgia, then you're "failing at the college experience." A woman at Tulane puts it succinctly: "Hookup culture," she says, "it's college."

Up north, a student at Cornell confirms: "We go to parties. And then after we're good and drunk, we hook up. Everyone just hooks up." "At the end of the day," boasts a student at Yale, "you can get laid." Nearby, at Connecticut College, a female student describes it as the "be-all and end-all" of social life. "Oh, sure," says a guy 2,500 miles away at Arizona State, "you go to parties on the prowl." "A one-night stand," admits a student a few hundred miles north at Chico State, "is a constant possibility." Further up, at Whitman in Walla Walla, a female student calls hookup culture "an established norm."

Students like these almost certainly overestimate how much hooking up is going on, but they're not wrong to feel that hookup culture is everywhere. And while the exhilaration and delight in their voices is real, so is the disappointment and trauma. In response, many students opt out of hooking up, but they can't opt out of hookup culture. It's more than just a behavior; it's the climate. It can't be wished away any more than we can wish away a foggy day.

I learned this from first-year students themselves. In the first year, the fog is thickest. Most incoming students think that casual sex in college is expected, encounter impressive amounts of (often free) alcohol, and are away from their parents for the first time. The average student reports hooking up more in the first year than any subsequent year. It is in this year, as well, that they are at highest risk of sexual assault.

The students whose firsthand accounts fill this book were enrolled in either an "Introduction to Sociology" or a sexuality-themed writing intensive course taught between 2010 and 2015 at one of two liberal arts colleges, a secular school in the American Southwest and a religious one in the South. Somewhere between introductions and the overview of the syllabus, I stood in front of their loosely arranged desks and announced that each student would collect data about sex and romance on campus, writing as much or as little as they liked about their own experiences or those of the people around them. The project would last through the semester, with their data or "journals" to be submitted each Tuesday. I also explained that I hoped, with their consent, to include facts and quotes from their accounts in my own research that I expected eventually to publish, although I would not know whether any student had consented until all grades had been safely recorded. All but nine of the 110 students gave consent. I promised to keep their identities confidential, so while I stay true to the stories their lives tell us, their names, some identifying information, and other details have been changed and sometimes dramatized.

Some students were thrilled by the opportunity to tell the world about their experiences, but I'll admit that some were skeptical. More than a few worried that they'd have no sexual activity worth writing about. Others weren't sure they wanted to tell their professor the details of their sex lives. I encouraged them to disclose only what they felt comfortable sharing. They didn't always lead with their most harrowing memories but, with time, many chose to disclose their deeper secrets.

The documents they submitted—varyingly rants, whispered gossip, critical analyses, protracted tales, or simple streams of consciousness—came to over 1,500 single-spaced pages and exceeded a million words. As the semester progressed, we talked about their insights and experiences, interpreting them together, testing theories, and reading what other scholars had found. In their journals, they described their hopes and dreams, exposed their insecurities, lamented their disappointments, and celebrated their victories. As the semesters progressed, their insights became keen. They were able to see their environment increasingly clearly and explain it with sometimes gut-wrenching clarity.

Consistent with existing research, I found little difference in the hookup cultures of the two institutions where I collected data. With the exception of evangelical and Mormon campuses (and my second school was neither of those), the sexual attitudes and behavior on secular and religiously affiliated schools look remarkably alike. In any case, only a handful of students at either school emphasized that their faith was an important part of why they made the choices they did.

All of my students were very recently out of high school and all but five lived on campus. Twenty-two came from a working-class or poor background, and fifteen were the first in their families to go to college. Sixteen identified as a sexual minority and another three hadn't quite decided how to identify. Reflecting gender disparities in college enrollment and those who opt to take social science classes, twenty-six of my students were male and seventy-five were female. None identified as trans or non-gender binary. Fifty-six students were white; thirteen were Asian or East Indian, ten were African American, fourteen were Latino or Latina, and seven identified primarily as mixed race. No students were Native American.

Some arrived on campus with lengthy erotic resumés; others were still awaiting their first kiss. A few had grown up feeling uninhibited and comfortable with their sexuality, while others struggled to do so. Some were questioning their sexual orientation, coming to terms with what they already knew, or shouting it from the rooftops. Four were dating much older men, usually in secret for reasons that will have to remain between them and me.

Some of the students in my study reported brutally traumatic life events. Eleven had been victims of sexual assault or abuse before arriving on campus. Two were in mourning for a girlfriend or boyfriend who had been murdered; one lost a sister at sixteen, and another had lost a father the previous year. Two students struggled to support family members fighting life-threatening illnesses, and the parents of one were being threatened with deportation. Among my students, there was a pornography addiction, a suicide attempt, and diagnoses of bipolar disorder, depression, anxiety, and anorexia.

Drawn in by their stories, I took my research on tour. I've traveled to speak about hookup culture at twenty-four colleges and universities of all types in eighteen states. I visited Ivy League schools such as Harvard, Yale, and Dartmouth; religiously affiliated schools such as Loyola in New Orleans and Pacific Lutheran University in Tacoma; private universities such as Tulane; liberal arts schools such as Carlton in Minnesota and Westminster in Utah; as well as large public universities in California, Idaho, Illinois, Indiana, Kansas, Louisiana, Missouri, Ohio, West Virginia, and Wisconsin.

At all of these schools, I presented my research, interacted with students, probed them with questions, and got their responses. I met them over lunch, dropped in on clubs, or hosted discussions in classrooms. I brainstormed with graduate students interested in embarking on sexuality research and had the pleasure, too, of talking to college employees: residence life advisors, counselors, faith leaders, Title IX officers, other faculty, and more. Together, these informal interviews and focus groups added up to hundreds more little bits of data, an opportunity to learn something new or confirm a theory. At only two of the schools—both commuter campuses with fewer than 10 percent of students living in residence halls—did students question whether they were in the fog of hookup culture.

As the project was coming to a close, I conducted follow-up interviews with twenty-one of the students featured in this book, all but one out of college by then. I asked them to reflect back and fill me in on the intervening years. We laughed a lot and cried a little. "You couldn't pay me enough to be an incoming freshman again," was a common sentiment, but so was the sense that they'd been indelibly formed by their experiences.

I bring my students' stories into dialogue with the hundreds of well-crafted scholarly and news articles that have been published in the last ten years. Hookup culture has been surveyed, observed, queried, experimented on, and more. I also take advantage of publicly available data from the Online College Social Life Survey. Designed and generously shared by sociologist Paula England, the OCSLS is a survey about college students' sexual behaviors, experiences, and attitudes. Between 2005 and 2011, over 24,000 students at twenty-one four-year colleges and universities submitted responses. Finally, I scoured hundreds of firsthand accounts of sex on campus written for student newspapers and other media outlets. I include quotes and the occasional story from these students as well, revealing the influence of hookup culture across many types of institutions in all regions of the country.

Bringing all this together, I make a case for why hookup culture makes so many students unhappy. I offer an anatomy of the hookup and explain where it came from and why it dominates the college setting. I show what it feels like to opt in or opt out and, for those who choose to participate, I discuss what they're in for: the emotional landscape of hookup culture, politics of its pleasure, punishing expectations of physical perfection, intimidating games of status, and possibility of becoming a victim or the agent of a sexual crime.

◆　　◆　　◆

We no longer need to speculate as to what students are or aren't doing. We know. And it's time that everyone knows. Students need to know so that they can find a way to wrest pleasure and joy from hookup culture, while acting fearlessly to remake their environments from the inside out. Former students need to know so that they can reflect on their time in college and be able to imagine a way forward that is healthiest and most productive for them. Parents need to know so that they can prepare and support their grown children as they navigate hookup culture's more treacherous features. And college staff, administrators, and faculty need to know so that they can intervene to make for a more humane residence life.

In fact, the lessons students have to teach us are something we all need to know. The inevitable churn of history has brought us a brave new world. College students are at its brink, but all of the problems with hookup culture are problems off campus, too. The fog, in other words, isn't just on college campuses; it's everywhere. It has infiltrated our lives, obscuring our ability to envision better alternatives: sexualities that are more authentic, kinder, safer, more pleasurable, and less warped by prejudice, consumerism, status, and superficiality. We need to understand what's happening on college campuses because what's happening there is happening everywhere.

First-year college students might seem like unlikely candidates to teach anyone about sex, but I think you'll be surprised. They are at a moment of heightened reflection, exploring and experimenting, attempting to discover a way of being sexual that is forward-thinking and feels good. Simultaneously conformists and critics, they put our sexual culture into stark relief. These are their stories.

1

Hooking Up, a How-To

The goal is to look "fuckable," Miranda said, her voice buzzing with excitement. She and her roommate Ruby were tearing through their tiny closets, collecting a pile of "provocative" items to consider wearing to that night's party. The theme was "burlesque," so they were going for a classy stripper vibe. Bridget offered her two cents as she headed back to her own room: "Lacy bras, corsets, fishnet stockings—anything that hints at being sexy underwear!" Ruby pulled on tights, short shorts, and calf-high boots. On top she wore a bright yellow bra and a see-through white tank top.

Miranda plumped her breasts and contemplated her outfit, a black crop top and a cherry red skirt with a zipper running down the front. She unzipped it a bit from the bottom and, then, a bit more. Ruby finished her "sleepy, drowsy, sexy eye look" with a splash of yellow to match the bra, just as Bridget walked back in balancing three shots of Smirnoff. "Let's get some dick tonight, ladies!" she yelled. They tossed back their shots and headed out. It was approaching midnight.

Across campus, Levi sat down at his computer and googled "burlesque party," trying to figure out what to wear. The search returned mostly women in corsets. He turned to his friend and motioned to the screen. "It doesn't matter what you wear," his friend said sharply, "you're a guy." So, he put on a pair of "jeans and a nice green button-down shirt" that his mom had given him for Christmas. Satisfied, he looked at his reflection in the tall mirror tacked up on his dorm room closet: "I'd shaved recently, so I looked pretty sharp," he thought. His roommate smeared some gel through his dark hair, tugged on the front of his polo shirt, and swallowed the last of his beer. "Ready?"

Two blocks over, the party was spilling out of the college's coed fraternity. Slipping past a couple sharing a smoke on the front step, the guys wedged themselves into the crowd. "It was almost impossible to move," Levi observed, comparing it to sardines in a tin. He described turning his right shoulder forward to squeeze through a hallway lined with people on both sides. As he shuffled through, he dodged the arms, legs, and eye contact of people "reaching across to try to flirt with each other." On his left, he passed an open doorway revealing a "make-out room" filled with couches covered in twisted limbs. His eardrums pulsed heavily to the music. "Any sweet talking was impossible over the din," he reported. Students lifted their red cups to their lips and used their bodies to communicate instead. The whole party was "tastefully dark," Levi wrote. "Dark enough to be sexy."

"It's fair to say," Miranda wrote after, "that I was completely shitfaced." It was one of the first parties of the year and, by her estimation, people felt "as if it was their chance to go crazy." By 3 a.m., she would be passed out cold and Ruby, the girl in the bright yellow bra, would be in bed with Levi. It was a proper hookup.

◆   ◆   ◆

Step 1: Pregame.

"You don't walk out of the house without your shoes on and you don't walk into a party without a couple of shots of vodka," insisted one of my students. "It's real." The first step in hooking up is to get, as Miranda put it, "shitfaced."

Party-oriented students believe that drinking enhances their experience. Destiny, for example, gushed about how it felt to be a bit drunk at a college-sponsored concert:

> I honestly think I would not have had as much fun as I did if I wasn't intoxicated. . . . I couldn't care less about what people thought about me and felt free enough just to do whatever I wanted and to be bubbly and carefree. That night I didn't have a care in the world and it felt absolutely fantastic.

Students also tend to think that alcohol improves their personality. Getting drunk, they argue, brings out their "intoxicated self," one that is freer, more relaxed, less anxious, and generally more fun to be around. Destiny emphasized how alcohol made her feel carefree three times in as many sentences. Others believe that it gives them confidence. "I rely on mixed drinks and shots," wrote another female student. "They are not lying when they call it 'liquid courage.'"

When everyone is being their intoxicated self, students collectively bring into existence a thing called "drunkworld." This is the word that the Ohio University sociologist Thomas Vander Ven uses to describe a typical college night out in his book *Getting Wasted: Why College Students Drink Too Much and Party So Hard*. Drunkworld is an alternative reality in which it's normal for people to "fall down, slur their words, break things, laugh uncontrollably, act crazy, flirt, hook up, get sick, pass out, fight, dance, sing, and get overly emotional," where "taken-for-granted human abilities (e.g., motor skills) are challenged and everyday interactions take on a dramatic air."

Because drunkworld is a group accomplishment, everyone needs to be on board. Hence, the pregame: a get-together immediately before attending a party where students get ready and get sloshed. All parties on and off campus involve pregaming, especially the dry ones. "When the school hosts a dance with no alcohol," wrote one observer, "*of course* all of the students arrive drunk out of their minds."

It's important to pregame because students who are standing around waiting to get drunk—and, even worse, students with no intention of getting drunk at all—offer nothing to drunkworld. They're freeloaders. They suck the energy out of the room with perfect diction, inside voices, and coordinated dancing. Also, everyone in drunkworld needs to be drunk to ensure that there's no one left to enforce regularworld norms. Sober people are a threat. Miranda and Ruby's friend Bridget tried going to a party sober once: "It was as if I was committing a crime," she wrote. "I got *a lot* of questions and weird stares and comments about me not drinking."

Being at least a little drunk, then, is the entry fee to college parties. In a study of non-drinking students at Central Michigan University, some admitted that they pretended to drink and faked being drunk to try to fit in. "Almost every single activity revolves around booze," complained one student. On his campus, said another, "not being drunk is unnatural and abnormal." The study even documented bullying of students who chose not to drink: men who painted the word "pussy" on a known non-drinker's car, a girl who was called "miss prim and proper cunt," and more than one student who had beer thrown in their face. "As someone who doesn't drink, I have always felt incredibly judged and out of place," confirmed a student at UC Santa Barbara.

My students didn't mention harassment, but they did learn rather quickly that going to parties sober was against the rules and unpleasant, too. While Destiny's description of attending the campus concert intoxicated was borderline transcendent, a few of the students who went to the same concert sober turned in reports that were much less glowing. "The environment came off as gross," a male student recalled. "I never noticed how annoying dances are because I've been intoxicated for all of them." One of my students described being sober at a sorority party as "absolutely awful." The sorority required a few sisters to abstain so that they could prepare the party, monitor the festivities, and clean up. She described this role as "a fate worse than death." It wasn't "the cleaning or anything," she clarified, "but rather having to be an outsider and watch all your friends do crazy disgusting things."

She was referring to the party's "gross stage," a phrase repeated by many students describing a certain point in the night. It's the stage at which an attendee can look in "any random direction and see people hooking up." Another student described it as a sexual "mosh pit." At one such party, she wrote, "people were rubbing against one another and everyone was sweaty and it was just gross." In that sexual mosh pit is grinding.

◆   ◆   ◆

Step 2: Grind.

"If you can't dirty dance," insisted one of my female students, "then you can't dance at all." Grinding is the main activity at most college parties. Women who are willing press their backs and backsides against men's bodies and dance rhythmically. "It is a bestial rubbing of genitals reminiscent of mating zebras," Laura wrote scornfully after attending a party. "Guys were coming up behind women on the dance floor and placing their hands on their hips like two wayward lobster claws, clamping on and pulling them close."

One of Laura's earliest memories was of her mother ripping up a school flyer inviting her daughters to try out for cheerleading. "My girls are going to play sports," she had said sternly, tossing the bits of paper into the recycling. By high school, Laura was writing essays about *The Feminine Mystique* and the popularity of tranquilizers among 1950s housewives. So, she'd arrived on campus with a feminist consciousness and an eyebrow already skeptically raised at hookup culture.

When she decided to go to the party, she brought a friend for moral support. They both thought the whole display absurd. "We started to imitate this mating dance," she recalled, "laughing and violently circling our booties and puckering our lips like Bratz dolls." They each lifted one hand up toward the ceiling and swung their heads from side to side, twisting their bodies to the sound of the music. "My friends and I have done this many times," writes a female student at Davidson College, describing how all they need to do is move their hips "until a male arrives." It works. Laura's friend shrieked when, "almost instantaneously, a man attached himself to her like a barnacle." She jumped like she'd been goosed, grabbed Laura's hand, and pulled her out of the party to retreat somewhere that didn't inspire mating metaphors.

Students are straightforward about what it is. Levi described grinding as "clothed sex with a stranger," and Bridget called it "dry humping standing up" or "pushing a guy's crotch with your butt."

Our colorful witness, Laura, described it as an exercise in "ignoring the awkward jabs of men's hapless boners."

At Stanford University, an undergraduate student named Shelly Ronen analyzed the written observations of seventy-two of her peers who wrote about their experiences at a college party. They described women who invited grinding by forming a circle and dancing with one another, advertising their availability to men. Women summoned a man onto the dance floor by holding eye contact or "angling her bottom toward him." Sometimes two or more women "mimicked heterosexual grinding" but, Ronen noted, this is "often accompanied by jokes and laughing with each other," assuring male onlookers that what women really want is men.

Reflecting twentieth-century gender roles, women can be overtly receptive, but the men choose whom they approach. "There's girls dancing in the middle, and there's guys lurking on the sides and then coming and basically pressing their genitals up against you," wrote one University of Pennsylvania student. "They rarely *ask* a girl to dance," a student of mine clarified, though sometimes they'll make eye contact before approaching. A verbal inquiry is so off-script that one male student reported that his female friends reacted with "incredulity" when he inquired as to whether they wanted to be asked to dance: "They said you should just walk up, say hi, grab her, and start grinding without any discussion of intentions." One of my students called it the "sneak attack."

Because men generally come up to women from behind, sometimes the identity of the man whose penis abuts their backside is a mystery. In that case, instead of turning around—for reasons that will soon become clear—they peer over to their friends for an indication as to whether they should continue. As one of Ronen's students at Stanford observed:

One woman mouthed to her single friend dancing across from her, "Is he hot?" The female friend mouthed back "No" and the woman grimaced. She then gently disentangled herself from the man's hands around her hips and began provocatively dancing with her friend.

My students also use this tactic. One woman explained: "We look to our friends for approval." Describing such a situation, she wrote: "One of my friends even mouthed to me, 'Is he cute?'" The Davidson student described a hand signal system that women used across the circle: an open hand means a five on a five-point scale, a single finger means bail.

It is essential that he be "cute" because the ultimate goal in hookup culture isn't just to hook up, it's to hook up with the right person. Or, more specifically, a *hot* person. Hotness, says one female student, "is the only qualification one needs to be considered for a hookup." "Average guys just don't cut it," another wrote:

> Sure, it's not a social tragedy to hook up with an average-looking guy. But hooking up with someone attractive is a social asset for sure. It raises your standing in the hierarchy of potential partners. It makes you more attractive.

About a guy she actually quite disliked, one of my female students said plainly, "I want to hook up with him for the social status." Hooking up with students who are widely considered hot was a way to get some of their status to rub off on you. "In our room," one of my male students wrote, "sex is a commodity, which, like gold, increases a man's social status, especially if he 'scores' or 'pounds' an especially blonde girl." Blonde is hot.

Bragging about sexual exploits is traditionally the purview of men, and such conversations continue to be a central way in which they bond with one another. As one University of Wisconsin student quoted in *Guyland* put it:

> When I've just got laid, the first thing I think about—really, I shouldn't be telling you this, but really it's the very first thing, before I've even like "finished"—is that I can't wait to tell my crew who I just did. Like, I say to myself, "Ohmigod, they're not going to believe that I just did Kristy!"

At the University of Northern Iowa, another student explained it this way:

> It's like the girl you hook up with, they're like a way of showing off to other guys. I mean, you tell your friends you hooked up with Melissa, and they're like, "Whoa, dude, you are one stud." So, I'm into Melissa because my guy friends think she is so hot, and now they think more of me because of it.

"It's totally a guy thing," he added, but I'm not so sure. Many of my female students were also quick to brag. "The whole point of hookups," wrote one, "is get some and then be able to point the person out to your friends and be like, 'Yeah, that guy. That's right. The hot one over there. I got that.'" "It's almost bragging rights," revealed another, "if you hook up with a guy with a higher social status." Athletes on certain teams and members of high-status fraternities tend to be considered hotter than other men on campus, all things being equal. As a Bowdoin student said, "He's on the baseball team, so it doesn't even matter who he is." One of my students noticed that women who hook up with certain kinds of men would make a point to emphasize it. "She will say, 'I just hooked up with a frat guy,' or 'I hooked up with a guy on the football team,'" she noticed, "instead of just simply saying she hooked up with a guy." It makes a difference, she wrote: "It automatically sounds better." One of my male student athletes couldn't help but notice the same: "I have seen multiple times that girls tend to not want to hook up with a guy who does not play a sport." Or, more succinctly, from a woman at Duke: "Frat stars and athletes—those are the only ones that matter. I mean, honestly."

Using indicators like hotness, blondness, fraternity member-ship, and athletic prowess, students form a working consensus about who is hookup-worthy, and that guides their decisions. "So many hookups," confirmed one student, "are dictated by how our peers view the potential partner." She admitted that she usually asked other people what they thought of guys before getting together with them. "I am unable to separate my opinion from those of my friends," she wrote frankly.

Let me be careful to distinguish this from the idea that peo-ple seek sexual contact with others they find attractive. Nominally, at least, this idea acknowledges that people have individual tastes. Beauty, they say, is in the eye of the beholder. In hookup culture, though, beauty is in the eyes of the beholders, plural. A body's value is determined by collective agreement. It's crowdsourced.

So is ugliness. In her focus groups with students at the Uni-versity of Southern California, sociologist Jess Butler asked: "Are there some types of people you just would not hook up with?" The answer was a clear yes. "I'd say the really heavy girls," replied one of her students, and then everyone chimed in together: "Fuglies!" They laughed. "Which means?" Butler inquired. "Fat and ugly," replied one student. "Or fucking uglies," said another. Both men and women used the term and it was applied generously to students of both sexes. As one of her students explained:

You wanna be hooking up with somebody that you not only think is attractive but that you also—like, that if you go and tell someone about it that they're not gonna be like, "Oh, what?!" Someone that you think your friends would approve of as well. You almost want attractiveness on a broad level—cuz you might be able to say, "Well *I* think she's cute" but then if you can't spin that into a good story, that's not gonna work.

Just as hooking up with a hot student can increase one's own popularity, hooking up with one widely considered unattractive can harm it. Because of this, students who are collectively categorized as unhot are sexual hot potatoes. Students fear being burned.

Kendra, for example, quite enjoyed her hookup. "I had fun," she remembered, "and it was a learning experience, and it made me feel good about myself because I felt attractive to someone." But, when she saw him in the harsh light of the cafeteria the next morning, she was suddenly embarrassed: "He wasn't attractive to me. At all. In any way," she wrote, as if squirming with discomfort. "He was scrawny. I mean, really scrawny, with glasses, and just not stereotypically masculine." Revealing that her regret was more about what other people might think than her own experience, she explained, "He wasn't the guy you're *supposed* to hook up with."

When she told her friends later, she exaggerated her level of inebriation, wanting to make "the fact that I hooked up with a relatively unattractive guy okay." By hooking up with someone that others might not approve of, Kendra was doing hookup culture wrong. "Because the point of hookups is to get with someone hot," she insisted, "and if you don't do that, you should have a damn good excuse."

Drinking alcohol increases the likelihood that students will hook up with someone that'll harm their social status, and they know that. "I know I'm going to be really drunk," said a female student to a friend, "so you need to stop me if you see me hooking up with someone who isn't cute." Though that might be kind of great for the not-so-cute guy. Perhaps that's part of what makes hookup culture so gripping for some students: there's always the possibility that they'll hook up with someone above their social station and always the risk of hooking up with someone below it. Social mobility is real, and that's both exciting and scary.

Ensuring that they are seen dancing and potentially hooking up with just the right person, all while super drunk, takes careful planning, consideration, and decision-making. It is a delicate ballet, a calculated grind. Men hope to approach and be welcomed by the buttocks of women who are considered to be as hot or hotter than them. Women, in response, make their own judgment call—or let their friends make one from across the circle—and respond by grinding with feeling, with indifference, or skittering away.

If one or both partners seem uninterested, the dance may be short-lived. If both partners are into it, the physical contact can escalate quickly. A Stanford student observed that "men are allowed to touch women in such ways that would otherwise be deemed inappropriate." My students said the same: it's "a license to grope," one woman remarked. If things get especially hot and heavy, it's perfectly within the rules to reach underneath a woman's clothes and even into her body. Fingering occurs with some regularity at college dance parties. It's "a common thing," observed one of my students, echoing several others. Accordingly, students in monogamous relationships don't generally grind, except with each other; it's considered cheating. As a student at the University of Kansas clarified: "Girls who have boyfriends don't go to parties by themselves."

Grinding, then, *isn't* just dancing. It's explicitly sexual, and can quickly escalate to something students call a hookup.

◆　◆　◆

Step 3: Initiate a hookup.

"The classic move to establish that you want to hook up with someone," Miranda's friend Ruby wrote from a woman's perspective, "is to turn around to face him, rather than dance with your back pressed against his front." Initiation can come from behind, too. He may tug on her arm or pull one hip back gently to suggest she spin. Or, he might put his face next to hers, closing the distance between them such that, with the turn of her head, there might be a kiss.

If she spins around, Miranda explained, it "seals the deal." Turning around isn't just turning around; it's an advance, an invitation to escalate. Once students are face to face, it's *on*. This is why women look to their friends when a guy approaches them from behind instead of taking a look for themselves. Turning around is tantamount to agreeing to a "difmo"—a DFMO, or "dance-floor make-out."

Back at the burlesque party, Ruby would make exactly that move. The shots of Smirnoff had loosened her inhibitions, and she wasn't alone. "All around me," she wrote, "I saw the same thing happening—female friends of mine meeting guys and flirting, dancing, and then making out." She would join the dance floor shortly and, in the midst of the throbbing crowd, end up dancing with Levi.

They danced for a while, she turned around, and eventually Levi carried her piggyback the two blocks to his dorm. They fell into his bed, laughing, and "suddenly it was happening."

◆　◆　◆

Step 4: Do . . . something.

According to the Online College Social Life Survey, in 40 percent of hookups, Ruby's "it" means intercourse. Another 12 percent include only what we might call foreplay: nudity and some touching of genitals, while 13 percent proceed to oral sex, mostly performed by women on men, but don't include intercourse. A full 35 percent of hookups don't go any further than open-mouth kissing and groping.

When sociologist Danielle Currier asked students at Randolph College to define a hookup, they had a difficult time. Thinking out loud, one female student said, "I'm gonna say a hookup is something . . . It doesn't specifically have to include intercourse but, like . . ." She stumbled. "It's so difficult now to actually say what it is." A male student struggled as well: "I think . . . I mean I think that . . . I mean . . . hmmm . . . I don't know! I don't know how to define it, I guess." Others gave answers like "I know it when I see it."

"It's ambiguous," admitted a student at Tufts University. "When someone says they 'hooked up' last night, you would be wise to ask them to clarify." Such ambiguity is the case across the U.S. Students at Radford, Tulane, and Southern Methodist are on the record that it could be "everything and anything from kissing to consummating." "Out on the dance floor, either for like five seconds or like, all night long," specified a student at the University of Southern California. "Or you leave in the morning in his clothes!" countered her friend. It "could mean anything," says a Bowdoin student. *Guyland*'s Michael Kimmel calls the word "hookup" the "yada yada yada of sex."

This can be confusing. "I sometimes have a hard time distinguishing what a particular person means when mentioning a hookup," reported one of my students. Currier argues that the ambiguity is strategic, allowing students to exaggerate or downplay their encounters depending on what they want others to think. Specifically, she found that it allowed women to "protect their status as 'good girls' (sexual but not promiscuous)" and men to "protect their social status as 'real men' (heterosexual, highly sexually active)." It also has to do with how they feel about the person they hooked up with the next morning. Hookups with high-status people may be exaggerated and those with lower-status people minimized.

In any case, thanks to its ambiguity, the content of any given hookup is mysterious unless the participants get specific or it happens in public. The *purpose* of the hookup, however, is the opposite of ambiguous. Or, at least, it's supposed to be and this is where Ruby worried she might have messed up that night.

◆　　◆　　◆

Step 5: Establish meaninglessness.

The goal is "fast, random, no-strings-attached sex," Ruby explained, but she wasn't sure that's what had happened with Levi. In fact, they were already quite close friends. Both ran in the popular crowd and were squarely in the "hot" category. Levi had an easy way about him and, though he wasn't a member of a fraternity or an athlete, his time in high school sports had left him able to fit in with the men who were. Ruby was a favorite among the popular boys Levi hung out with. With light brown skin, a heart-shaped face, and wavy brown hair that fell to the small of her back, she had the kind of beauty that others eroticized as "exotic."

Ruby swore that she'd never thought of him as a potential hookup before that night. So, she was surprised at the turn of events. Uneasy, too. "I don't want hooking up with Levi to mean anything," she confessed nervously. "I don't think seeing someone naked should necessarily drastically change the way you think about them," she wrote, but she was concerned that it might affect their friendship.

> It's mostly me psyching myself out, telling myself that now that we've hooked up our friendship has to change. It doesn't— or at least I really don't want it to. But I can't help feeling so weird every time I see him since then. All I can think is, it didn't mean anything to me . . . but did it to you? Do you hate me now, because you cared and I didn't?

Truly, step 5 is the trickiest. How do two people establish that an intimate moment between them wasn't meaningful?

On the one hand, it's a familiar idea. The English language offers many ways to reference the concept: "casual sex," "meaningless sex," and "just sex." Likewise, cheating spouses often attempt to ease the impact of their actions with the phrase "It didn't mean anything!" On the other hand, while the phrase "making love" used to refer to any amorous attention, today only sex is described this way. It occupies a privileged position of being the source of our most cherished emotion, an activity that can purportedly generate it out of thin air. We talk about walks on the beach, candlelit dinners, and making music together as romantic, but none of these things, our language tells us, actually makes love. As one astute student observed, "Whether or not sex *has* to be a big deal is beside the point, because in our society there's no denying that it is."

College students know, then, that the wider culture imbues sexual activity with great emotional significance, and this belief overlaps considerably with what they think characterizes loving, romantic relationships for themselves as well. So, despite the language we have for dismissing the significance of sex in practice, establishing that a hookup was meaningless is a challenging personal and interpersonal task.

It's difficult logistically, too, because hooking up always involves actual people. In theory, as one female student maintained, "It doesn't really matter who you hook up with in hookup culture. The point is just to get some." Or, as a University of Michigan guy explained, "It's not really about the actual like person per se." It's just "sexual." In practice, however, people have to *choose*. When two students hook up, it means that they picked each other when they could have picked someone else. If the hookup is going to be understood as meaningless, all of these implications have to be nullified.

This is how they do it.

◆　　　◆　　　◆

Step 5a: Be (or claim to be) plastered.

When students talk about meaningless sex on college campuses, they are almost always referring to drunk sex. According to the Online College Social Life Survey, most casual sex occurring on college campuses involves alcohol; men have drunk an average of six drinks and women an average of four. "People who hook up casually are almost always drunk or have at least been drinking," a female student observed. "Thank god for vodka?" Levi asked rhetorically. "I blame it on the Cuervo," countered a student at Marist College. One University of Florida, Gainesville student half-joked, "If you don't remember the sex, it didn't count."

I was first clued into the symbolic function of alcohol in hookup culture while listening to students discuss "sober sex" when I visited campuses and talked to students in small groups. It was the hushed and reverent tone that got my attention. Sober sex is interpreted entirely differently from drunk sex. It's *heavy* with meaning. "A sober hookup indicates one that is more serious," explained a student. About sober hookups, students say things like "shit's getting real" and "it takes a lot of balls." "If you are sober," a female student described in more detail:

> It means you both are particularly attracted to each other and it's not really a one-time thing. When drunk, you can kind of just do it because it's fun and then be able to laugh about it and have it not be awkward or not mean anything.

This comment was made after she hooked up with a good friend. Like Ruby, she was worried that it would complicate their friendship—and later it would—but for the moment she was sure that it was "harmless" because it happened when they were drunk. "If we did it more or when we were sober," she clarified, "it'd be something more. It would make us more than friends and it would change our relationship." But because they were drunk, the logic goes, it meant nothing.

Sobriety is taken so seriously, says a student at Lehigh University, that some students who are attracted to each other think it's best to "only hang out when they're drunk or on drugs." Students use alcohol as evidence against the contention that any given sexual encounter meant something. It can even erase the implications of same-sex experiences involving people who identify as heterosexual. That this applies to women kissing in public doesn't seem too surprising—women (supposedly) kissing for male attention is a tried-and-true part of hookup culture—but among my students it also applies to women and men who have homosexual make-outs in private. Even same-sex hookups that proceed to oral sex are some-times dismissed with reference to levels of inebriation.

It goes both ways. One student described a gay male friend who had sex with a female friend, but claimed it didn't make her question his sexual orientation. "Even if you are gay," she surmised, it "doesn't mean anything" if a heterosexual hookup happens drunk after a party. Another confirmed her observation. He noticed that "some gay men, when highly intoxicated . . . hit on girls and otherwise act like straight men, which never happens while they are sober." He thought it odd that no one around him seemed to question their homosexuality.

Being drunk, then, is useful to students, and not only because alcohol is liquid courage; it also frames the sexual activity, boxing it into the realm of meaninglessness. It's how students show that they are being careless in both senses of the word: they aren't being careful and they don't care. If students are being careless, they can't be held responsible for *what* they did, but neither can they be held accountable for *who* they did.

Because Levi and Ruby were drunk, they could claim that there was no particular reason that they hooked up with each other that night instead of with someone else. They were both just there doing what people do at college parties. "With alcohol," Ruby confirmed with relief, "anything is funny and okay and just a joke."

◆　　◆　　◆

Step 5b: Cap your hookups.

"We've only hooked up once," explained a male student, "so . . . it automatically is not a big deal." A second trick for dismissing the significance of hookups is to limit how many times two students hook up together. One hookup, students argue, isn't anything to get serious about. "One and done," is what they say. A female student snorted when asked if she would hook up with a guy a second time. "No way," she said gruffly. She had "no feelings for him," so he was "not a viable hookup ever again." Based on the Online College Social Life Survey, we know that most people only hook up with any given person once and very few hook up more than two or three times.

Students believe that avoiding repeat hookups helps ensure that no one gets the idea that a relationship is on the table. They think this is simply the right thing to do. One insisted that it would be "extremely rude" to hook up with someone a second time if there weren't feelings involved. Critiquing the behavior of a female friend who kept creating drama in her personal life, another student complained, "She can't figure out that if she has sex with a guy multiple times, that gives off the message that she likes him."

Capping hookups also reduces the possibility of someone "catching feelings." "The number one established rule of hooking up," wrote a woman enrolled at Tufts, is "don't get too attached." It's a real risk, explained a student at Bellarmine University. "Sometimes you actually catch feelings and that's what sucks." Students, then, aim to hook up with someone that they don't particularly like and, from there, retreat.

If the relationship-averse generally agree that repeat hookups with the same person are risky, they're right. The Online College Social Life Survey shows that three-quarters of seniors have been in at least one monogamous relationship lasting six months or more and, even though hookups rarely lead to relationships, most relationships start with hookups. So, one must be vigilant to ensure that expectations for a relationship don't accidentally evolve.

One time, then, is generally agreed to be safe. Other students tolerate a higher cap, but cutting off a hookup habit before it becomes too comfortable is a common strategy. It's a way to ensure that everyone understands that it was just for fun and stays that way.

◆　　◆　　◆

Step 5c: Create emotional distance.

After it's all over, students confirm that a hookup meant nothing by giving their relationship—whatever it was—a demotion. The rule is to be less close after a hookup than before, at least for a time. If students were good friends, they should act like acquaintances. If they were acquaintances, they should act like strangers. And if they were strangers, they shouldn't acknowledge each other's existence at all. "Unless at the beginning you've made it clear that you want more than a hookup," wrote a male student at Bowdoin, "then the expectation is . . . just to pretend it didn't happen."

The logic gets wacky, but it goes something like this: an unrequited crush will probably be more damaging to a friendship than being temporarily unfriendly. After a hookup, then, when the possibility of romance is a specter that must be eliminated, acting aloof is the best way to ensure that students remain friends. "People act very strangely," one student commented, "to make sure, almost to prove, they're keeping things casual."

Plenty of students feel uncomfortable with this proposition, but hookup culture has a way of enforcing compliance. If the rule is to be unfriendly, then even the slightest kindness—essentially, any effort to connect or reach out—can be interpreted as romantic interest. So, if students are nice after a hookup, they risk making an impression that they don't want to make. As one male student remarked with regret, "I try to stay friends with girls I've hooked up with, or at least stay on a 'don't hate me' basis [but] . . . I've found that, in doing so, you sometimes run into trouble with leading someone on." A second student struggled with how to handle a guy she liked, but not "in that way." She wrote:

> I don't want to be rude by not answering his text messages and not being friendly every time I see him. He doesn't deserve that. But I guess he also doesn't deserve to be led on. . . . I have no idea what to do.

She knew he liked her and it felt terrible to treat him dismissively, but she was advised that "being mean was the best way to handle it." "Many guys I have spoken to," confirmed another student, "admitted to . . . not being nice to the women they hook up with to 'protect' their feelings." The more students value a person's friendship, the more essential they may think it is to be unfriendly after a hookup.

Ruby thought it essential. Since she and Levi had been close friends before their hookup, she temporarily demoted him to acquaintance. A few days later, Ruby filled me in:

> I've seen and interacted with Levi a few times—definitely much less than I would have in a normal three-day span. I've only spent about ten minutes alone with him, in which we joked and made casual small talk, graciously avoiding the fact that we've had each other's genitals in our mouths.

It worked. A week later, Ruby would happily report, "It's as if it never happened and I am perfectly good with that."

◆   ◆   ◆

That's the hookup: a drunken sexual encounter with ambiguous content that is supposed to mean nothing and happen just once. It's a scrappy little sex act, a wayward Cupid. Armed with dark of night and blur of intoxication, its aim is a fun, harmless romp, a supposedly free expression of one's sexuality, but within oddly strict parameters. It's spontaneous, but scripted; order out of disorder; an unruly routine. It is, in short, a feat of social engineering.

The hookup is not in itself new. It's been around for a very long time, at least as long as college has been around. It was around in the 1970s when students started experimenting with free love and psychedelics. It was around in the 1950s when coeds, in blatant violation of school rules, snuck past the house mother and out the windows of their dormitories to consort with boys. It was around in the 1920s when a quarter of college women engaged in homosexual activity. And it was around in the 1880s when certain men in fraternities discovered a carnal brotherhood.

In none of these decades, though, did students think they were *supposed* to be having casual sex. The imperative is the critical difference. "Casual sex was happening before in college," says Indiana University psychologist Debby Herbenick, "but there wasn't the sense that it's what you should be doing. It is now." It's the elevation of the hookup over all other ways of engaging sexually that has transformed campuses from places where there is hooking up to places with a hookup culture. Hookup culture *is* new. Where did it come from? And how did it get here?

2

How Sex Became Fun

Some people are fun but, by her own admission, Clare Hollowell was not. "I am not, and have never been, a fun person," confessed the gender studies professor. It wasn't an easy thing to admit. Being un-fun had been a source of insecurity for much of her young life. It felt like a "personal failure." She felt pressure to try to be fun and, failing that, to stay out of fun people's way. We aren't very nice to un-fun people. We call them names like "downer," "stick-in-the-mud," "wet blanket," and "party pooper." Un-fun people are "a drag," and Hollowell knew it.

When she got to college, the pressure to have fun was amplified. "Everyone was expected to have fun all the time," she noticed. "You have to be *up*," agreed a female student enrolled at Duke. "Because, like, if you're a 'terrible,'" she said, using the word as a noun, "no one will talk to you." Hollowell felt this threat intensely. Fun was more than something she was *allowed* to have; it was something she felt she was *supposed* to have. No one wants to be a "terrible."

The distress this caused her took on an ominous tone very late one night. The phone rang, waking her out of a deep sleep. On the other end of the line was a man who threatened to kill her. Her body was flooded with adrenaline, though she recognized almost immediately that it was a prank. Un-fun as she was, she reported the harassment to campus security, who laughed it off. It was probably just "boys having fun," they said, declining to pursue the incident further. Hollowell was stunned. "This was apparently the end of the conversation," she wrote. "As far as the (male) campus security staff were concerned, the problem was not that these boys' fun had involved deliberately frightening me, but that I had failed [to] identify this as fun."

Later, as a PhD student at Lancaster University, Hollowell interrogated the very idea. In individual interviews and focus groups, she asked female college students to talk about what they did for fun, to describe fun times they'd had, and to discuss the importance of fun to their lives. Very persistently, she found, fun was described as going out, drinking, flirting, and having sex. And fun was, as she had suspected, incredibly important to them. "That's like the main thing really," replied one woman. "Especially in the first year," said another, "it seems to be like the primary thing is fun and the secondary thing is work."

Hollowell's interviewees did have fun, but the imperative to do so also brought anxiety and guilt. They worried about fun, whether they had enough fun, if they were *really* having fun, if they were having the right kind of fun, and if other students found them fun. Ironically, though fun was described as a way to relieve the pressure of work and school, Hollowell found that it was "itself a pressure, something that one has responsibility to have."

◆   ◆   ◆

I went looking for Hollowell's work because the idea of fun peppered my students' journal entries. Students used the word over 500 times. Almost always they used it in a positive sense, but they expressed anxiety about fun, too. "I'm not anti-fun," wrote one student defensively. She didn't like to party the way her peers did, she explained, so she felt "like the weirdo who doesn't want to have fun."

Fun was a big deal to my students and, almost a third of the time, when they used the word they were using it to describe sex. "Fun," one of my students argued, "is what people are looking for when they want to just hook up." Sex was a "lot of fun," a "fun experience," and a "fun time." People wanted to have "one night of fun," "a little fun," and to "do it for fun." Sex was just "a fun thing that friends do sometimes"; something that should be "fun and taken lightly"; about "having the most fun possible"; and "tons of fun if both people are willing to have some fun." One student argued that casual sex was "fun and healthy." Another that it was fine to have sex for love, but only if "you have fun." "Everyone has sex in college," wrote a third. "This is going to be fun."

Many of today's college students believe that they're supposed to be having fun and that sex is a chief way of doing it, but not all students feel equally comfortable being so cavalier. Riley was among them. Riley started college with an adoring boyfriend to whom she lost her virginity. Recalling the tenderness of their relationship, she described one lazy afternoon during high school when they lay on her bed in an embrace, contemplating whether they should take their intimacy to the next level. Noses almost touching, he told her: "Your physical relationship should match your emotional relationship." When she fell in love with him, she knew it was right. "It was a symbol of how intimate we were with each other," she recalled warmly.

A few months into the academic year they broke up, as most couples do, but she remained very protective of her sexuality. Echoing her ex, whom she still admired, she wrote:

> I take it very, very seriously. I think it would be horribly damaging to have sex with someone I just met, or, for that matter, someone I wasn't completely in love with. I won't even kiss someone I don't know, because I think sharing your body with someone is a very personal thing.

Riley was very cautious.

Quickly, though, it became apparent that being in a monogamous relationship had offered her some protection from the social expectation to hook up. A petite natural blonde with a short, asymmetrical haircut, she got noticed by guys who liked girls who were a little plucky. Men started paying closer attention to her and, without a steady boyfriend, there was no longer anything between her and them.

Then, late one morning while she was waiting in line to buy an orange juice and thinking about how she might organize her "Elements of Logic" paper, she was ambushed by her friend, Tao, who excitedly informed her that Craig had said she was hot and wanted to "get with" her. Craig *who?* Riley asked. *Craig* Craig, Tao emphasized. It took Riley a minute to process and then she remembered him: a friend of a friend with whom she'd never actually exchanged words. Describing her reaction to this news she wrote, in what felt like a plot twist, "I haven't ruled it out."

> I am kind of curious as to what it would be like, but I also think it's kind of weird that Craig is (supposedly) so eager to hook up with me but doesn't even talk to me. . . . And I know

I'd feel gross about doing it the next day, because he doesn't really know me and I don't know him. And I don't like sharing my body with people I don't know.

Riley was pretty sure that she only wanted sexual contact with someone she knew well, but this feeling was complicated by a desire to be more "carefree." She continued:

I always feel like I'm not sexually open enough, or that I'm too private or conservative, and that I get too emotionally attached or put too much weight on things that aren't supposed to be a big deal.

She ran herself in circles trying to decide what to do about Craig: "I literally just have no idea what to do and it sounds so trite but it's on my mind all the time. I can't decide what I want and what I don't want."

Riley's conflict stemmed from a struggle between *what* she wanted (sex with people she knew and trusted) and *who* she wanted to be (someone who took sex a little less seriously). The phrase she used to chastise herself most often was "loosen up." "Sometimes I wish I could just loosen up and not care about things so much," she wrote. And then: "I should just try it out and loosen up." And, then, again: "I feel like I need to loosen up and not be so uptight." And then she'd go full circle: "WHY am I trying to convince myself to loosen up if I obviously don't want to!?!??!" But she knew why: Because "maybe," she conceded, "it would be fun."

As if she was channeling Hollowell, Riley used the word "fun" five times in a single paragraph describing what she felt the first year of college was supposed to be like:

People wanting to have a lot of fun. Many people say freshman year of college is the best year of your life. It's fun, you meet lots of people, go to parties all the time, have tons of freedom, and grad school barely looks at freshman year grades anyway! So, lots of people have the mentality that freshman year is going to be a huge free-for-all. My friend actually has a catchphrase: "College, no bedtime!" Implying that fun takes priority over sleep and rest, and most of the time, it does. The stories people tell of their fun, spontaneous experiences are glamorized and seen as "cool." . . . Thus, the college culture encourages spontaneous, free, fun-loving attitudes, not serious, reflective ones.

College, Riley was convinced, was supposed to be fun, not serious. This was the conclusion, too, of a counselor at Duke: "One of the worst labels a student can have . . . is being 'too serious,'" he said. "You can't lose cool points faster than taking anything seriously." Sex included.

But students *are* serious. They're serious about having fun. And fun *is* serious, tightly linked in our culture to a seriously important democratic entitlement: freedom. The Pulitzer Prize-winning political scientist Sebastian de Grazia, known as the "father of leisure studies," wrote of the conflation of fun with freedom as early as 1964. "Fun and freedom often seem almost synonymous," he argued. "When you're having fun, you're free and only if you're free can you have fun."

For students, the conflation of sex, fun, and freedom is all but perfect. My sexually eager students talked about anticipating the "imminent freedom that college presented," being "finally free to explore their own sexuality," and finding "freely engaging like-minded individuals" with which to do so. They talked about "free love," "free sexual expression," feeling "freer to explore," and the opportunity to "live their sexual lives freely." In the paragraph in which Riley invokes fun five times, she insists that freshmen are supposed to be "free," have "tons of freedom," and that college should be a "free-for-all." She obviously felt like sex was a seriously important part of what it meant to be free in college. That's why she was so preoccupied with it to begin with.

To your average college student, hooking up isn't just about a good time; it's about enacting one of America's most cherished values. How exactly did students come to think of sex this way?

◆   ◆   ◆

Or, perhaps the right question for the beginning of the twenty-first century is: How did *women* come to think of sex this way? Riley's fear of missing out on sexual fun is likely quite familiar to most men. According to the social rules that govern men's lives, it's downright compulsory to think of sex as a form of leisure; avoiding relationships is equally obligatory. It is required that men like women in the abstract, that is, but liking a particular woman will attract teasing. As the bullies on *The Simpsons* say when they catch Nelson Muntz in a romantic moment with Lisa, "Aw man! You kissed a girl! That is so gay!"

The bullies owe their attitude to the Industrial Revolution. Before this transformation, men, women, adults, and children all labored together on family farms. It was a tough life, but families worked as a team. As 20 percent of the American population began migrating from the country to crowded cities, work increasingly happened at centralized factories. These were much harsher workplaces than family farms, generally indifferent to the workers' well-being. The wages were low, the jobs were dangerous, and hours were brutally long. Friendly and familial relationships were replaced by competition among strangers. No one cared for one another. Bosses were driven by profit. Employees were disposable.

Commentators at the time were concerned that no part of life would be spared the indifference of capitalism. They scanned for a solution and the home, once a place of work, emerged as a haven from it. If the workplace was ruthless and competitive, the home would be kind and cooperative. If the workplace rewarded individualism and self-promotion, the home would be a place for togetherness and selflessness. If work was about profit, home was about care. And if women did anything resembling work in the home—if in their twelve-hour day they organized and completed errands, preserved and prepared food, made and mended clothes, cleaned and repaired the household, hosted and entertained company, and raised children to adulthood—it was no longer work, it was a labor of love.

Onto work and home were laid the now familiar gender stereotypes. Men were newly seen to be naturally suited to the workplace, whereas women, who had worked alongside men on farms for two hundred years at least, were thought to be too sentimental and physically frail for the harsh realities of capitalism. Likewise, while men had been actively involved in raising sons for most of American colonial history, they were now seen as insufficiently nurturing for childrearing. Men and women were suddenly "opposite sexes." That loaded phrase, with its exaggerated claim of gender difference, began outpacing previously common language like "other sex" and the "fair sex" in the first decade of the twentieth century. Now men and women were distinctly different, with complementary strengths and weaknesses. The era of "separate spheres" had begun.

Love and sex were mapped onto these spheres. Men were recast as helplessly carnal, subject to irrepressible vulgar sexual desires. Middle- and upper-class white women, the new keepers of anticapitalist values, got love. They were reimagined as naturally chaste, innocent of the desires that ravaged men. Poor women and women of color weren't put on the same pedestal of purity and, out of economic necessity, sometimes found themselves bridging the gap between the assumed sexual needs of wife and husband, doing for the now supposedly insatiable men what their wives presumably would not. By one estimate, in the mid-1800s New York City was home to one prostitute for every sixty-four men; in Savannah, Georgia, and Norfolk, Virginia, it was closer to one for every thirty.

The association of men with lust and women with love was a rather sudden ideological transformation. The Puritans had believed that women were the more sexual sex: weaker overall than men and, therefore, less capable of controlling their passions, sexual and otherwise. They looked to the biblical story for evidence, noting that it was Eve who couldn't resist tugging the apple from the tree. Now it was men who were supposedly powerless in the face of unspeakable passions. Had Genesis been written in 1900, Adam probably would have been the first sinner.

In just a few decades, though, the idea that respectable women were interested only in the content of men's hearts and not their pants would be stretched to the limits of believability. By 1920, half of Americans lived in urban locations, and these dense concentrations of people enabled the first mass modern entertainment: jazz clubs, dance halls, speakeasies, sports stadiums, amusement parks, burlesque shows, and an invention called the movie theater. It was a decade so exciting that we called it the Roaring Twenties. In France they called it the *Années Folles*, the Crazy Years. It was the era of flappers, surrealism, art deco, the Harlem Renaissance, ragtime, the excitement of early aviation, and much more. Arguably, it was more fun than anyone had had in generations.

Together in this exhilarating environment, young working

people invented the "date": a shared, erotically charged evening of entertainment arranged and paid for by men. As far as courtship goes, this was a dramatic reversal of power. Previously—and in rural areas and among the most privileged classes, even then—courtship was controlled by women. If a young lady had an interest in a young man, her mother or another female relative would invite him over for a snack and a chat. If things got more serious, if they "made love" with their conversation as we used to think people could do, the couple might be allowed to sit alone if a chaperone was close by. Marriage would soon follow. This practice was described as "calling." Women decided which men would come by and when. They provided the refreshments. They watched over the visit and decided when he would leave. If they liked him, they would invite him back and if they did not, that was that.

Dating took courtship out into the streets, where men were in charge, and this put women in a pickle. They earned only a fraction of what men earned, so if they were going to enjoy city life, they needed men to "treat" them by paying their way. This meant getting chosen by men who had their pick of women, which put women into competition for men's attention. And, because the goal was not to begin a relationship but—foreshadowing hookup culture—to go out with as many different people as possible, they had to attract over and over and over again.

In response, women began to do something that is so taken for granted today that it's hard to imagine it had a beginning: they tried to be sexy. Being sexy meant not only conforming to the standard of beauty at the time, but also signaling a certain amount of sexual availability and potentially offering physical favors. Sex became an exchange. Not just sex per se—though that certainly occurred, at least somewhat—but the company of a woman who, by virtue of her sexiness and sexual attention, made a man feel important. All this was so new that a word had to be invented to describe it. "Sexy" was first used in print to mean "sexually attractive" in 1923. Before then it worked grammatically more like the word "hungry"; it was used as we use the word "horny" today.

This new need to attract the attention of men is the origin of many of the aesthetic demands on women's bodies. It was the beginning, for example, of the "reducing diet" and the widespread use of makeup. During the Victorian era, wearing even modest makeup in public would have been equivalent to going out in clown makeup; only prostitutes painted their faces. By the 1920s, however, women were being told that makeup was essential, not immoral. Some of the biggest companies in the business—Maybelline, Max Factor, and Revlon—came to life in this era. Sales of cosmetics more than octupled in just ten years.

Then came the Great Depression, and on its heels hundreds of thousands of young American men were killed in World War II. Almost as quickly as the crazy years had come, they were gone. Men were dead, families were devastated, and the future of the American woman was in peril. In 1945, the *New York Times* reported ominously that 750,000 young women would likely never marry. *Good Housekeeping*, not to be outdone, warned that 6 to 8 million women would lose out to the "male shortage." *Esquire* added fuel to the fire, warning American women that their GIs were "romantic heroes" to the world and, if they didn't get their act together quickly, foreign women would be happy to take their place at the altar. Facing this kind of uncertainty, women dropped dating in favor of monogamous relationships with men that potentially led to matrimony. They called it "going steady."

In 1938, the newspaper for the all-female Radcliffe College mocked women who were "pinned" to just one man; just a few years later, they were bragging about the proportion of their graduates who were already married. In 1957, the president of Amherst suggested that a female student who wasn't paired off by junior year was an "old maid" and a male student who was still single as a senior was "more or less 'on the shelf.'" Knowing that women paired up quickly, men made locking down a steady date a priority. "During my first two weeks at Smith," wrote one woman in 1957, "I felt rather like a display in a shop window. Boys from Amherst, Yale, Williams, and Dartmouth swarmed over the campus in groups, looking over the new freshmen for one girl that they could tie up for the next eight Saturday nights, the spring prom, and a house party in July." The men called it "social security," a guarantee that they'd have a date when they wanted one.

Grownups criticized going steady, calling it "premature monogamy." They mostly thought it sounded boring. "Does going-steady spoil dance fun?" asked a reporter for a local Florida newspaper. "Lakeland teen-age misses feel that the dance has lost much of its dazzle now," she concluded. "What's the use to 'dress to the teeth' for somebody who's used to seeing you in shorts and pedal pushers?" At Vassar, administrators tried to enforce partner-swapping at dances as a matter of policy. At least one high school threatened to expel any student who insisted on dating only one person. In tried-and-true fashion, academics studied the "going steady craze," debating whether this newfangled culture of sex was good or bad, and for whom.

There was real concern, too, that getting close to a single person might facilitate intimacy. And it did. Instead of getting to first base with lots of people, like many of the youth of the 1920s had, many young people in the 1950s got to all the bases with just one. Half of women had premarital sex, the age of marriage dropped to a one-hundred-year low, and the number of babies born less than nine months after the wedding—excuse me, "premature"—reached a one-hundred-year high. Sex was still something women gave to men, but now it was in exchange for a marriage proposal.

Before long, the glaring contradictions that characterized American society during the decade quickly started to rupture the social order. Premarital sex was strongly condemned, but the rate of teen pregnancy had reached an unprecedented level. Suburban housewives were supposedly living the dream, yet they were popping tranquilizers like candy. Hugh Hefner invented the "playboy," making it hard to tell anymore if men who resisted marriage did so because they didn't like women or because they liked them a little too much. Responding to this ideological chaos, activists ushered in an anti-establishment movement that rejected authority in all its forms. We saw antiwar protesters, hippies and free love, the women's and gay liberation movement, and civil rights victories.

More permissive attitudes toward sex were just part of this wider abandonment of conformity, obedience, hypocrisy, and the status quo. Journalists began heralding the death of the going-steady craze as early as the mid-1960s. "Something is happening," wrote a Lawrence, Kansas, journalist in 1966, reporting that the number of young people going steady had dropped by half in just two years. He interviewed sixteen-year-old Sandy, who explained that she didn't prefer it: "I don't believe in being tied to anyone. I need to be free to do what I want when I want." Thirteen-year-old Pat agreed. "I think it's stupid," he said. The comparatively mature fifteen-year-old Mark argued that "one should not be tied down to someone outside of marriage."

Kids were a-changing, as they always do. Meanwhile, feminists were fighting the Victorian stereotypes that excluded women from the world of work. They began dismantling the legal and cultural barriers that allowed men to bar women from politics, workplaces, sports, military service, and more. And they fought for recognition of women's sexuality, of their right to be sexual without social stigma, and to have sex for pleasure like men. They wanted, in other words, to be able to give away sex for free instead of in exchange for men's resources. Economic independence was an essential part of this new contract, as was the decriminalization of contraception in 1965 (for married people) and 1972 (for single people) and the 1973 Supreme Court decision that made certain restrictions on abortion unconstitutional.

Feminists also questioned the idea that the things women had been held responsible for—things related to love, like raising children, maintaining a safe and comfortable home, and nurturing others as wives, mothers, nurses, and teachers—were somehow less important than what men were expected to do. Feminists wanted women to be able to do the things in life that were valued, things associated with men, but they also wanted everyone to sit up and notice that the things women had been doing all along were valuable, too. They hoped to collapse the Victorian binary, to give men and women equal access to both work and home, profit and care, and sex and love.

They would get half of what they wanted.

◆　　◆　　◆

Sociologist Emily Kane sat across the table from the father of two preschool boys and asked him how he felt about them playing with girl toys. "If they asked for a Barbie doll," he replied, bringing to mind the most iconic girl toy of all, "I would probably say no, you don't want [that] . . . boys play with trucks." Another father, when asked about his five-year-old, expressed concern about his tendency to cry. "Stop crying like a girl," he would say to his son when he wept out of desire for a toy or a later bedtime. "If you decide you want [some] thing, you are going to fight for it." "If he was act-ing feminine," said a mother who was posed the same question, "I would try to get involved and make sure he's not gay."

At about the same time that today's traditional-age college stu-dents were children, between 1999 and 2002, Kane interviewed almost four dozen parents about their children's gender perfor-mance. She found that they were generally apprehensive about boys who were a bit girlish. Some parents didn't approve of boys who strayed too far from stereotypical masculinity; other parents were just well aware of what comes to boys who do. As one mother explained, "He's not the rough-and-tumble kid, and I do worry about him being an easy target."

This is a reasonable fear. As boys become men, being seen as appropriately manly translates into social opportunities: getting invited to parties, making cool friends, and attracting the atten-tion of desirable women. It's also how they avoid being a victim of emotional and physical abuse. In many fields, manliness will be vital for pulling off a job interview and standing out for promotion. For men to deliberately wave off the imperative to prove their mas-culinity is akin to deliberately sacrificing social and occupational success.

It's not particularly surprising, then, that parents recognized the value of masculinity for boys; what's really interesting is that they saw it as best for their girls, too. When Emily Kane asked a father about his hopes for his young daughter's personality, his answer was clear: "I never wanted a girl who was a little prin-cess, who was so fragile," he said. "I want her to take on more masculine characteristics." Another day, across another table, a mother said about her daughter, "I don't want her to just color and play with dolls, I want her to be athletic." The parents of girls interviewed by Kane didn't express the same concern regarding cross-gender behavior that parents of boys did. They were more than tolerant of their girls' boylike behavior; they were *tickled*.

We tell our girls, from the time they're in diapers, that being "girly" is okay, but being a little bit "boyish" is pretty great. A girl might be encouraged when she discovers a fascination with backyard bugs or engineering toys. Getting ready for elementary school, she may be signed up for a youth sport. Her coach may praise her once in a while for not throwing "like a girl," an obvious jab at femininity. In middle school, she might join her teammates in cracking jokes about the girls in cheerleading. Even if she's somewhat jealous about the attention they get from boys, she's sure that what she's doing is more badass precisely because it's less girly.

In high school history class, the women her teachers talk about are all ones who broke out of traditional gender roles: Joan of Arc, warrior; Sojourner Truth, activist; Marie Curie, scientist; Amelia Earhart, adventurer. Likewise, our contemporary feminist icons are overwhelmingly women who are admired for succeeding in male arenas of life: Hillary Clinton, politician; Oprah Winfrey, media mogul; Sonia Sotomayor, Supreme Court justice; Pussy Riot, rebels; Danica Patrick, race car driver. As the famous saying goes, "Well-behaved women rarely make history." This is a lesson easily learned by any child paying a modicum of attention.

Most girls in America today grow up being told that they can do anything, and they know when this is emphasized that what it really means is that they can do anything *boys* do. So, today's young women are quick to incorporate masculinity into their personalities and lifestyles. They do this in a myriad of ways, picking and choosing the mix that works best for them. Some girls major in computer science, some aim to ascend the hierarchy at a Fortune 500 company, some brag about a taste for hard liquor, and some have sex for fun. We shouldn't be the slightest bit surprised. It's exactly the kind of choice they have been rewarded for every day in essentially all realms of life.

Feminists wanted this for women. They wanted them to have the right to put themselves first, to build impressive careers, and to have sex freely. And they got that. But they also wanted men to embrace having sex for love. They wanted to share with men the beauty of a life driven by empathy, care, and tenderness. That's not what happened. Instead, the average woman became more masculine, and so did the average man.

In the midst of the sexual revolution, a Stanford psychologist named Sandra Lipsitz Bem developed what would later be called the Bem Sex Role Inventory. It was a survey that asked respondents to evaluate themselves on sixty traits, many of which were gendered ones, such as aggression, warmth, self-reliance, competitiveness, and sincerity. The result was a quantitative measure of the extent to which a person's personality was stereotypically masculine, feminine, or balanced between both. The Bem Inventory was first used in 1971 and, as is typical in the field, used repeatedly in studies done all around the U.S.

Decades later, in the mid-1990s, another psychologist decided to use it to look back through time. Jean Twenge, then at the University of Michigan, amassed and compared all of the studies that had used the Bem Sex Role Inventory to see if men and women had changed. They had. Both were increasingly likely to claim masculine traits as their own. Women's scores, especially, had shifted, and their personalities were measuring as masculine as men's.

Women came to embrace the same self-concept that men had once claimed for themselves because American society has continued to value the masculine over the feminine. It's why women flock to male-dominated occupations, break into male-identified sports, and adopt masculine fashions, but men generally aren't doing the inverse. Because of this asymmetry, when women adopt masculine ways of life, they're doing more than just breaking out of their gender role; they're breaking into a better one. They're liberating themselves. Many women apply this logic to sex, too, adopting a stereotypically masculine approach that puts sex before love.

"I railed against the idea that women were needy, dependent, easily heartsick, easily made hysterical by men, attention-obsessed, and primarily fixated on finding romance," one of my female students explained insistently. "I did this by proving how very like a boy I could behave." She engaged in what she called "sexual tomboyery":

> I figured the best way for a girl to reject oppressive sexism would be to act in exact opposition of what our sexist society expects of a decent woman; to get exactly what she wants from men, whenever she wants it. In essence, objectify them back.

She wanted to prove that she could do so just for fun. "I had an aversion to the idea that all girls were left in mushy little puddles of attachment," she wrote. She was going to show the world otherwise.

Many of my female students feel the same. They argue that hooking up is a way to "reject oppressive sexism," "pursue sexual liberation," and challenge the idea "that women are supposed to be passive." They're not alone. The hookup is "the road to sexual emancipation," asserted a woman at the University of Florida. "My friends and I are like sexual vultures," bragged a woman at Syracuse. "I'm a true feminist," insisted a student at the University of Pennsylvania about hooking up. "I'm a strong woman. I know what I want."

Hookups are described by women as sexual liberation itself, but also as a way to protect their ambitious trajectories. As recently as the 1980s, college women were "mobbed by romance," prompted at every turn to find a career-minded boyfriend so that they could quickly get engaged, settle down, and start a family. Schoolwork took a back seat to steady boyfriends, leading women to revise their career ambitions in favor of planning to be a supportive wife. Young women today resist this path. In fact, 28 percent of women believe that romantic love brainwashes women, tricking them into investing their time and energies in someone else; another 19 percent think that it might.

Almost half of female students, then, think that love might bring them something bad instead of something good. "Right now," explained a female student at Princeton, "I have to focus on my career, getting through medical school, establishing myself." "Based on my own experience," wrote a Wesleyan University alum, "this new sexual paradigm has given women the freedom to focus on their own lives and careers." "I know it sounds hyperbolic," wrote a female senior at Northwestern:

> but I mean it when I say that getting married right now would ruin my life. I want the chance to pick up and move to a new city for a new job or for adventure, without having to worry about a spouse or a family. I need to be able to stay at the office until three in the morning if I have to and not care about putting dinner on the table.

This is Hanna Rosin's argument in *The End of Men*. In her estimation, hooking up is liberating women from reliance on men in both the short and long terms. "Feminist progress is largely dependent on hook-up culture," she writes, arguing that a "serious suitor" is as dangerous to a woman's future today as an unintended pregnancy was to an unmarried girl in the nineteenth century.

I'm not so sure that hookup culture is unequivocally good for women, but Rosin is certainly not wrong to notice that they make this argument. Many young women today think that hitching themselves to a man, even a successful one, is a bad idea and backward to boot.

♦   ♦   ♦

For quite specific historical reasons, both men and women who are coming of age in America today believe that sex is and should be fun. They easily dismiss the Puritan idea that it's sinful outside of marriage. They also soundly reject the Victorian insistence on female purity. The sexual double standard isn't widely endorsed on college campuses anymore, at least not explicitly. Only 12 percent of students believe that women should be less sexually active than men and an equal amount endorse a "reverse" double standard, admitting that they judge men more harshly for their sexual behavior than they do women.

Ironically, if their children are going to be sexually active, many parents probably prefer that they "go steady." Such premarital monogamy was unheard of before the 1950s, and parents of the time thought it sounded both dull and dangerous. Now adults of all ages tend to think it sounds safe. It's not, of course. Decades of feminist activism have shown us that monogamy is no protection from mistreatment and violence. Hookups expose students to emotional trauma and physical assault, to be sure, but relationships do not protect them from these things.

Still, going steady never went away and many students are attracted to love relationships. Plenty, though, are oriented toward sex in the same way that the working youth of the 1920s were oriented toward flirtation. They're surrounded by attractive others and eager to enjoy the opportunity to have a sexy, good time. And if the women of that sparkling decade were reluctant to go "all the way," they are less so now. Today's young women—in principle at least—have effective means of birth control, a limited right to an abortion, and the ability to support themselves and a baby if they need to.

The feminist movement brought them those things and also insisted that women should not have to feel ashamed of their sexuality. In this brave new world, hooking up is what it feels like to be free. Young women have embraced this new reality; they are no longer willing to play the angel to men's frisky devil. They flatly reject the idea that they should be our society's moral compass, *especially* in college. After all, as everyone knows, bad girls have more fun.

3

Sex in Drunkworld

Mara and Naomi sat reclined on the wide porch of a three-story, 126-year-old house near Penn State. Naomi gazed out across the lawn, her fingers resting gently next to a red cup at her right, and pointed to one of the fraternity brothers playing catch. He threw a chin nod her way. Nonchalantly, she mentioned that she'd had sex with him the night before on a bathroom floor. Tossing back her long, newly blonde hair, she raised her scraped knees so that Mara could see. "He's the ultimate douchebag," she said, "and I *hate* frat boys. But his body was too good to pass up." Mara peered at him without much interest. "A shirtless guy with sculpted abs and sunglasses," she observed. "He was clearly pretty hot, so it was like it was an accomplishment or something."

The two women had been best friends since sixth grade. Both had been a little wild in high school, bonding over drinking, smoking, and a slightly twisted sense of humor. Mara had looked up to Naomi. "She was the one that did all the drugs first," she wrote, "she was super sassy and ran a super fast 60-meter sprint." When college acceptance letters came, she was sad that they'd be parting ways, but it had been her dream since she was twelve to move to California. So, Mara left Lancaster, Pennsylvania, for a small liberal arts college and Naomi went to State.

Sometime in the spring, Mara caught a plane to spend a long weekend with her best friend, but Naomi wasn't the same person she remembered. She'd become the "type of girl," Mara wrote, that she used to "make fun of." All of her female friends, she noticed, were "super hot and blonde" and they went after boys with a ruthlessness that she found unsettling:

> Spend any time with [them] and you'll hear how much they talk about sex: how Naomi banged this one guy, how their backs always hurt after doing doggy style, how [this girl] had sex with some guy while everyone else was in the room, the list goes on. . . . It all just seemed so centered around sex it was overwhelming.

Mara expressed discomfort with how Naomi spoke about the men she hooked up with: "Belittling," she wrote, offering as an example the way that Naomi and her friends would crudely compare the "quality of men's dicks" and how she said all the guys she slept with were "gross." She felt like Naomi was taking things to an extreme. "It just seemed so weird," she reflected, "my best friend . . . so perfectly fitting into the slutty college girl persona."

Mara herself was no slouch. She was an active participant in hookup culture. She drank. She went out most weekends and looked for boys to kiss. She vaguely remembered losing her virginity in the first few weeks of school, under questionable circumstances, to a football player with whom she had a one-night stand. "It's not like I'm really one to judge her for hooking up with hot guys and having fun," Mara admitted about Naomi, acknowledging that she'd done her fair share of just that.

And Mara had changed in unexpected ways, too. Earlier that year she'd been sitting with her own new friends at a late-night eatery complaining about feeling excluded from the college's nightlife. "Like it or not," said her friend Priya, who was gearing up to make a case that they should rush a sorority:

> most parties around campus are either Greek mixers, Greek formals, Greek sponsored, or hosted by upperclassmen with connections in the Greek system. This means that first-semester freshmen have to know someone, or know someone who knows someone, to get invited to parties.

It was true, Mara noted. Nobody wanted to let a "herd of freshmen" into their house. "Who do you know here?" the party hosts would ask, and then turn them away. Mara used the word "mortifying." Meanwhile, the get-togethers in her dorm seemed just like high school and the on-campus rules regarding noise and alcohol were very strict, making her feel like she was still a kid.

When Priya suggested that they all rush, Mara was skeptical. "I've always been kind of against it," she wrote. She thought frat boys were "sleazy" and sorority girls were "materialistic and shallow," but Priya made a strong argument. "If girls rush sororities," she said, sounding certain, "the game changes." She explained:

> First, they are already guaranteed invites to the events that involve their organization . . . Second, they meet upperclassmen women who will invite them to parties . . . Third, girls who rush sororities get to meet and form bonds with guys in fraternities sober (in addition to drunk).

Number three was a particular selling point, insisted Priya, because without being in a sorority "there is virtually no way to make connections with upperclassmen besides than to hook up with them." She figured that joining was one of the only ways for women on campus to make friends with men "without needing to use their sexuality" to do it.

Mara caved. She was tired of having nothing to do. So, she rushed. "I've never done so much girl-flirting in my life," she laughed.

◆   ◆   ◆

Neither Mara nor Naomi intended to get involved with the Greek system, but they did. In part, it was because they were primed by the mass media to want to party, get drunk, be crazy, and have casual sex in college. In pop culture, lust looms large and unfettered on campus, leaving many students expecting, as a student named Kariann put it apprehensively, a "big four-year orgy." "Like most people I knew," Kariann wrote, "I believed that college was a wild, sexual party scene, and that to fit in, you had to be into alcohol, weed, and sex." All of these features of her imaginary college life intimidated her, and being a virgin made it all the more daunting. "I thought that only nerds, religious nuts, and momma's boys were untouched when they started college."

"I couldn't even begin to list all of the movies that I have seen that depict a live free, party hard, and sexually overloaded college scene," another student wrote about his expectations:

Stations such as MTV, Comedy Central, and Spike all showed, in one way or another . . . college life as a party atmosphere where the flow of alcohol never stops, drugs are frequently

consumed, and women enjoy exposing themselves and having
sex with many different partners.

A student who watched the Spike network show *Blue Moun-
tain State* wrote that it left her with the impression that college
is "filled with crazy parties, hot jocks, and sexy/slutty girls who
always flash boys."

If college students tend to overestimate how much sex their
peers are having, the media might be part of the reason why. Some
of my students certainly came to college with outlandish expectations. Recalling his high-school-senior self, one student wrote that
he expected that, once he was in college, "not a week would go by
in which I would not have sex at least a dozen times." A female
student, explaining why she intended to stay single in her first year,
wrote that she "thought it would be more fun" if she had the option
of "being sexual with each boy I met."

Among their influences, students mentioned movies like
American Pie, *Old School*, *Superbad*, and, of course, *Animal House*.
No single portrayal of college life has had a greater impact than
the movie that introduced Delta Tau Chi. The comedy hit theaters in 1978, introducing us to a set of fraternity men who remain
among the most iconic in American history. The fraternity brothers' sheer ridiculousness made it one of the most profitable films
of all time. Students still mention it as a formative influence.
As recently as 2012, two Mount Allison University psychologists tested the proposition, finding that watching clips of *Animal House* increased the likelihood that students would express
positive attitudes toward substance use and negative ones toward
studying.

Colleges themselves have largely accepted that they have to sell
their institutions to attract students, confirming the pop-cultural

depictions of college as a place where young people go to have fun. After *Animal House* was filmed at the University of Oregon, for example, the university's tenuous link to the party lifestyle became a part not only of its implicit appeal but of its advertising. A more systematic analysis of college recruitment materials found that campus life was presented as mostly social. Brochures highlighted leisure time, student clubs, residential perks, and athletic activities. Half failed to include even a single picture of a student studying. It didn't matter if the school was Ivy League, a regional state school, a religious college, or Big Ten; the buildings changed, but the message was the same.

To stay in business, colleges need students' tuition dollars, and telling a story about how much fun they'll have is one way to get them. As reporter Caitlin Flanagan wrote for the *Atlantic*:

> The entire multibillion-dollar, 2,000-campus American college system . . . depends overwhelmingly for its very existence on one resource: an ever-renewing supply of fee-paying undergraduates. It could never attract hundreds of thousands of them each year . . . if the experience were not accurately marketed as a blast.

Thanks to everything from pop culture to propaganda, when students arrive on college campuses today they expect—with varying levels of inclination and trepidation—to have a *really* good time. But that is not why Mara became a sorority girl and Naomi ended up on the bathroom floor. To really understand that part of the story we have to go back, back three hundred years at least, to when college was not fun at all.

◆   ◆   ◆

During the colonial era in the U.S., college was, as one historian, described it, a "veritable straitjacket of petty rules." Essentially every detail of students' lives was controlled: how they kept their room, how they dressed and wore their hair, what they could do, when and what they ate, where they could go and when. There were substantial penalties for deviance and they came swiftly.

Except for a few hours in the evening, students obeyed a strictly regimented schedule. Most of their professors were ministers, so they rose at dawn to be led in morning prayers and attended a religious service before bed. Between visits to the chapel, they studied a curriculum that can safely be described as dry: proficiency in Latin and Greek, lots of mathematics, a little science and philosophy, some spelling and grammar. It was dreadfully boring to most.

Early college students did not sit in the back row with a baseball hat pulled over their eyes, sleeping off last night's keg—a sight most college professors today would recognize. They were expected to recite ancient prose on demand and engage in vigorous debate. Student performance on these tasks was often met with withering criticism. A good verbal thrashing was the pedagogical strategy thought most effective, and professors encouraged peers to join in. Avoiding taunts was often the only motivation to study. Instead of being fun, college was menacing.

At the time, most students were relatively humble middle-class men studying to be ministers like their professors. They were generally obedient, but as the eighteenth century came to a close, colleges were increasingly filled with wealthy sons of elite families. These young men weren't as interested in higher education as they were in a diploma that would ratify their families' hoarding of wealth and power. Predictably, they had a much lower tolerance for submission.

As a result, higher education became a battleground. Between the mid-1700s and the mid-1800s, there were student protests and uprisings at every school in New England and most of those in the South, with students objecting to everything from the quality of the food to the rigidity of schedules to the content of the curriculum. They sang, yelled, and blew horns late into the night to torture their sleeping professors. They set fire to school buildings, smoked faculty out of their offices, and rolled flaming tar barrels across campus. At Yale students detonated a bomb, occupied buildings, and drove back a local militia. People got killed in campus riots. Somebody lost an eye.

In 1836, for example, University of Virginia students rioted after the faculty informed them that their muskets would be confiscated. That night dozens of students descended upon campus buildings to do as much property damage as possible. They threw rocks till "scarcely a pane of glass in the professor's houses . . . was left unbroken"; they occupied buildings and destroyed furniture; they produced a "continuous roar of musketry." They used those muskets—alongside an impressive collection of pistols and rifles—to create an intimidating chaos. Faculty members feared for their lives and a militia was brought in to quell the violence. Sixty-six students were expelled.

Expulsions were common. After one riot at Harvard, 62 percent of the graduating class was expelled. Princeton once expelled more than half its student body. In an effort to make the punishment as powerful a deterrent as possible, college presidents agreed among themselves not to admit students who had been kicked out of other institutions. There was one lone exception: Eliphalet Nott, the president of Union College in Schenectady, New York. Defying the consensus, Nott took in the errant sons of the other colleges, which may be one reason why, in the year 1825, Union College became home to one of the biggest rebellions of all: Kappa Alpha, the first social fraternity.

Greek life is thoroughly embedded in higher education today, but at first the two were at odds. The men who started fraternities did so specifically to cultivate values that their professors opposed. They rejected the religious values held by their pious professors and lauded the skills they believed would be useful for winning in *this* life, not the next. Instead of humility, equality, and morality, fraternities promoted status, exclusion, and indulgence. At a time when the declaration that "all men are created equal" was still freshly penned—however imperfectly it was applied—fraternity men lauded hierarchy. They used their clubs to isolate themselves from and claim superiority over "blue skins," their slur for their middle-class peers. Their attitude was summed up by one nineteenth-century Virginian. "I am an aristocrat," he said. "I love liberty; I hate equality." Fraternities, with their rules about who could and couldn't join, seemed decidedly undemocratic, even unAmerican.

Wealthy young men loved the idea of starting exclusive clubs in defiance of their professors, but faculty and administrators did not. "I would incomparably rather resign my place," wrote the president of Brown University in the mid-1800s, "than allow young men the right to meet in secret when they choose without knowledge of the Faculty." College presidents were worried that nothing good could come from young men conspiring out from under the careful supervision of their elders.

In 1863, the third president of Amherst confidentially asked his fellow college presidents what they thought of the societies, and the consensus was resounding. "They have led to greater unkindness and ill feeling than almost any thing else in college," replied one president. "Their general effect is to sow dissensions and produce factions," wrote another. They were described as "evil" and a "plague"; eliminating them would be "a great blessing" and "an occasion to rejoice." College presidents made valiant efforts to close them down, but they consistently failed. In just a few decades, there were 299 chapters of 22 fraternities at 71 colleges.

Infused with a rebelliousness that was their birthright, fraternities incubated a lifestyle that revolved around recklessness and irresponsibility. Members encouraged one another to neglect their studies and mocked those who were earnest about getting an education, disparagingly calling academically hardworking students "digs" and "grinds." Nicholas Syrett, the scholar who penned the definitive history of white fraternities, wrote that by the early 1900s it was "glaringly obvious" that, "for the most part, fraternity men did not study much, dedicating themselves instead to extracurricular activities, camaraderie, athletics, and having fun."

To these preoccupations, fraternities would eventually add sexual conquest. Before the 1900s, fraternity men had sex mostly with prostitutes, poor women, and women they enslaved. Early fraternity men enjoyed these activities—"I did get one of the nicest pieces of ass some day or two ago," wrote one brother to another in 1857—but it wasn't a *game*. The women they had sex with weren't their social equals, so they had little power to negotiate sexual terms. Since men needed no skill to get access to the women's bodies, there was little basis for masculine rivalry.

By 1930, though, women made up 40 percent of the national collegiate population and college was becoming a place where young men and women of the same class mingled relatively unsupervised. This changed the way fraternity men thought about sex. Once recreational, it became increasingly competitive. Extracting sexual favors from women who weren't supposed to give them out became a primary way that frat boys earned the respect and admiration of their brothers.

Partly in response, the criteria for membership shifted to reflect the social and sexual functions of fraternity life as much as its economic elitism. As a dean at Princeton put it in 1931, frats still preferred to pledge rich men, but they mostly just wanted members who weren't "personally unattractive" or, in the parlance of the time, "wet": "The question of family will enter in only if he wishes to make the most exclusively snobbish upper-crust fraternities or clubs," the dean wrote, "and even there family cannot prevail over 'wetness.'"

The modern frat boy was born.

By this time popular interest in college life had reached a fever pitch and the fraternity man was at the center of the story. His way of doing college was so frequently depicted, so relentlessly glamorized, and so ceaselessly centered, that it had become impossible to imagine college without him. And, rather quickly—and here is where his story meets the stories of so many college students in America today—his way of doing college became *the* way of doing college.

Soon it seemed as though everyone sailed through higher education as flippantly as the frat boy. In the newly popular college-themed novel, characters of all types socialized with the other sex, drank alcohol illegally, and danced jauntily to a music called jazz. Party-focused exposés of student life were so ubiquitous, and so thoroughly void of any discussion of academics, that the dean of men at the University of Wisconsin complained that college students were unfairly portrayed as "low grade morons with flapping sox, fur coats, rickety Fords and not an idea in their heads beyond necking, booze, and sex literature." Frat culture had become what *Life* magazine dubbed "youth culture," and it was all about having fun.

For a while, college administrators continued to try to control students, employing curfews, adult residence hall monitors, punishments for drinking and sexual activity, and other rules and practices meant to protect students from themselves. Rules were especially strict for women. Eventually, the baby boomers put an end to that control. Chafing under the restrictions on their freedom, they demanded to be regarded as the legal adults they were, and they got their wish.

By the time the sexual revolution was in full swing, colleges were treating students more or less like adults. For the first time, they were free to do just about whatever they wanted, so long as it was legal, with no institutional sanctions. Things got wild. As the civil rights leader Malcolm X observed in 1965, "I imagine that one of the biggest troubles with colleges is there are too many distractions, too much panty-raiding, fraternities, and boola-boola and all of that."

When *Animal House* was released in 1978, the alcohol industry saw an opportunity and aggressively ramped up marketing on campus. They started advertising in school newspapers, erecting massive inflatable beer cans at sporting events, promoting drink specials at nearby bars and clubs, and hiring students as representatives of their brands to give beer away for free. They spent millions in the 1980s to convince students that "it's naturally part of college life to drink."

Between the vision of college life promulgated by the alcohol industry and the founding of Kappa Alpha more than 150 years before, college life had steadily transformed. Nothing emerged to stop or slow the march toward more and more fun, until 1984. That year the U.S. government initiated an effort to reduce highway deaths, informing states that it would cut their transportation budget allocation if they didn't raise the legal drinking age from eighteen to twenty-one. By 1987, all states had complied and campuses were held accountable for policing underage drinking in residence halls.

Still, collegiate life was far too drenched in drink to be derailed by such a little thing. College drinking didn't slow down during Prohibition, and it didn't slow down in the 1980s. The new drinking age succeeded only in driving much of the drinking off-campus. Today, if students want to party—and they do—they're probably going to do it in rented houses, bars and clubs, sorority functions at local businesses, stadium parking lots, or fraternities.

That is how Naomi and Mara ended up going Greek.

◆   ◆   ◆

When Naomi enrolled at Penn State she discovered that, like many students today, she was required to live on campus for her first year. She was eighteen and it was well past 1987. She couldn't legally drink, and her resident advisor enforced the rules. She likely felt comfortable pregaming in her dorm, but the real raucous all-out partying and drunkenness couldn't happen there.

Her best bet was to go to an off-campus, private location. As a freshman, her networks were limited mostly to other first-year students who also lived in dorms. Like Mara, she probably didn't know many juniors or seniors and, if she did, she didn't know them well enough to get invited to their house parties. There were also obstacles to drinking in bars: namely, obtaining a fake ID and the fear of getting caught (in Pennsylvania, the penalties were a $300 fine and up to ninety days in jail). The National Panhellenic Conference forbids sororities from serving alcohol in their homes, so partying at sororities wasn't an option either. Fraternities were among the few places Naomi could party like she believed college students should.

At colleges like Mara's and Naomi's, the men of Greek row are able to corner the market on college partying. In fact, membership in old-line social fraternities and sororities—those whose members are still mostly heterosexual, white, and wealthy—soared after the drinking age was raised. Raising the legal drinking age also resulted in an increase in patronage of nearby drinking establishments.

This is where Alondra, another eager partier, went for fun. Fraternities weren't allowed to have houses at her college, so students got drunk and danced at an eighteen-and-over bar and grill called Murphy's that billed itself as the "number one college bar in America" and a club with the motto "Leave your dignity at the door." Hookups at Murphy's were so common that students referred to them as "Murphy make-outs." "It's the center point of it all," one wrote. "Girls and boys alike who want an easy hookup can go to Murphy's and almost have that guaranteed." Perhaps especially on 50-cent shot night. Inside, other than the fact that students had to (barely) buy drinks, the scene was hardly distinguishable from a traditional fraternity party. Alondra reported one night that she "saw at least fifteen couples making out on the dance floor" and a couple "doing questionable acts" in a booth. There was "lots of *very* dirty dancing," she emphasized, and "men on the prowl."

Most colleges have an adjacent strip of bars and clubs that draw in underage students with drink specials and make a ruse out of checking IDs. The University of Wisconsin has State Street and Louisiana State University has Tigerland, a cluster of bars that offer $3 pitchers, host midget wrestling, and spark fistfights. "Tonight's forecast," read a recent tweet from one of the favorites, Reggie's, "low standards, and poor decisions with a large chance of beer showers." "If you're a freshman," says an LSU student about the place, "you must experience this place or you can't really say you were a freshman."

At UC Santa Barbara—a campus on which Greek life is only moderately prominent—students just party in the streets. On a four-block drive colloquially called DP, houses with up to fifteen rooms rented by groups of students serve as a de facto Greek row. Just as students know they can skirt liquor laws and campus rules at a fraternity house, they know they can go to Del Playa Drive and party pretty much as hard as they want.

At Princeton, students congregate in on-campus "eating clubs," all mixed-gender since a 1990 court order. At Harvard, there are single-sex social organizations called "final clubs," now under pressure from the university to integrate. Writing about both, journalist Bryce Sopher explains, "The clubs have a monopoly on spaces where underage students can consume alcohol without fear of legal repercussions." The final clubs occupy mansions in Harvard Square and some host parties that allow only members and conventionally attractive young women to attend. The eating clubs occupy mansions on Prospect Avenue, or "the Street," and throw large parties open to everyone.

Locations vary, but wherever the party occurs, it's at least a little inspired by those first fraternity boys. Their lifestyle has become a part of college life for all. Excited to live it up, lots of students arrive on campus ready to go wild, break the rules, and flirt with peril. Like those errant men almost two hundred years ago, they want their partying to smack of revolt.

◆   ◆   ◆

In *Getting Wasted*, sociologist Thomas Vander Ven describes the typical college party as a good, frothy mixture of "dramatic drunkenness, human wreckage, and primitive behavior." It's mayhem, "temporary derangement," an excuse for "a few hours of insanity." Vander Ven was the one who coined the term "drunkworld" to capture the sense that a college party is a world apart, a different universe with disorienting and disordered laws. "Things get out of hand," Vander Ven observes, "but in an entertaining sort of way."

A Duke student described college partying as a "whirlwind of drunkenness and horniness." Those are the two main ingredients. In fact, students from Bowdoin, the University of Pennsylvania, and the University of Illinois at Chicago have all used the phrase "hand-in-hand" to describe the relationship between partying and hooking up. "That's the culture," wrote one of my students. "You go to a party together, everyone gets wasted, and the goal of the night is to get some." It's "more than just a norm," insisted another, "it is near an obligation!" Sex and alcohol, she continues, are the two essential ingredients for any college party that is deemed "fun," and the potential for sexual contact is quite often "the only reason students socialize." It's "what *all* the parties are about," wrote a third with finality.

Of course, some students absolutely love this. At the University of Pennsylvania, an enthusiastic female student wrote, "Sometimes, we just want to have sex for sex's sake. What's wrong with that?" At Princeton, a woman found hookups to be "rewarding, mutually fulfilling and memorable." "From a single guy's point of view," explained a student at Yale, "I find few things more fun than going out at night and seeing what I can come home with." One of my female students put it like this: "Practically unlimited and uninterrupted sex whenever I feel like it? I don't think I could pass that offer up." She was delighted by hookup culture.

Students who are on the fence about whether to hook up, though, can find that doing so can feel, as four of my students separately intoned, "inevitable." It certainly felt that way for Mara. She described five hookups in her first year, but only a couple of times were they intentional. The rest were "happenstance." One night, for example, she found herself stranded at a house party at a college across town. Her two girlfriends had disappeared and she watched as the first floor of the house slowly emptied out.

She found herself alone with an acquaintance who lived there. When she told him that she wasn't sure how to get home, he gestured hospitably to a threadbare tan couch that she remembered seeing someone spill beer on earlier in the night. "At this point it was very late and I was very tired," she recalled, "so I figured I just had to take my chances."

She accepted his hospitality, but she didn't take the couch. Not because it was less than inviting, which it was, but because she felt obligated to hook up with her host. In her mind, she owed him a hookup because he was "providing shelter." Sleeping on the couch was akin to having bad manners. They hooked up but it was "low-key," she reported, and they went to sleep pretty quickly. "I was VERY lucky that this guy ended up not being creepy," she wrote in retrospect.

Mara may have been lucky, and sexual coercion by peers is a serious problem on college campuses, but her story reveals a different kind of coercive pressure. In fact, she specified that she generally didn't feel pressured by men. She knew that she could say no, and felt capable of doing so, but hookups were so powerfully built into the party script that it seemed wrong not to go along. Saying no to a hookup at that stage of the night was like going for a jog in a tuxedo or taking your cat to the park. It was just *weird*. She wasn't always motivated enough to make things weird. "It was only worth making a scene if I really didn't want to [do it]," she explained. "If I didn't really care, it would just continue." So, there were several instances in which she hooked up with a guy because it felt like it was just the thing to do.

Temptation, opportunity, and "happenstance" accumulate over time. Another student named Sondra described how she just "let a kiss happen." "He introduced himself to me," she elaborated, "and we suddenly realized we both were from Montana, so we spent the whole night talking and drinking out of red cups." That was the first night. She could tell he was interested in hooking up, but she wasn't attracted to him. So, they chatted and nothing happened. They chatted again for the next few weekends. "We'd drink and talk," she recalled, "and he would hit on me but I would leave before anything happened." Then, about a month after they met, they had a hookup that proceeded to intercourse. "I finally gave in," she wrote with resignation. Sooner or later even students who aren't inclined to hook up drink a little too much, have a night where they feel like celebrating, or run into someone who is really cute, and the next thing they know, they've hooked up.

If hookups sometimes sound like the inevitable fender bender, other times they sound like high-impact collisions. "I arrived on campus with my innocence in my left hand, my morals in my right. I dropped them within two weeks of my arrival and they fell to the ground and crumbled," recalled one of my female students. "I have always been a very sexual person," worried another, "but I had values. College seemed to strip them away from me." "It is the fact that college students are so bluntly given the opportunity to change that makes it so tempting," observed a male student. For young people who are still learning how to manage sexual desire, college parties combining sex with sensory overload and mind-altering substances can be overwhelming.

It was certainly overwhelming to Arman. He was a deeply spiritual student who had come to the U.S. for college only to discover a way of life that seemed intensely foreign, frightening, and enticing. Hookup culture shook his religious belief to its foundation. "It's been a major shock," he wrote. He described overhearing elaborate and explicit hookup stories, watching students flirt on the quad and grind on the dance floor, and getting bold and assertive sexual signals from women. It was, he wrote, "beyond anything I have experienced back home." Arman was unnerved.

He was deeply torn as to whether to participate. He was "stuck," he wrote, "between a sexually conservative background and a relatively sexually open world." Should he "embrace, accept and join in?" Or, he wondered, using the past tense like a Freudian slip, should he "remember who I was and deprive myself of the things I actually and truly want deep down inside?"

He struggled. "I find myself in conflict with myself very often," he wrote. "Always having to internally fight the desire to do sexual things with girls is not easy. The temptations are high." Eventually, he admitted to having "occasionally succumbed." One night he went to a party, drank, and kissed a girl on the dance floor. When the alcohol wore off, he was appalled at his own behavior. "How much shame I have brought onto myself," he recalled with anguish, though he had only gone so far as "groping" and "deep kissing." Ultimately, his feelings were of the deepest ambivalence. "I felt more free and unbounded," he confessed, "but at the same time, guilt beyond imagination." He would lose his virginity to a girl he hooked up with later that semester.

◆　　◆　　◆

In some ways, residential colleges today aren't that different from the colonial colleges of the 1700s. They still coordinate groups of young people, organizing their lives in sometimes rigid ways. Many colleges are, in other words, still "total institutions," planned entities that collect large numbers of like individuals, cut them off from the wider society, and provide for all their needs. Prisons, mental hospitals, army barracks, and nursing homes are total institutions.

So are cruise ships, cults, convents, and summer camps. Behemoths of order, these organizations swallow up their constituents and structure their lives.

Each year, millions of young people are swallowed by thousands of college campuses. They are sequestered in dormitories. Their food, rest, and work is bureaucratically regimented. Rooms and roommates are assigned. Classes are scheduled. Minimum units are specified. Work study is doled out. The gym doors are opened. Cafeteria hours are posted. Food is prepared. And activities are organized.

When students move into dorms, they are truly *in* the institution. To live on campus is to be a part of something wholly, which is part of the appeal. Students are free to leave, but there is no need to do so. Most everything essential is provided for them and, barring that, there is a campus store with clothes, school supplies, electronics, hygiene products, and any other essentials they could possibly want.

In both large and small ways, though never completely, students become one with the institution. Its rules, scripts, languages, logics, technologies, timetables, and architectures become their own. Like the nun who recites traditional prayers, the soldier who reports for breakfast at 0500 hours, and the cult member who tends the garden, students' lives play out within a structure that they don't control, but largely accept and even embrace.

Because many colleges are total institutions and hookup culture is totally institutionalized, colleges don't just control what students learn, when they eat, where they sleep, and how they exercise; they also have an influence on whether and how they have sex. Thanks to the last few hundred years, most colleges now offer a very specific kind of nightlife, a drunkworld that is also the site for sex.

Drunkworld incites sexual activity. The delighted, the willing, and many of the reluctant go along. And while students can always break the rules or rewrite the scripts, in general hookups follow the logic of the institution: they occur at predetermined places and on particular days of the week, allowing students to fit sex into their schedule in a way that is compatible with the college's needs. Sex is now a part of how students do higher education. That's why it can feel inevitable.

Of course, one way to avoid the inevitability of hooking up is to refuse to get off the boat, to stay buttoned up tight in one's cabin and in bed by nine. And people do. Many do, in fact. They opt out. Like the reluctant cruise vacationer, they're on board but not on board. They've paid for their ticket and they're along for the ride, whether they want to be or not. As one student wrote forebodingly, "Even if you aren't hooking up, there is no escaping hookup culture."

4

Opting Out

Emory was a romantic in both the literary and interpersonal sense of the word. He was majoring in creative writing with the hope of becoming a novelist and thought of himself as a student of the human condition. Intensely interested in people, he wanted true connections, not furtive hookups. "I am . . . soft-hearted and hypersensitive," he explained, "more interested in the timeless and seemingly archaic ideals of romantic love and relationships than in the more fast-paced, modern, 'fuck and run'—to quote Liz Phair—thoroughly unromantic, sexual lifestyle."

Though college men have the reputation of being quite keen to have casual sex, many college men are not. In fact, the Online College Social Life Survey shows us that men and women are equally likely to report zero hookups upon graduation. Certainly some students just never get lucky, and maybe more men than women are in that category, but most students who don't hook up do so by choice.

"I simply cannot behave that way," is how Emory put it, referring to the hookups he saw all around him. He's not the only guy who feels that way. One man at the University of Houston, for example, insisted that sex was "super personal and super intimate," not something he engaged in with just anyone. "It would be so uncomfortable to have sex with someone I don't know or with a friend," agreed a guy at UC Santa Cruz. "I prefer building a relationship and talking," said a student at the University of Florida in reference to hooking up, "so something like that wouldn't work for me." "For me, [sex is] definitely something you build up to," explained another at the University of Georgia.

These men, like 34 of my 101 students, opted out of hooking up. I call them "abstainers," students who decide that they'd rather have no sex at all than obey the rules of hookup culture. Most of my abstainers opted out because casual sex didn't appeal to them. One planned on saving sex for marriage. A few were facing family crises that took up their time and energy. Some had simply had enough of hookup culture in high school. One identified as asexual. Some of these abstainers wavered, but most, like Emory, were confident that they were making the right choice for themselves.

Not all abstainers saw it strictly as a personal choice, though. Some simply couldn't easily take advantage of the idea that sex should be fun. Jaslene, for example, a devout black lesbian who purposefully chose to attend a religious school, was one of them. "I do not fuck, make out with, or even kiss my friends," she wrote early in our semester together. Statistically speaking, I was not surprised.

Hooking up isn't "for black people," she stated bluntly. Like other nonwhite students, despite being quite beautiful, Jaslene was disadvantaged by the "erotic marketplace." She was frank, saying, "Black females do not fit the conventional standard of beauty." Both academic research and data from online dating sites suggest she's right. There is a hierarchy of sexual desirability. White men and women, black men, and Asian women are at the top of this hierarchy; black women and Middle Eastern and Asian men tend to fall to the bottom.

Consistent with the erotic marketplace, the Online College Social Life Survey shows that black women hook up less often than women and men of other races, with the exception of Asian students of both sexes. Asian women likely opt out voluntarily, as both men and women tend to prefer them, all else being equal, but many Asian men feel like they're not even considered as potential sexual partners by their peers. Asao, a student of Japanese and Mexican descent, who was interviewed for a study of raves, felt so discounted by his peers that he left campus altogether when he wanted to party. At raves, he said: "You can be anybody. Black, white, Mexican, Filipino, you can be an alien, it don't matter." An Asian male enrolled at Occidental College agreed. Raves are "something that you don't have to, like, be accepted to go," he explained. "You can just pay and have fun without racial discrimination."

Among my students, those who were privileged in the erotic marketplace sometimes expressed sexual preferences that reflected the hierarchy. They said that they were "not attracted to Asian men in the slightest," "mostly attracted to white people," "just really into white chicks," and "only . . . attracted to Caucasian men." Some of the students who expressed these preferences were white themselves and others were not. Students who weren't at the top of the hierarchy noticed. "Even the Asian girls that I liked," Asao said with frustration, "they would always like white guys." "I have noticed a lot of guys going after white girls," reported one of my African American female students. "Girls here, especially white girls," one of my Latino students observed, "would rather hook up with other white guys."

Of course, some of the race differences reflect the fact that students of color are less inclined to hook up to begin with. Compared to white students, black students are more actively religious, have more conservative views about sexuality, are more likely to be virgins, report stronger gender egalitarianism, and have lower rates of alcohol consumption, none of which makes them well-suited to the kind of casual sex happening on campus. "It's just not how I was raised," insisted a black man enrolled at the University of Southern California. Black men at Middlebury College and Ohio State felt the same. "I know we don't do what the white kids do," one said. "If I started hooking up," said another, "my friends would be saying I'm, like, 'acting white.'"

In some ways, hookup culture *is* a white thing. Men of color are stereotyped as hypersexual, even dangerously so, prompting one black man to abstain from hooking up because he didn't think he could get away with the same level of sexual aggressiveness as white men. Similarly, women of color have never been able to fully embrace the logic of sexual liberation that is captivating to so many white women. At the same time that middle-class white women were put on pedestals as an example of asexual wholesomeness, women of color were hypersexualized as "Jezebels," "hot Latinas," geishas, and "sexy squaws." So, for students of color, embracing hookup culture threatens to reaffirm stereotypes about their race, not break apart stereotypes about their gender.

Students of color are also more likely to be low-income, and poor and working-class students of all races hook up less than their more affluent peers. This may be because they are already on campus against all odds. Unlike middle- and upper-class students, who can get away with getting into trouble, they usually have to be squeaky clean to get to college at all. Low-income teenagers, for example, are more than twice as likely to be arrested for drug crimes as middle-class youth, despite significantly lower rates of drug use, and if they get pregnant, they're less likely than more affluent youth to have an abortion.

Roslyn, a part-white part-Latina student from a humble economic background, recognized these realities. "Some of us with serious financial aid and grants or scholarships," she wrote, "tend to avoid high-risk situations." She continued, thoughtfully:

> I feel like students on less or no financial aid have grown up in lives where everything is purchasable and there are not as many consequences: tickets and citations get paid for, your education is paid for, and your drugs and alcohol are paid for, too. I'm not a goody two shoes or anything, and neither is my cousin, but we are very serious and grateful for the opportunities we've been given and don't want to lose them.

Low-income young people who get to college may be more averse to risky behavior than middle- and upper-class ones, and they may retain that cautionary approach to life even after they get to campus.

Working-class students may also be studying harder to make up for a substandard high school education or working to make ends meet, which leaves less time for partying. Or they might be living at home to save money. The family of one commuting student, Kim-Li, had only one car, so she got a ride to school every day from her parents. They dropped her off just before 7 a.m. on their way to work and picked her up at 6:15 p.m. on their way home. As you might imagine, she spent a lot of time hanging out in the library and was almost never on campus after dinnertime. "Dreadful," is how she described it, "because that is the time when all of the exciting things begin to happen on campus."

For Jaslene, though, religion was the biggest factor. "I want to be faithful to God," she said simply. Religious students aren't any less likely to hook up than non-religious ones (Muslims and evangelical Christians hook up a little less, Catholics hook up more), but regular attendance at services does appear to correlate with lower levels of casual sexual activity for women. In contrast, men who attend church are actually more likely to hook up than non-religious men.

If her race, economic background, and religion hadn't soured Jaslene on hooking up, though, it is likely that her sexual orientation would have. It depends on the school, but hookup culture is usually indifferent to or unwelcoming of non-heterosexual students. Recent profiles of sex on campus in *Rolling Stone* and *New York* magazines make sex at Syracuse, Tulane, NYU, and Bard seem like an experimentalist's dream, with demi-sexuals, queers, non-binary genders, and a general distaste for labels, but I suspect they're overstating their case.

Wren, for example, described her secular, left-leaning campus as "quietly oppressive." She identified as pansexual and was hoping for a "queer haven," but she was let down. People weren't overtly homophobic very often, and in classrooms her peers eagerly dismantled the gender binary and theorized queer sex, but outside of the classroom, and especially at parties, they "reverted back into gendered codes" and "masculine bullshit." When night fell, students weren't feminist or queer at all. Everything, she observed, was "superhetero." She wrote transfer essays and almost didn't come back after her first year.

In contrast, when Lanie arrived on campus, she didn't even try to integrate into the wider hookup scene. "I definitely like girls," she said right away in her journal and immediately joined the LGBTQ club. "Quickly," she wrote happily, "I was flirting with multiple girls, and even hooking up (no strings attached) with one of them." She met lots of women she liked and enjoyed being openly gay for the first time. Her group of friends brought more and more women into the fold as the year progressed and there were some sweet stories of lesbian sexual debuts. Lanie didn't opt out of hooking up, but she arguably opted out of hookup *culture*. She kept to a close-knit group of out lesbians who built their own community. Accordingly, she had a different experience than Wren.

Queer-friendly niches exist on many campuses, to be sure, but they're niches, an alternative scene to a much larger, more prominent, and strongly heterocentrist one. Most big parties are not particularly friendly to non-heterosexuals, while queer-friendly ones are less frequent and usually don't attract many non-queer students. Likewise, conversations about same-sex hookups don't pervade campuses the way talk about heterosexual ones do. Queer students often thrive in college, but they generally remain on the margins and exert a negligible social impact on the larger culture.

Meanwhile, lesbians like Jaslene and Lanie, and pansexuals like Wren, often don't feel comfortable in the dominant gender-conformist heterosexual scene. It "just screams so much like prostitution to me," said one. "You know, even if [girls are] not literally having sex with the guys, it's just like they're . . . selling their flirtiness for beer or something, and that's just so not me." A UC Santa Barbara student who identified as bisexual reported that being out about her sexual orientation at parties attracted a kind of attention that she didn't want. "If a guy finds out I'm bisexual," she said, "it's all of a sudden like, 'threesome?'" Having one's identity sexualized for the benefit of heterosexual men can make the typical college party unpleasant for bisexual and lesbian women.

Parties can be overtly hostile, too. The only same-sex behavior that routinely goes on at college parties is girl-on-girl kissing, an activity that is premised on the assumption that their desire for one another is pretend. It only works, in other words, if the heterosexual women involved feel confident that there are no *actual* queer or queer-curious women at the party. Ironically, one study found that college women who participate in girl-on-girl kissing are more homophobic than women who don't. The irony is not lost on women who are attracted to women, some of whom find it quite obnoxious that heterosexual girls can kiss other girls in public without the risk of reproach, but they can't. "It's making a mockery of us," said one.

◆　　◆　　◆

As a God-fearing black lesbian, Jaslene had little interest in hooking up, but it still felt like a sacrifice. "I feel like I'm missing out on the 'whole college experience,'" she wrote in her journal one day, explaining:

> As much as I hate admitting it to myself, I feel incredibly left out . . . because all my friends want to do is hook up and are hooking up with other people, but all I can do is watch or go back to the dorm and do G-rated things.

Jaslene had opted out of hooking up, but she was still in hookup culture and, since her college was a total institution, there was little opportunity to get out. She was having, in other words, the experience of being an "outsider within."

The concept was first used by sociologist Patricia Hill Collins to describe the place that black people have historically held in a white supremacist society. Black people were not allowed to fully participate in white life, but they were still inextricably inside of it. They chauffeured white businessmen, and were privy to the most secret of negotiations. They cooled the foreheads of dying patients, at their bedsides in their final moments. They even nursed white babies, sharing their body's milk with the children of their oppressors. They were literally inside of white bodies, but never an insider. To be an outsider within is to find oneself embedded in a society that isn't for you and is unresponsive or even hostile to your needs.

Hookup culture is not on a par with white supremacy, but the idea of being an outsider within is useful for understanding what it felt like for Jaslene to be inside hookup culture, but not hooking up. It was a feeling that many of my abstainers expressed. Jimena's experience was probably the most extreme illustration of this phenomenon.

Jimena used the phrase "culture shock" to describe her first year in college. Growing up with strict Nicaraguan parents, she had been forbidden to wear makeup and required to wear long skirts and cover her shoulders. They'd told her, and she strongly believed, that "sex is a serious matter" and that bodies should be "respected, exalted, prized." For her, sex was inconceivable in the absence of love, so it's no surprise that hookup culture was jarring. She also just so happened to be placed with the most sexually inconsiderate roommate in all of my students' journals: Cassidy.

Cassidy was very likable and Jimena enjoyed having her as a roommate. She was funny and sweet. She made the school dance team and Jimena, being too coltish for dancing herself, admired her coordination. They got along well, generally speaking, and sometimes had long conversations about trouble with their families. In some ways, they could really relate.

In other ways, though, they were as different as different could be. On their second day on campus, while Jimena was unpacking boxes in their room, Cassidy sat cross-legged on her bunk with her phone up close to her face, narrating Tinder. She swiped right and left and left and right and before long she matched with another new student named Chad. She suggested they all meet for dinner together and they did, after which Jimena went back to her room alone. A few hours later, Cassidy returned, reporting that she had gone back to Chad's to have sex. "I was astounded," Jimena wrote, but Cassidy was just warming up.

Cassidy routinely brought men back to their shared room and it quickly became clear that she was perfectly happy to have sex with her roommate present. The first time it happened, Jimena was watching TV on her computer in bed. It was about four in the afternoon, sunny outside, on the second Saturday since they'd moved in. Cassidy and a guy named Declan had been drinking most of the day and had just come back in from smoking weed. Someone said something about dinner (again) and Declan turned to Cassidy, pulled down her navy blue leggings and underwear and exclaimed, "Dinner's right here!" Cassidy squealed and laughed, falling back on the bed. He climbed on top of her as Jimena spun to face her computer and the wall. "What's happening!" she cried. Cassidy replied: "Sex is happening!"

Jimena froze with her back to the pair. "I was in shock," she said when I asked her why she didn't flee the room. She had never seen two consenting adults having sex before and she was afraid to look. Leaving seemed like the obvious thing to do, but climbing down from her bunk, collecting her things, and getting out the door would have required her to open her eyes. It was strangely easier to just wait it out. So, that's what she did, catching reflected glimpses of Declan's bobbing buttocks each time her screen went black between commercials.

Cassidy would have sex in front of Jimena three times that semester. By the third time, Jimena had figured out how to spot the early signs and quickly gather her things and get out. Students call it being "sexiled," though usually they are given fair warning to get out or stay clear.

When she explained to her roommate that this made her uncomfortable, Cassidy would agree to be more respectful and her exhibitionism would die down for a while, but it was never gone for good. In any case, even when Jimena was spared the front-row seat, Cassidy was eager to share all the details of each and every sexual encounter. "It irritates me," Jimena wrote, but she was a conciliatory person and wanted to get along.

Most abstainers did not have a roommate like Cassidy, though many found themselves occasionally sexiled. Even those who didn't have sexually active roommates felt surrounded by hookup culture, if less explicitly. Petra's experience was more typical. Like Jimena, she had no interest in going to its parties. She and her roommate, she wrote, "do not like to drink or smoke." Nor was she interested in what she knew happened as the night progressed. "How *could* someone!?" she wondered.

She spent most evenings in her dorm room and, especially on Friday and Saturday nights, hookup culture swirled around her. It was routine for her to shuffle in her slippers past women taking selfies in miniskirts. She would brush her teeth alongside women applying eyeliner and listen to them rev one another up for the hunt. She complained gently about the noise: "You can hear every conversation occurring in the hallway even with your door closed because of the cinderblock walls and tile floors." For hours, she wrote, she would listen to the "click-clacking of high heels."

Eventually the women in heels would leave, rowdily, and there would be a reprieve. But they'd come back drunk and disorderly, now with arguments, toasts, crying spells, and elated congratulations. Petra documented one particularly sleepless night. She was jolted awake by someone exclaiming "I am so fucked up right now!" outside her window. It was 3 a.m., the house party had been shut down, and the revelry had moved to the small courtyard between one wing of her residence hall and the other. Students were laughing, chasing one another like schoolchildren, tackling each other on the lawn, and tripping into the bushes underneath Petra's window. Their voices rang across the courtyard as they squealed, called out to one another, and belted out drinking songs. "They were totally wasted," Petra recalled.

Sometimes overhearing her dormmates' excitement about partying and hooking up made her question her priorities. "I feel like I am kind of a weirdo," she wrote late one night. Like Jaslene, she wondered if she was missing out. Other abstainers worried, too, calling themselves "outcasts," "losers," and "prudes." Many said that they felt "lonely," "isolated," or "pathetic." One wrote that hookup culture "effectively forces people to have sex or be seen as some sort of pariah."

◆　　　◆　　　◆

Some of my abstainers' sense of exclusion came not from the decision to abstain itself, but from the fact that they weren't part of hookup culture's conversation. Remember that most students aren't hooking up much to begin with, so it wasn't just the hooking up that made abstainers feel left out. It was their inability to take part in the *talk* about hooking up.

On campus, sexual speculation abounds: Facebook stalking, Instagram hearting, Snapchatting, swiping right, flirting, whispering, relaying messages, and deciphering cryptic texts. Students spend the week planning the weekend. Which parties will they go to? Where do they think other people are going? Who do they want to hook up with? Who do they want to avoid? "Every conversation that my friends and I have," one of my male students wrote excitedly, "revolves around sex in some way." "Hookup culture is all over the place on campus," wrote another. "Every conversation, every meeting is used to create a platform for a potential sexual encounter to occur," wrote a third.

Sometimes the subtle flirting and not-so-subtle propositioning turns into real action. Or, to put it another way, it becomes fodder for the "recap." Mornings after big party nights, there's a ritual retelling of the night before. Students fill their friends in on blurry memories, reassure one another that they didn't act too crazy, stroke the egos of disappointed friends, and brag.

At the University of Southern California, students call it the "morning debrief." It "takes up, like, half our day," said one. "Talking about it is, like, the best." "Who did you hook up with last night?" is the "common question" asked every Sunday morning at Tulane and Connecticut College. "Romantic entanglements at this school," wrote a woman enrolled at Whitman, "end with some juicy new gossip to share at brunch the next morning."

"Most hooking up happens so that someone can say they did something," confirmed one of my female students. Being able to answer yes to the simple question "Did you get some?" prompts a dramatic play-by-play. Doing things outside of students' everyday sexual repertoire is especially exciting, earning others' awe and envy. Anything out of the ordinary—sex in the laundry rooms or in the baseball dugout, sex with ice cubes or erotic toys, threesomes or foursomes, anything new or audacious—can mean an hour or more of story time.

Students go back to their rooms after brunch to edit and upload photos and stories to social media. "I think a lot of our hookup culture and party culture is glamorized," wrote one student, referring to sites like Instagram and Facebook. "A big part of these parties," another explained, "is also taking mobile pictures," and their "sole purpose" is so one's whole social network can see that one is having a GREAT time at college."

For at least one of my abstainers, this had a fortunate upside. Marisol described her previous educational experiences as "freakishly sheltered." She attended private religious schools that, she laughed, were "this sort of rare institution that many believe went extinct right along with orange lipstick." Students were taught that putting on makeup in front of a man was equivalent to undressing in front of him and watched a film in which Ted Bundy, the serial killer, attributed his murderousness to pornography. "To my high school," Marisol wrote, "sex was the sole reason for teenage corruption."

Despite all the fear-mongering, she fell in love with a boy in her sophomore year of high school. Then the unimaginable happened. One night he asked very nicely if he could put his fingers "inside" her and she was struck by a great terror. "A panic gripped me so deeply I couldn't breathe," she recalled. "I started saying NO very loudly repeatedly and then burst into tears." In that moment, memories of being sexually molested as a small child came flooding back to her.

Marisol was devastated. She tried to reconcile the messages she had received her entire life—that sex was "terribly immoral" and that sexually active girls "would be punished by God"—with the sudden realization that she had been touched sexually and perhaps penetrated. She looked around at her high school friends and felt a painful and isolating shame: "All of these girls were completely sexually pure and I had unwillingly experienced sex." For years Marisol held these feelings close to her chest, in silent pain.

Arriving at college changed this. If her high school friends had had positive or negative sexual experiences, Marisol didn't know, but her college friends weren't so reserved. On campus, she wrote, women talked "openly and freely about sex" and many of them, like her, had stories of rape, abuse, and molestation. Being around these women gave Marisol a new way to think about what had happened to her. "I have met many girls here who have been sexually assaulted, raped, and molested and have lived through it," she explained. "I have been able to truly realize that being molested is simply something that happened to me, it is not and never will be the person I am."

For some abstainers, being around people who were open about their sexual activity was quite good. Marisol needed a different way of thinking about what had happened to her, so the explicitness of hookup culture was helpful. Other students, though, with other crises, found the culture's dominance on campus to be suffocating.

This was true for Laura. About a month after she described grinding as a "bestial rubbing of genitals," she learned that her mom had been diagnosed with breast cancer and she was immediately gripped by an all-consuming and intolerable dread. "In my mind," she said of the day she found out, "she is the way I saw her last at the airport." She wrote in present tense, as if to hold the memory close:

> She hugs me twice ferociously, her collarbones chafing at my neck, a feeling that has come to mean love. I see the chance of rain in her eyes and give her a sideways look. "Mooom," I say in the voice of an exasperated six-year-old girl and she rearranges her face. I tell her I love her for the second time in ten seconds and it feels urgent. She rejoins quickly and then she is in the car. I am walking away and in spite of my bags and my irrational fear that there is no way I can make my plane, I am turning, looking back.

The reasons for her mother's urgency at the airport had become all too clear, but the semester marched forward, not yielding to the life-and-death battle being fought 1,000 miles away. The week her mother underwent surgery, Laura's writing started to sound hollow, as if she were witnessing college life from far, far away.

I learn about infants' ability to comprehend the continuity of objects in cognitive science class and my mind rebuts, "but my mom is in the hospital." I try to sleep and my mind protests, "Do you know that your mom is in the hospital?"

Numbly, Laura entertained her friend's dalliances in hookup culture:

My friend Kelsey twirls in her new skirt, worries about a stain, clips it with a pin because it is too loose. Do I think that it will look okay if she wears it "with a tight shirt"? She is very, very worried about a kind-of-date she has with an older boy.

Laura encouraged Kelsey to be herself and have a good time. "I listen while she complains about him and the way he says Priuses are 'girl cars,'" she wrote, and she conceded, "Priuses may be girl cars, but does she know, has she heard that my mom is in the hospital?"

Overwhelmed with anxiety and worry, her friends' sexual and romantic flings seemed trifling, yet she felt obligated to indulge them. She pretended to care about their small interpersonal dramas, suppressing the voice inside her that was ever more insistently reminding her that her mother was sick. It was exhausting. "Even the frivolous superficiality of the hookup culture," she wrote, "does not come without a stifling, unbearable weight."

◆   ◆   ◆

Abstainers were at risk of being in "interpersonal purgatory." Those who couldn't or wouldn't talk the talk could be invisible, unintelligible. Jimena tried adding her two cents, for example, but her words bounced off the collective conversation. "When I speak my mind," she wrote, "people laugh at me." She was one of the few students in my sample who would say out loud that hooking up wasn't morally acceptable, for her or for anybody else. Her peers would respond with what came to sound like a refrain: "But this is college," "This is how college *is*," and "This is the time to do this." One guy said, mockingly: "Oh what? You're saving yourself for marriage? That goes out the window when you get to college." Then he offered to hook up with her if she would consent to a threesome. Her ideas didn't fit, so neither did she.

Other much less conservative students, like Violet, had a similar experience. Violet had no moral qualms about hooking up; she just felt "awkward" about going to parties because she had a boyfriend who lived across town, so she had nothing to contribute to the conversation on campus. She felt, moreover, that more party-oriented women were suspicious of her opinion of them: "I often feel like the other people feel like I'm judging them for drinking or hooking up," she reported, though she wasn't.

This left her feeling disconnected from her peers. She had exactly three friends: her roommate and the two women who lived next door. "We stay in our dorm rooms most of the time," she confessed. She suspected that there were other women like her outside of her immediate environment, but she didn't know where they were. She was diagnosed with clinical depression in the spring and attributed it partly to the lack of "fun" and social support.

Near the end of the year she tried to get up the courage to go to a party. It was one of the biggest dances of the year and "everyone kept talking about it." Alone in her dorm room, she picked out an outfit: a fitted heather-grey shirt with cap sleeves and black pants atop short slouchy black boots. She liked what she saw in the mirror, but she wasn't sure what to do. "The problem was," she explained, "I didn't have anyone to go with." She thought about going by herself, but was nervous that she wasn't dressed quite right. Without a bunch of women to pregame with, she couldn't know what anyone else was wearing and she didn't want to stand out. She looked at herself in the mirror again and lost heart. She flounced down on her bed, pulled off her boots, and put her pajamas back on.

Like Violet, many students felt that their sex life and their social life were one and the same. They said so often and explicitly: "I feel that if I don't engage in the party scene," wrote one, "I am excluded from making friends with many of my fellow classmates." Partying and hooking up, insisted another, "is the only way to make friends." "Hookup culture = social life," another concluded, simply making an equation. "If you do not have sex," one student wrote forcefully, "you are not in the community."

But why didn't Violet make friends with Emory, the romantic; Jimena, Laura, or Petra; or any of the other abstainers who lived more than a dorm room away? A third of students opted out, certainly enough to build a vibrant alternative community. If abstainers were lonely, it wasn't because they were alone.

This flummoxed sociologists Elizabeth Armstrong and Laura Hamilton, too. For their research, they secured a room in a residence hall and put together a team of graduate and undergraduate students to occupy it. They stayed throughout the academic year, becoming a part of the lives of the women who lived on the hall. They found students like Violet at their college as well, ones who didn't make friends with either their party-oriented peers or one another. They came to call students like these "isolates."

Eventually, they concluded that isolates were *so* isolated that they didn't even realize that other isolates were out there. One of their students, for example, said, "I would hear things going on . . . and kind of feel left out because all the other women were friends," revealing by her choice of words that she believed she was uniquely friendless, the only person on the floor who didn't bond with her dormmates.

Students who are actively partying and hooking up occupy a lot of psychic space. On the quad, they're boisterous and engage in loud greetings. They sunbathe and play catch on the green at the first sign of spring. At games, they paint their faces, throw their hands in the air, and sing fight songs. They use the campus as their playground. Their bodies—most often white, slim, athletic, and well dressed—convey an assured calm. They move among their peers with confidence and authority. "For some reason," observed one of my Latina students, "they exude dominance." All that click-clacking up and down the hallway, hooting and hollering about hookups, and uploading, tagging, and liking online make them hypervisible. Everyone else fades in comparison.

◆　　◆　　◆

Imagine for a moment Mara, Naomi, and the guy with sunglasses on the lawn of that 126-year-old frat house. These are the ones who say yes, who are eager or at least willing to sample what hookup culture has to offer.

Zoom out and you can see the entire university: classrooms, labs, offices, and administrative buildings; theaters, auditoriums, and galleries; sports fields, stadiums, and gymnasiums; health clinics and counseling centers; and residence halls, cafeterias, bookstores, and student centers. Pull a little farther out and you'll see the late-night eateries, drugstores, coffee shops, and entertainment options that serve the campus community, where students buy cold medicine, study, volunteer, catch movies, fall in love, and make friends. Zoom out that far and you can see the total institution with its myriad functions: fun, yes, but also education, research, art, athletics, sustenance, wellness, and jobs that help pay the bills.

In that mix is Petra listening to her floormates get ready for parties; Wren seeking a queer erotic community; Jaslene doing G-rated things; Asao attending raves; Jimena ducking out of her dorm room; Riley trying to loosen up; Kim-Li waiting for the library to open; Alondra dodging Murphy make-outs; Laura agonizing over her mom's illness; Emory happily waiting for love; Roslyn wondering if rich students study; Violet holed up in her dorm room; and all of the other students who animate this book. Zoom out and you see the whole range of personalities and experiences.

There is a wide range of students on campus, but the diversity is sometimes invisible because of the nearly exclusive focus on the ones who flock to the parties to hook up. For better or worse, they have been held up as the model for what college life should be like ever since *Life* conflated fraternity culture with "youth culture" in the 1920s. And still today, since they make for much more salacious stories, they're usually the only students who appear in the news and opinion pages, whether the spin is positive or negative.

When we zoom in on wherever it is that students like Mara, Naomi, and men in sunglasses go to party, we lose sight of a full third of the college population: the abstainers, the romantics, the devout, and those who are too worried to have sex for fun. And they pay a price. To not hook up can mean missing out on friendships, adventures, and the collective conversation. It can feel like they're missing out, even, on the "whole college experience."

The other two-thirds of students are not willing to miss out. They decide that social irrelevance is too considerable a penalty to pay. Or they're curious about casual sex. Or they get swept into the "inevitable" hookups. Or they believe that college is the time to go a little wild. And, so, they do.

Opting In

The gay liberation movement began on a Friday. It was summer in New York. It was 1969. The event was routine, a police roundup of the motley crew that frequented the Stonewall Inn, one of Greenwich Village's known gay bars. But that night the bar's regulars had had enough. "The scene became explosive," reported the *Village Voice*. The gay, trans, and genderqueer men and women of the bar fought back. They pelted the police officers with pocket change, beer cans, and bottles, shouting, "Gay power!"

The police were forced to barricade themselves inside the bar. "The sound filtering in [from outside didn't] suggest dancing faggots any more," recalled a reporter inside with them, describing it as "like a powerful rage bent on vendetta." They set the place on fire. When more officers arrived, they were able to temporarily beat back the rebellion and snuff out the flames, but there was no stopping the revolt. The next night more than a thousand people returned to protest on behalf of gay rights. The civil disobedience lasted several days.

A few weeks later, members of the queer community in New York formed the Gay Liberation Front. On the first anniversary of the Stonewall rebellion, the first gay pride parades were held in New York, Los Angeles, Chicago, and San Francisco. Before long, the American Psychological Association would retract its claim that homosexuality was a mental disorder. Four years later, there were almost eight hundred gay and lesbian organizations in the United States. Inspired by "black is beautiful," "gay is good" became a rallying cry, and gay men and lesbians began coming out in record numbers.

This was the political context in which gay enclaves in places like Lower Manhattan, West Hollywood, and San Francisco came to thrive. People living in less welcoming parts of the country were drawn to these "gayborhoods," where they could work, shop, and play in gay-owned businesses with gay employees alongside other gay people in their own sort of total institution. Gay and bisexual men were especially likely to fill up these neighborhoods, as women were still fighting for the freedom to be able to live as independently from men as men could from women.

For gay men living in these places, sex was about more than pleasure. Since homosexuality was taboo and even criminal, being sexually active, especially wildly so, felt like liberation. It was a way to reject the degradation that they had lived with their entire lives. It "was very liberating because it removed shame," said a man interviewed for the documentary *Gay Sex in the '70s*. "It replaced shame, in fact, with great joy and self-discovery of your body and other people's bodies and loving each other and, I mean, all the good stuff about free love." With marriage an impossible dream and HIV an as-yet unimagined nightmare, they saw no reason not to embrace their freedom wholly.

◆   ◆   ◆

"The hookup culture is a gift from the gays to the straights," laughed a senior at Georgetown. She may be right. If the young people living it up in cities in the 1920s are the hookup generation's ideological grandparents, the gay men of the 1970s might be their two dads. Gay men arguably invented the lifestyle; we may be seeing it in colleges today because young students on residential campuses are situated similarly to those who fled to gay enclaves during the height of gay liberation.

Today's students can technically marry anyone they want, but to many it feels like the wrong time to be thinking about commitment. Traditional-age college students are in what Clark University psychologist Jeffrey Arnett calls "emerging adulthood," a period during which they focus on their own personal development. Their lives are unstable and unpredictable. They may move frequently to take advantage of educational opportunities or spend time exploring different occupations. They face a series of institutional hurdles that will take years to clear.

Many students take this period of their lives very seriously, and they are right to do so. For young people without family wealth and connections, there is no guarantee that they'll land in the shrinking middle class. Compared to their parents, today's college students will make less money, have less in the bank, and go into greater debt. More of them will face unemployment and poverty. They'll likely have to work harder and maintain their focus for longer.

If they are successful in landing a white-collar job, they will face the challenge of persisting in their occupation. More than half of full-time salaried workers put in more than forty hours a week, and one in five puts in more than sixty hours. That's twelve hours a day five days a week. If they do that for long enough, maybe at some point they'll be able to pay off their student loans and think about making adult purchases and grown-up decisions. They'll be the lucky ones.

Partly because of these demands, the average age of marriage today is twenty-seven for women and twenty-nine for men; among college graduates, it's even older. The average college student will see ten years pass between their freshman year and their wedding day. In that light, the first year of college can seem like the wrong time to think about settling down or, even worse, being "brainwashed" by love. "It's not that dating relationships don't occur," a male student explained, "but . . . a lot of people look at it as something that they would never do."

Katie Coyle, a female student enrolled at the University of Illinois, tried to put it into perspective, writing:

> We were the generation of high schoolers pressured to do everything: get good grades, have a job, volunteer, participate in clubs, go out, stay in, have friends, have a significant other and exercise, while making sure to have a clean room, get enough sleep and do chores. Now that we're in our own little bubble of just people our age, with no parents to dictate our schedules to us, we're still capable of doing all that, just like we were trained to, but the level of intensity has increased. Classes are harder and clubs are more time-consuming. Just getting enough sleep is hard sometimes and going out and having friends is necessary to blow off some steam, but having a significant other doesn't need to be as important.

"So that's where you get a hookup culture," she concluded. "Let society be aware of that one, because it's not entirely our fault." Excelling in everything, a goal that seems essential to guarantee long-term success, just doesn't leave time for romance.

In the meantime, residential college students are living in dense, relatively homogeneous groups not unlike the gay enclaves that men enjoyed in the 1970s, to which they bring a similar sense of sexual freedom. "At college, there are no parents!" exclaimed one female student, both excited by and a little nervous about the possibilities. A male student wrote gratefully that he was "free from fear that my parents will find out and I will get into trouble." Perhaps for the first time in their lives, young college students don't have to tell someone where they're going or when they're coming home; they can come home drunk or high and no one's going to care; or they can not come home at all. It's quite dramatic to go from living at home to living in a dormitory in just one day. Students notice.

This sense of sexual freedom is not particularly inhibited by concern that they might contract a sexually transmitted infection. The gay men of the 1980s would be shocked to know just how casually many students treat their sexual health today. AIDS ripped through their communities, decimating many gay enclaves. In response, gay men were the first people in history to normalize condom use, to make it a taken-for-granted, non-stigmatized practice, even a moral responsibility. It was one of the fastest and most effective public health campaigns the world has ever seen.

Today's students, though, seem to think they're not at much risk of HIV or any other sexually transmitted infection. Fewer than a third of my students who were sexually active even mentioned STIs, and usually it was in the context of discussing past sex education classes. One did so only jokingly, saying that a friend had told her, "If you don't get an STD in college, you haven't done college right." There were four diagnoses among my students, and one had a friend who discovered that he was HIV-positive.

Students are significantly more concerned about pregnancy—

or, at least, the women are—and many women are using hormonal birth control. If students think they're protected against the possibility of pregnancy, they tend to rely on their intuition to decide whether someone is likely to be disease-free, a process which is primarily based on stereotypes and familiarity and, according to neurologists, takes only "milliseconds." Since most of the people they hook up with are fellow students, they evaluate them optimistically. There is little motivation for them to use condoms if they feel protected from pregnancy and their partner seems "clean."

Add the embrace of an emerging adulthood to a laissez-faire attitude about STIs and the belief that college is a good time to be a little bad, and you have a recipe for sexual abandon. "It's almost like a free zone," wrote one, "where nothing a person does has real impact on their life." It's a place, explained another, where "society does not completely frown upon young adults being promiscuous, drinking underage, and completely misbehaving." For women, there is the added sense that having sex is a rejection of old-fashioned and restrictive sexual mores. Suddenly the parallel with the gay men of the 1970s feels quite close indeed.

Students who opt in to hooking up often believe that having sex in college is, as the abstainer Jaslene bemoaned, part of the "whole college experience." The alternative—not having sex—can make no sense at all. Of the twenty-nine of my students who started college as virgins, only one persisted in planning to lose her virginity on her wedding night. Arman had wanted that in high school, but changed his mind in the course of his first year. So did Omar, whom we'll meet in a moment. None of the other twenty-six virgins had intended to wait in the first place.

Some students were more eager to drop their virginity status than others, but most agreed that, if they hadn't lost it already, it was about time. As one woman explained:

I've reached the age where my lack of sexual experience is getting to be a setback, if not a full-blown problem. There's a line . . . between innocence and ignorance, and in the months between my senior year in high school and my second semester in college, I've crossed it.

In the 1990s, half of 18- to 35-year-olds had at one time or another thought of their virginity as something precious to give to a carefully chosen person. Many college students today continue to think of it this way, but if they haven't had a chance to give it away to someone special by their freshman year of college, they are increasingly likely to just look for someone cute. A third of students now report that their first time having intercourse was during a hookup. "I mean it's whatever," wrote one of my male students who lost his virginity this way, "like I know it's supposed to be 'special' but honestly it needed to happen." She was "good-looking and a nice girl" and that was sufficient cause for him.

One of my students' female friends said that "she wanted to just 'get it over with,' but not to just anyone." She wanted to make sure that she lost it to someone hot. So, she picked out a guy she liked the look of and worked on getting introduced to him. They exchanged numbers at a party and texted "for about a day." Then, after a week or so of hearing nothing from him, he sent her a text very late on a Saturday night and "she decided to 'just do it.'" She never heard from him again, but she was happy that she'd lost her virginity to someone she had a "crush" on.

In the *New York Times*, Kate Taylor profiled a first-year student at Penn State who decided to lose her virginity to a guy in a hookup. "I could be here for four years and not date anyone," she observed, so she didn't imagine she'd have the chance to make it special anytime soon. She picked someone who was "superhot" and "nice."

They had sex, it was a one-time thing, and she felt great about it. "I came back with the biggest smile on my face," she said. "All of my friends are jealous, because I had such a great first experience."

If virginity doesn't make sense to some students, voluntary abstinence among non-virgins is even less intelligible. With the all-important initiation no longer standing between them and sexual activity, there are few culturally understandable reasons not to go for it. My pansexual student, Wren, expressed this kind of uncertainty and I was rather surprised. With a straight back and sleek, chin-length hair that came naturally to sharp points at her earlobes, she seemed extraordinarily self-assured, far more than any first-year student had the right to be. She had come out nonchalantly to her dad in high school, waiting until the commercial break in the baseball game he was watching to tell him that she'd been on a date with a woman. "Oh?" he said, indicating no concern. "How'd it go?"

Wren felt no consternation about her sexual identity, but she was anxious about her level of sexual activity. Before arriving for her first year, she assumed that "college kids were having the best sex of their lives, were crazy and wild, and had sex all the time." She wasn't entirely certain that this was an accurate portrayal of college life, and yet she still felt compelled to compare herself to it. "I *know* that I should want to have sex all the time and should take advantage of it when I get the chance," she wrote anxiously in her journal. After declining a hookup with a friend of a friend, she chastised herself:

> I started to feel like it was something that I should have done, and because I didn't, I felt like a loser, or uncool. As confident in myself [as] I am (or so I thought), thoughts kept running through my head like, "You're at college and you're not having sex. What's wrong with you?"

She wondered if she was a prude. "I'm so embarrassed by that," she wrote, contemplating the possibility that she wasn't into hooking up. "I feel as if by not voluntarily taking part in it, I am weird and abnormal."

◆   ◆   ◆

Wren did take part a little. She was among the thirty-six students I call "dabblers," students who hooked up but did so ambivalently. Some were curious, convinced, or swept into the scene; some were crossing their fingers for a relationship; and some just mustered up a sort of "when in Rome" attitude. There were lots of reasons to go for it.

Setting out to measure students' motivations, sociologist Jeremy Uecker and his colleagues surveyed over five hundred students at Duke University who'd hooked up at least once, asking them to indicate whether they did it for excitement, for pleasure, to fit in, to find a partner, or because they were too busy for anything more. They found that half of their students were what they called "utilitarians," students who were hooking up in the hope that a committed, monogamous relationship would evolve. They made a bargain with hookup culture, an acceptance of its terms in exchange for the possibility of emerging with a boyfriend or girlfriend. "I wanted to find love," confessed a student at George Washington University. "Hopefully it's something more than a hookup," said a utilitarian at Stanford. Many of my students expressed something similar. "I've been going about it how I usually do," wrote a bisexual woman, "which is to hook up with them and hope the feelings come out of it."

Burke was a utilitarian. He wasn't attracted to the idea of hookups, having always been a relationship-oriented guy, and he didn't want his interactions with women to be distorted by drunkenness, but being asked on dates made his peers feel uncomfortable. "It's harder to ask someone out than it is to ask someone to go back to your room after fifteen minutes of chatting," he observed wryly. Meanwhile, living in a residence hall made it "extremely easy" to hook up. He was keenly aware of the absence of parental figures and the "close quarters" he shared with women. Plus, he was nice-looking—tallish with blond hair and a baby face—so women looking for someone who seemed safe found him appealing.

With one of these women he had what he called a "mutually exclusive attraction" or "fling" that lasted a couple weeks, but he never wanted it to be just a hookup. "My intentions were for things to lead towards a solid relationship involving more than partying together," he wrote. With traditional dates off the table, Burke "inevitably" found himself in the occasional hookup in the hope that it would turn into something more.

If half of the students polled by Uecker and his colleagues were hooking up in the hope of a relationship, another quarter were doing it for less strategic reasons. Reflecting the fact that these students didn't articulate any single or clear reason why they liked hooking up, Uecker's team called them "uninspireds" and "unreflectives." I prefer "experimentalists." These were students who weren't exactly enthusiastic about hooking up or mainly interested in a relationship, but were willing to try it out. First-year students were especially likely to be in this category.

Riley, the girl who chastised herself to have some fun, may have been an experimentalist. Once she knew that Craig wanted to hook up with her, the anticipation of kissing an attractive stranger began to crowd out her anxiety about what might happen if she did. Then, on a warm day in March, she decided to do it. Sitting down to write that week's journal, she typed:

Right now I'm in my room writing this on my computer and staring out onto the lawn. Craig is playing Frisbee with his friends in the sun with cutoffs and high-top sneakers and Ray Bans on. He totally fits this image of the cool guy that I could just hook up with a couple times and be kind of coy about. It's this totally big fantasy of, like, how I see "the teenage years."

"I want him," she confessed. "I literally can't stop staring out of my damn window." Partly out of attraction, partly out of curiosity, and partly out of the desire to be a "carefree, coy, 'powerful' girl," she made a conscious decision to have a sexual experience with someone that she had no intention of making her boyfriend. Riley dabbled.

Omar dabbled, too, much to his surprise. He was a light-skinned African American with freckles, naturally red hair, and a comically huge smile. He had never perfected the air of nonchalance that made men seem mysterious. He had become a born-again Christian in ninth grade and had spent all of high school intensely involved with the church. He was a dutiful believer, too. "I accepted everything that my pastor told me," he wrote, "like 'abstaining from sexual sin' and 'watching out for the devil's sex tricks.'" Quite serious about his faith, he pretend-bragged that his most salacious behavior involved surprising his friends with "promiscuous slick booty slaps."

When I met him in his freshman year, he had never kissed a girl. He was waiting for love, he said, but also confessed that he was a "closet freak." "My hormones were literally raging," he wrote. Over the course of his first semester, he started to reconsider the limits he had placed on his behavior and he found the process significantly less stressful than Arman had. He decided that masturbation was acceptable within reason ("my roommate enjoys it a little *too* much") and he'd changed his mind about kissing. "I don't see any harm in it," he decided. "At parties here people do it all the time and there are no repercussions."

Then one day in his journal, he made an announcement: "I have FINALLY KISSED A GIRL!" The star of his story was a shy brunette. They were both "extremely drunk" and Omar had walked her to her room after the party. She lived in a quad with three roommates and so, to avoid disturbing them, they went out on the balcony. They were drunk enough to just plop down on the concrete and he tried out a line he'd been practicing for months. "Look girl," he said, "give me a kiss right now." They bonked their foreheads together in their eagerness and they laughed. Omar thought it was perfect.

"My first kiss made me feel like I was on cloud nine," he wrote later, ecstatic. "I could not wait until the next weekend when we would get drunk again." And they did. This time there was no forehead bonking. They got horizontal. "Even though I had this religious background and a strong desire to save my virginity for marriage," Omar wrote breathlessly, "I was willing to throw it all away that night."

Omar wasn't 100 percent on board with what happened in hookup culture, but he was willing to dabble. "I hope to meet more women," he wrote, "and explore them sexually, enjoy the art of foreplay, without the actual play just yet." At the end of his first year he announced half-jokingly that he had gone from "not being open to anything to basically open to a full-blown orgy."

◆   ◆   ◆

Students like Omar and Riley found hookup culture hospitable enough, but there are also students who, like the man interviewed for *Gay Sex in the '70s*, are truly enthusiastic about the "free love" that hookup culture promises. These are students motivated almost entirely by fun, excitement, and pleasure. Uecker and his colleagues called them "uninhibiteds"; the final fourth of their sample fit the description. A similar proportion of my students, 23 out of 101, did as well.

I call them "enthusiasts." Enthusiasts said things like "I jumped at the opportunity" and "It was everything that I wanted." Owen was an enthusiast at the beginning of his first year (though not at the end). Mara's friend Naomi, the girl with the scraped knees who bragged about sleeping with the guy in sunglasses, was an enthusiast too (and she would remain so years later). Miranda, our intrepid guide at the burlesque party, certainly was. "I consider myself an active, often enthusiastic participant in hookup culture," she had declared with satisfaction, spontaneously using the word.

Enthusiasts came in all types. Hiro was an enthusiast. He was a square-jawed, white and Japanese American, with an intense gaze. While queer men in my sample tended to feel at least a little uncomfortable in hookup culture, Hiro was an exception. Being bisexual, he actively partook of the whole range of hookup options. "Anything that moved," he wrote with zeal. His journals sometimes just took the form of a delighted list of people he danced with, kissed, or slept with that week. He preferred his hookups to be "clean" and "emotionless" and, much of the time, that's what he got. "Overall," he wrote mid-year, "embracing the college hookup culture has been incredibly exciting and fun."

Esther had been an enthusiast since she lost her virginity at the age of fourteen. Her parents embraced her precocious sexuality, making sure she had the tools to keep herself safe and giving her permission to be as sexually active as she wished. She'd never been told to feel guilty about her sexual activity and she didn't. In college, she proceeded quickly to intercourse in hookups and slept with a handful of some of the most desirable men on campus. She had "amazing sex," she said, and also enjoyed being thought of as an "amazing fuck." Definitely an enthusiast.

Petra was one of the few students who started their first year as an abstainer and left it as an enthusiast. When we last saw her, she was wavering, sitting in her dorm room feeling like a "weirdo," wondering if abstaining was the right thing to do. Spring break would put an end to her uncertainty. She spent most of it at home in South Dakota with her family, but on Friday, she went to Brookings to spend the weekend with her friend Sesapa, who was enrolled at State. That night, she and Sesa went down to a boy's room and they poured Petra her first ever alcoholic drink. It was vodka and lemonade. She had "one cup" and it made her feel giggly. She remembers flirting with the boys, getting tickled, and being in bed by 1:30 a.m.

The next night she and Sesa found themselves at a house party that was significantly less low-key. This time they drank vodka and orange juice and Petra was feeling a bit more brave. In the basement she noticed a boy playing beer pong who she thought was "really cute." His name was Wyatt and when his game ended, she "scootched over on the couch to make room for him." He took the invitation, squeezed in, and they starting talking. "When Sesa got up and made more room on the couch," she wrote, "I made sure to not scootch away." One thing led to another and, at the end of the night, Petra claimed her first hookup. The next morning she flew back down south. "I could not stop smiling," she recalled. "Wyatt was sooo cute . . . I had a really fun night, and don't regret a thing."

Back in her own dorm room, Petra had a different outlook altogether. "During my entire first semester and first half of second semester, I stayed away from parties and college dances because

I had no desire to go, put myself out there, and meet new guys," she wrote in her journal. "However, when I was in South Dakota, something changed." It was Wyatt, she said (and probably the vodka). He gave her butterflies.

The next Saturday she talked her roommate into going to their first college party. Like clockwork, two guys "pulled our butts against them," she reported, and just like that, Petra had opted in. She hooked up that night with a guy from her calculus class. Wyatt was "really cute," but this guy was "super hot." He was the second of five hookups in the last two months of her first year, including one with the "hottest" guy in her dorm. "I don't know that the party scene fit like a glove," she said later, "but better than I thought it would."

Students with the most casual sexual experience are the most likely to report that it brings them unadulterated pleasure. Enthusiasts such as Hiro, Esther, and Petra are probably having as good a time as they claim. A study at Cornell found that, for enthusiasts, casual sex was associated with high self-esteem and low rates of anxiety and depression. This was certainly true for Hiro. Having so many people interested in him made him feel fantastic. "My ego was inflated to astronomical levels," he remarked with glee.

◆　　◆　　◆

While most enthusiasts had no trouble finding at least a few people to hook up with, some, like Luke, struck out completely. Luke, to his own horror, was a virgin. In large part, this was because he'd grown up in a conservative town in the American South. His mother was a homemaker and his dad spent most of his career in elected office. Being the son of a politician made coming out more difficult than usual, and there didn't seem much point in doing so anyway since there weren't any other out gay students at his high

school. So, even though he had known he was gay since he was fifteen, he waited until he started college to say so.

He was probably also inhibited because he didn't yet know how
likable he was. He was endearing, his face more kind than handsome. He was a bit awkward: tall, lanky, and noticeably nervous.
But instead of being offputting, his features and quirks made him
seem humble and sincere, which he was.

Luke had always been a bit doleful, but as a freshman he was
more so than ever. He tormented himself with crushes that were
"obsessive and poorly managed." All of his loves were unrequited.
"I felt repulsive," he said, and he figured that this state of affairs
would "continue in perpetuity."

Coming out as gay to his peers didn't bother him at all, but he
hated coming out as a virgin. The most traumatic of these admis-
sions happened late on a Friday night when his friend Adriana
burst into his dorm room, grabbed his arm, and pulled him three
doors down the hall. Nine students were stuffed into her room,
sitting on the bed, on chairs, and on the floor, all people Luke
was familiar with from the queer student group. They cheered and
raised their red cups as Adriana pushed him through the door.
They were playing Hot Seat, a confession-based drinking game
that usually devolved into a contest over "who can uncover the
most embarrassing things from their peers about their sex lives."
Students were thrust into the circle and peppered with questions.
It was Luke's turn.

He knew, he recalled, that it would be "highly unpleasant." The
last thing he wanted was to make his nonexistent sex life the center
of attention. He tried to retreat, but the crowd was persuasive and,
despite his protests, the interrogation began. The first question was,
"What is something that you do every time, without fail, during
sex?" Luke stammered and floundered. He wasn't sure whether to

lie or tell the truth. His brain raced to think of a thing, something, *anything* people do during sex. His friends started to notice his discomfort and started throwing out suggestions. "Like, close your eyes," Adriana offered. "How about wear a condom!" said the safer sex advocate of the bunch. When he spit out that he'd never actually had sex, everyone was suddenly silent. "It was a very uncomfortable experience," he wrote. "Once again, I was the only virgin."

They tried to make him feel better. "Well, it's nice to wait," one of the other gay men in the room said, his voice wavering at the end of the sentence. But Luke wasn't waiting, he was *involuntarily* virginal, and that just made him feel worse. "I sat in this room with a bunch of other queer people," he wrote, "and I can see on their faces that they are wondering what's wrong with me." He bolted. He went back to his room and cried.

Luke was in the small category of students I call "strivers": ones who opt in but feel shut out. His agony would come to an end, as we'll see later, but for the time being he was part of a group for whom hookup culture can be especially cruel. It's hard enough to feel excluded, but to fear that it's because others find you sexually unappealing is a twist of the knife. "As someone who hasn't opted out of hookup culture," Luke wrote, "but rather someone who is excluded by virtue of his awkwardness and definitive lack of allure, I definitely feel a bit victimized." He apologized for the dramatic language, but I don't think calling his experience victimization is too far off the mark. Social psychologists call it a "microaggression," a remark that, intentionally or not, reminds the listener that they're an outsider. It hurts.

Like Luke, strivers may be shy, self-conscious, or socially awkward. Xavier was one of those. He described being obsessed with sex in high school but always unable to "seal the deal." College didn't turn out much different. "I was scared to go out and party and things like that," he confessed, because he remembered all the rejections he got in high school. He spent the year on the margins of hookup culture. "I think the hardest thing for me to do at this point," he wrote at the end of the year, "is to accept the fact that I'm an eighteen-year-old rising sophomore virgin."

Students who are physically disabled or neurologically different also often face exclusion. A combination of others' discomfort with disability, stereotypes of people with disabilities as asexual, and a social hierarchy that rewards "perfect" bodies and socially adept interactions puts most disabled students at a disadvantage in one way or another. The Occidental College alum Carrie Wade, who only coincidentally shares my last name, wrote about her experiences with sex as a lesbian-identified woman with cerebral palsy—specifically, that there was none of it. "[One of the] difficult things to do when you have a disability," she wrote, "is get somebody to fuck you."

There has been no research, to my knowledge, on the experiences of trans students in hookup culture, but it's probably safe to say that those who want to hook up have less luck than the average non-trans student, since we know that they often face harassment and marginalization even in the course of routine interactions. There were no trans students in my sample but one of my students, Hiro, wrote about one. He was the bisexual student who said he would hook up with "anything that moved." It turned out that he wouldn't.

He met Malia at an event held for queer students. "Our interest in each other was obvious," wrote Hiro, who didn't yet know that Malia was trans. They texted back and forth for a while and late one night Malia invited him over to watch a movie, an invitation that functions much like "Would you like to come upstairs for a cup of coffee?" used to. It is, in other words, a widely understood way to initiate a hookup. Hiro took the opportunity.

Malia, quite understandably nervous, interrupted the hookup before it began. "So I wanna talk to you about something," she said seriously, standing a safe distance away. "Shoot," Hiro replied, and Malia asked: "So I'm assuming you wanna hook up with me?" Hiro chuckled and said, "Yeah." "Well then I have to tell you something," she explained, "and it's a secret. A pretty big secret, like if I tell you, you can't tell anyone."

"Okaaa-aay," Hiro replied, starting to feel uneasy. Malia took a deep breath and let it out: "I'm trans." "Oh," Hiro said. "What does that mean, I mean, what does that entail?" Malia explained that she'd been born male but had been taking hormones every week for years and had breast implants. "There aren't really any scars," she said reassuringly, hopefully. Then, carefully suggesting that she hadn't had surgery below the waist, she admitted, "Well, the sex wouldn't be like normal sex."

From Hiro there was an uncomfortable silence and Malia jumped in to close it: "I totally understand if this makes you not want to hook up. But we don't even have to have sex. I like giving blow jobs, we could be make-out and blow job buddies." Hiro looked uncertain. "I think you should think about it," she said, perhaps trying to avoid an outright rejection. "Yeah," Hiro agreed. "I'll think about it."

"I was out of the room within ten minutes," he told me in his journal. "While I'm a very accepting and open person and not at all prejudiced against transgendered individuals, this was too much for me to handle, and so I sadly didn't let anything happen further." Hiro, the bisexual enthusiast who hooked up with "anything," drew the line at Malia. Even in the best-case scenario, then, when a potential sexual partner is nondiscriminatory and bisexual, trans students may face rejection.

Even students who have bodies that barely deviate from the

extremely narrow standard of attractiveness endorsed by their peers can feel excluded. Roslyn, the mixed-race Latina who was careful to protect her scholarship by not partying too hard, was one of the students who worried that her body stood between her and hooking up. Though in some journal entries she sounded like an abstainer, in others it was clear that she felt rejected by her peers.

Tall and strong, she was proud of her athletic body, but she knew it meant that she wasn't the fragile type that men seemed to idealize. She was also keenly aware of the contradictions that her racial background posed. She had lighter skin than most Latinas and "good hair," but she was no blonde Barbie. Then again, she was constantly told that mixed-race people were beautiful, and yet, she didn't feel that she was. It made her unsure if being part Latina was an advantage or a disadvantage in the erotic hierarchy.

"I am worried that no one finds me attractive enough," she proffered nervously. Earlier that semester she'd gone outside during a sweaty house party. When she pulled her shirt up off her belly to expose it to the cool air, a guy she knew huffed in disgust and walked away. The same guy later interrupted her and a friend at a party with a look she interpreted as "'time to move on bro' with a side of 'she's not hot, dude.'"

By the end of the semester, she was the only girl in her friendship group who hadn't hooked up. After one night in which a guy friend tried to hook up with everyone but her, she found herself frustrated:

I almost felt like waving my arms around screaming "HEEEYYY, I'm right here!! Did you even think to look in this direction????" I wasn't even interested in hooking up with this guy really, but the fact that he didn't even seem interested in being with me in the slightest was actually hurtful. I could basically feel his scorn without him saying anything.

Roslyn never figured out if her lack of luck was because of her appearance, her race, her tendency to stay relatively sober, or something else, and it never stopped hurting.

◆　　◆　　◆

Even among the men in the gay enclaves of the 1970s, there were surely many emotional reactions to the opportunity to have casual sex. No doubt many, like Esther and Hiro, did it for the sheer thrill. Some, like Burke, yearned for a stable relationship. And many, like Riley and even Omar, probably just figured that it was a good time to have some fun. I imagine there was a striver or two, though I doubt it would have made Luke feel any better to know it. College students, in their educational enclaves, have a range of responses to the opportunity to hook up, but most do. They opt in. What exactly are they in for?

6

Careless and Carefree

Sometimes, for its own mysterious reasons, our body hijacks our higher functioning. It bathes our brain in a chemical cocktail designed to make us happy, tortured, and stupid all at the same time. Our heart pounds and our tongue ties. We're nervous. We're elated. We're a gooey, sappy mess. It feels awesome. And awful. It's like a drug. No, it *is* a drug. It's oxytocin and dopamine, serotonin and adrenaline, vasopressin, and norepinephrine. These are the chemicals that make us feel, and our frontal lobe, however "evolved" and "higher-functioning," doesn't stand a chance against them.

Hookup culture, though, tells students that their frontal lobes are in charge, that they can be logical about sex and control their feelings if they choose to. Not just the pleasures and pangs of love, as the above example implies, but *all* of the feelings that sex can spark: insecurity and fear; ambivalence, regret, and confusion; happiness, transcendence, sadness, and misery; loathing and awe. Hooking up, they claim, can and should be *emotionless*.

"It's always nice," one of my students put it plainly, "to have a clean, emotionless hookup." It does sound nice, in a floating-in-a-vacuum kind of way, but it's nonsense, of course. Saying we can have sex without emotions is like saying we can have sex without bodies. There simply is no such emotion-free human state. We have emotions when we hear our morning alarm, have our first sip of coffee, sit in traffic, watch the clock tick toward quitting time, or think about exercising. Feelings are part of our basic biochemical operating system. We don't get to set them aside at will.

Students do think that emotionless sex is possible, though. In fact, they think it's *typical*. When two College of New Jersey psychologists asked students what they thought their peers felt when they were in the midst of a typical hookup, students listed emotions as wide-ranging as excitement, embarrassment, regret, fear, anxiety, confusion, and pride, but the most common answer—mentioned by a whopping two-thirds of their sample—was lust. "Overwhelmingly sexual desire and lust," said one woman. "Sexually aroused, driven only by physical forces, not thinking much—just doing."

Lust so dominated the emotional landscape of hookup culture that the next most common answer wasn't even an emotion at all. It was "nothing." Not "no answer"; literally nothing, the absence of emotion. Nothing came in a very distant second, offered by 17 percent of respondents, which means that students generally believe that hookups are about lust, only lust, and nothing else. My students call it "unattached, unemotional crazy one-night stands," "fast, random, no-strings-attached sex," and "emotion-free sexual abandon," or, simply, "meaningless sex."

◆   ◆   ◆

In hookup culture, "hot" is the preferred temperature. People are hot, sex is hot, hot people make for hot sex, and hot sex is good sex.

Women worry whether they're hot and reassure one another that they're hot. They ruminate over which clothes are hot and wonder how to look hot when it's cold. Students debate about who's hot, who's hotter, and who's "super hot and cool." There are many categories of hotness: people who are "fucking hot," "too hot," "recently got hot," and people who "didn't know they were hot" or "would have been hot" under other circumstances. Students talk about hot teachers, hot haircuts, hot underwear, hot tits, hot cum, who they have the hots for and, of course, "hot and steamy sex" or, better yet, "hot, head-banging, screaming sex."

But God forbid they be warm. Students may have spent hours or even weeks working up to a hookup by taking opportunities to interact, being attentive and flirtatious, offering compliments, and getting to know each other, but once a hookup is in progress, it's time to get down to business. No sissy stuff. No niceties. Everything must be hard and furtive. Expressions of tenderness—like gentle kisses, eye contact, holding hands, cuddling, and caresses—are to be avoided. "Cuddling is for people you love," insisted a student, adding, "if you hold hands during sex, you're making love. If you make eye contact during sex, you're making love." Hooking up is not making love.

It makes sense, when you think about it. If students accept the idea that casual sex is meaningless, then essentially everything else—no matter how small—carries more meaning. "That little touching definitely signifies something," wrote a student about holding hands, "something a little more than just fucking." "To me," another divulged, "holding hands and cuddling is something that people participate in when they actually care about someone." This sentiment was echoed in a *New York Times* article about students at Yale in which "several men say that they found holding hands more intimate than getting a hand job."

Even *not* having sex often seems more intimate than sex. "From the stories I have heard," one of my female students reported, "the only guys that do not pressure girls are the ones that actually might care." "He likes me," said another girl, explaining why she and a guy friend had never hooked up. "I'm the kind of girl that he would date for years . . . not someone you just hook up with once." In this topsy-turvy world, you have sex with people you don't like and don't have sex with people you do.

Emotions, though, are leaky and intimacies often sneak in despite students' best efforts to ban them. Such an experience was recounted by Lincoln, an extroverted Asian-American enthusiast. One night, students had been celebrating the last weekend of the semester with a marathon of parties. When Lincoln got home, his floor had turned into a giant pajama party. Everyone, he recalled, "was dancing like there was no tomorrow." He began flirting with Terrell, a friend that he had "always got the gay vibe from," and before too long they were alone in his dorm room.

"For a little while," Lincoln wrote, "we just sat in silence looking at each other, very close to each other." Lincoln's comforter was bunched up messily, indicating a rushed or absent-minded morning, and the expanse of taut, bare sheet made the hookup seem imminent. Lincoln leaned in and asked him, "Have you ever been with a guy?" Terrell shook his head. "So do you think you're gay?" he asked. Terrell said, "I really don't know." Lincoln went in for the kiss:

> It was actually really sweet and very different from past hookups. We didn't immediately dive into making out, but kept the kiss going. I could kind of feel him melt, as cheesy as that sounds. I felt really happy that I was helping him figure things out.

Eventually they did dive in. In his journal, Lincoln skipped straight to what happened afterward. He got out of bed to show Terrell to the door and they hugged goodbye. This—the hug—gave him pause. It was "something I've never done after a hookup before," he noted, adding the all-important caveat, "although I obviously didn't have feelings for the guy."

Obviously? Terrell *melted*, for goodness sake. He succumbed to his attraction to men for the first time in his life and, of all the men in the world, he decided to share that precious moment with Lincoln. There are lots of appropriate emotions here: the tenderness that a mentor feels for an apprentice, the care we feel for someone when they make themselves vulnerable to us, the gratefulness we feel when we know someone could have picked someone else and picked us instead, or the closeness we have with someone with whom we share a secret or treasured experience.

I know Lincoln recognized it as a significant leap for Terrell and I do think he was touched by it—he described it as "sweet"—but feeling something for others is against the rules and so he made sure to specify that no feelings were involved. In hookup culture, there are no tender initiations, even when there are.

◆   ◆   ◆

Once the sex is over, the rule is to go from hot to cold. This is part of the demotion rule described in the Hookup How-To: after a hookup, students are supposed to be cool. To be cool, writes philosopher Susan Bordo in her book *Twilight Zones*, is to be "aloof rather than desirous," "blasé rather than passionate," and "self-contained rather than needy." The power of cool is in needing no one. Cool people are detached and invulnerable, indifferent toward you, everything you stand for, and what you think of them. They are certainly too cool to think *you're* cool. This is why high-fashion models never smile. A smile is an invitation, a plea. It says: Let's be friends. Models don't smile; they gaze at you with a total absence of interest.

On college campuses today, being cool means being chill. To be chill, NYU alum Alana Massey explains, is to have "a laid-back attitude, an absence of neurosis," and no discernible passion about anything or anyone. Whatever you do, she says about the aftermath of a hookup, "Do *not* make anything a *thing*." Accordingly, the most stigmatizing label on college campuses today is no longer one that references sexual behavior like "slut," or even the more hookup culture-consistent "prude"; it's "desperate."

As one student explained, "The two worst things a boy can say to a girl is that she is fat or that she is clingy." Clingy, desperate, and needy are extremely effective insults, invoking all the things that students don't want to be: weak, insecure, unable to control one's emotions, and powerless to separate sex from feelings. For men, it's the antithesis of masculinity. For women, it's a failure to be liberated, modern, strong, and independent. In a society that values masculinity over femininity, it is pathetically *feminine* for either men or women to actually like someone.

Students aim, then, for aloofness. "Hookup buddies never should talk about emotions or anything too personal," one student insisted. "You can never show your true feelings and insecurities to the partner," explained another. "You assume that another person feels a certain way," wrote a third, "so you behave in what you assume to be the protocol." Being unchill is way uncool.

But being uninterested is also a relative state. The idea is not just to not care, it's to care *less*. Lack of interest is a moving target and the direction is down. So, after a hookup, students monitor each other's level of friendliness and try to come in below the other person. Each time one person takes a step back emotionally, the other takes two. They can end up backed into their respective corners, avoiding eye contact, and pretending the other doesn't exist. Massey, the NYU alum, calls it the "blasé Olympics."

Most students seem to think that men are better at this game. "It's a contest to see who cares less," said a female student at Boston College, "and guys win a lot at caring less." It's true that women report having a somewhat harder time separating sex and emotions, but gender stereotypes also accelerate this downward spiral, putting women at an even further disadvantage.

Since the Victorian idea that women are motivated by love persists even alongside the more modern idea that they want to have sex for fun, women's efforts to stay cool are less credible than men's. So, no matter how good women are at pretending to be uninterested—indeed, no matter how uninterested they actually are—many men simply *assume* that the women they hook up with want a monogamous relationship.

It was Deanna's story that brought this point home for me. One day her regular hookup partner met her at a picnic bench nestled into an alcove outside of her building. It was a sunny day but Reid looked glum and it quickly became clear why he had dropped by: he had fallen for someone else. "So I think we need to stop sleeping together," he said, his voice soft and serious-sounding.

Deanna let the news wash over her and watched Reid's face contort gently as he told his story: how they hadn't been exclusive (she knew), how the hookup had just happened (as they do), and that he hadn't meant to like this new girl (but he did). For a moment, she felt a tight sensation in her chest that was familiar—she hadn't been chosen—but she didn't feel that way about Reid anyway. She wasn't heartbroken. Instead, she was "genuinely happy for him." She said so and told him that she was flattered that he hadn't ended their hookups sooner.

But Reid's face didn't relax. He continued, still looking concerned, stressing what a lovely person she was and how he hoped she wasn't too upset. "You too will find love someday," he said reassuringly. Deanna started to get annoyed. "He more and more drastically emphasized asking if I was okay," she recounted, "as if he had somehow damaged me, seeming to expect a flood of tears." She reiterated that she wasn't hurt and failed to collapse into a blubbery mess, but he wouldn't let it go. "Although this started out subtly," she recalled, "by the end of our talk it was awkwardly apparent that there would be no way that he would believe me when I said that I was fine."

This experience was a wakeup call. Deanna had thought that their hookups had been about exploring sexual attraction as equals, but this incident revealed that he didn't and hadn't ever thought of them that way. Reflecting on their encounters, she wrote:

> The stigma attached to women being the emotional creatures in the relationship and the men being the physical ones had never been so apparent to me. . . . He clearly thought that he was the one with the power to hurt and I was the one that was expected to cry with anguish.

It was ironic, she commented, because Reid's concern for her feelings was "a far more womanly trait" than any feelings she had for him, but there was no convincing him otherwise. "The hardest part of the whole affair," she wrote, was "seeing in an equal's eyes their opinion that I was inferior."

Several other women told stories of men who seemed to fabricate the woman's affection for them on the basis of gender stereotypes alone. "I felt no attachment to him whatsoever," Netta wrote matter-of-factly, but he came by her dorm room drunk the next day anyway, sloppily blurting out that he thought she was too "attached to him." She was "completely insulted" by his assumption that she was the more "desperate" of the two.

Ebony had a similar experience. After a few days of "being a dick," a guy she'd hooked up with got coarse with her, telling her that he didn't want a "real relationship." She stared back at him blankly, confused. They weren't "technically dating" and she'd never asked him to be her boyfriend. She was "pretty stoic" about hookups and hadn't developed any feelings. Yet, there he was, telling her to back off.

This is called "benevolent sexism," a phenomenon in which a positive trait stereotypically attributed to women is used against them. In this case, women's gentle hearts are believed to make it impossible for them to have sex without falling in love. So men—with their more lustful but less laudable ways—forever have the upper hand. The man can feel confident that the woman always wants him more than he wants her because women are just so darn sweet. The stereotype portrays him negatively and her positively, but he still has all the power in the end.

On the assumption that all women are knock-kneed with feelings, men are *even more* standoffish than they might be otherwise. Women, for their part, try to avoid being seen as that kind of girl, the desperate kind. They pretend not to care at all, knowing that the slightest friendliness might make them seem like they are begging for a boyfriend. Both these decisions—men's stiff arms and women's stiff upper lips—make the aftermath of a hookup even less friendly. "Like friends with benefits," explained one of my students, "without the friendship maybe." Hookup culture isn't carefree; it's care-less.

◆　　　◆　　　◆

In fact, it's people in loving relationships, not people who hook up, who are expected to be kind to each other: to show interest in and support for their partner's goals, to help with getting through the daily grind of life, to provide an ear and a shoulder during trying times and reassurance that they are good, worthy, and attractive, among other kindnesses. When people don't provide these things to their partners, it is considered a breach of contract. But caring relationships, argues sociologist Mimi Schippers, are also almost exclusively understood to be monogamous ones. So much so that words like "relationship," "serious," "commitment," and "romance" are usually used as synonyms for monogamy.

Students simply flip this logic around and conclude that non-monogamy involves no kindnesses at all. These arrangements, they argue, are supposed to be "easy" and "simple." "Clean," as one student said. Students see two categories of engagement—hard and easy, caring and careless, emotional and emotionless—and nothing in between. But this isn't as functional as it might sound. It's one thing, after all, to have casual sexual encounters with someone with whom you are not in love, but it's entirely another to do so with someone who may have no positive regard for you at all. In hookup culture, it can be hard to tell the difference.

It was Macy who articulated the most clearly how this felt. In high school, she'd had an enjoyable sexual debut with her boyfriend. They waited over two years to have sex and, once they did, their sex life was energetic and adventurous. "We used whipped cream," she remembered, "tied each other up, played strip blackjack or poker, had sex in the shower and bathtub, and other things." When she arrived on campus, newly single, she was hungry for more and she brought not an ounce of trepidation. "I am very comfortable with releasing my inner beast," she purred.

An excellent flirt with a sexy vibe, Macy was one of the most sexually active of my students. She was matter-of-fact about it—"I slept around," she said with a smirk—but she became increasingly frustrated. Plenty of men were willing to sleep with her, but no one seemed to want to be her *friend*. "Many times after," she wrote, "they just act like I don't exist." They avoided her or pretended not to know her at all. At Lehigh University, it's called the "Lehigh look-away." Macy knew her own college's version of it well. "None of the guys here want to be my friend," she complained, "only my fuck buddy."

Over the course of the semester, Macy's disillusionment with hookup culture reached a higher and higher pitch: "They only want to fuck me and then be done," she wrote. "I am sick and tired of this shit. I am more than just a vagina . . . I am a human being." Men's treatment eventually began to eat away at her self-esteem. "Fuck my life," she wrote exasperatedly. "It's pathetic. *I* am pathetic."

Women at other colleges are having similar experiences. Guys "act as if nothing happened," wrote a Marist College student. He "shuffles by you without a second glance," complained a student at Indiana. Men treat women like "disposable beings," said a student at Tufts. "I was not worth being acknowledged, spoken to, or smiled at," recalled a student at Davidson College about the aftermath of her first hookup. "Girls feel that they should not even expect a text message from a guy after hooking up with them," wrote a student at Cal Poly in San Luis Obispo.

Women are particularly disgusted by how coldly men treat them, but men don't necessarily enjoy it either. One male student hooked up with three women in a row, only to be treated with indifference afterward. "I am depressed, frustrated, and feel unrespected and worthless to the opposite sex," he wrote dejectedly. My gay male students sometimes had the same complaints. One said that his hookup partners "invariably never speak to me again."

Lincoln didn't mention how he treated Terrell the day after they shared Terrell's first kiss, but I suspect it was with a proper degree of indifference.

Casual sex, though, doesn't have to be cold. If partners are invested in mutual consent and pleasure and are gracious and friendly afterward, one could say they have been nice to each other. But somewhere students lost sight of this possibility. Instead, non-exclusive relationships are assumed to lack not only love, but all the kindnesses that come with it, both small and large. Students, then, are given "two and only two choices," concludes Schippers, "hookups with 'no strings attached' or monogamous relationships that come with interpersonal responsibility and fairness."

The irony is that most college students actually want to be in a caring relationship. Of the students who filled out the Online College Social Life Survey, 71 percent of men and 67 percent of women said that they wished they had more opportunities to find a long-term partner. Despite their claims to be too busy and focused on their careers, students overwhelmingly find the idea of a committed partnership appealing and, in fact, many of them get what they want. Over two-thirds of college seniors report having been in at least one relationship lasting six months or more.

Most of these relationships start as hookups. Rachel Kalish, a sociologist who studied student dating for her dissertation, found that dates do occur between college students, but the dates almost always come after they have been hooking up together for a while. Dates aren't how today's college students get to know each other; they're how the transition from casual sex to a potential monogamous relationship is signified.

Hookup culture, then, has co-opted the process of relationship formation. When Kalish asked her students how they might form relationships without hooking up first, many were at a loss. "If you don't want to hook up before getting into a relationship," said one of her female interviewees, "good luck finding a relationship. Sad, but very true." "They're probably fucked," said a senior guy. "This is college, get real."

At some of the campuses I've visited, they call it "backward dating." "You have sex with a person," said a student at Dartmouth, "then if you like the sex, and you kind of like their personality, you ask them out." Or, as one of my students quipped, "It all begins with fuck buddies." One of my students, describing the beginning of a relationship between two of her friends, explained, "It began as a sexual thing and they had to work backwards." "All of the relationships I'm aware of started with a series of hookups," admitted one of my male students, including his own.

Among my 101 students, nine formed new monogamous relationships in the course of their first year. Students do form caring, committed relationships, but they do it delicately, having devised a whole series of baby steps designed to help them. Between the hookup and a monogamous relationship is "talking," "hanging out," being "exclusive," "dating but not in a relationship," and a whole host of other statuses. "I just don't know if, like, we hook up sometimes or like, we're 'hooking up,'" wondered a male student one day about a girl he liked. "Hooking up" implies an ongoing arrangement, while "hooking up sometimes" suggests that any further hooking up is random instead of intentional. "Talking" and "hanging out" suggest that two people who are hooking up may also be seeing each other on purpose, in daylight, when they're sober. To be "exclusive" is to be hooking up only with each other but without emotional attachment or accountability. As far as I can tell, "dating but not in a relationship" is an actual monogamous relationship between two people who don't want to use the word, or it might be a pre-relationship status. Most of these terms are purposefully vague.

This happened to Mason in his first year. He started hooking up with a good friend with no intention of getting serious. "My instinct was always to steer away from commitment," he said, having had plenty of experience with hooking up in high school. But the bond between them "got intense" and when she asked him if he wanted to be exclusive, he agreed. "We fell in love just like that," he reminisced. They stayed together for about two years.

Mason and his girlfriend had "the talk," but sometimes students don't communicate about the state of their engagement at all. One of my students watched a couple form and have a lovely relationship without ever admitting that that was what they were doing. She observed that they "sleep in the same bed every night and dote upon each other affectionately even in front of their friends." They were quite clearly in love, but they never described their arrangement as anything other than casual. "It is as if the conversation about making their relationship serious is preposterous," she wrote, so it never occurred. She thought it quite odd, but characteristic of hookup culture. "It is as if they are dating in secret," she wrote insightfully, "except that the secret is only to themselves, as the entirety of the outside world sees it for what it is."

A University of Kansas woman describes her story of relationship formation as "really frightening." After the first time she had sex with a guy she really liked, she said, "Listen . . . obviously there are feelings here . . . but I'm not ever, ever, ever trying to be in a committed relationship." She later laughed at herself. "Clearly it was exclusive," she admitted, "but I was still pretending like it wasn't a thing." She held firm until one day the guy sat her down and said, "Listen, I know what we are and I know this is committed, so I don't need you to call me your boyfriend, but [my mom] does. For her sanity, can we just have the fucking title?" So they became boyfriend and girlfriend, but they laid the blame on his mother.

Students do sometimes navigate the transition from a hookup to hooking up to talking to hanging out to exclusivity to dating but not in a relationship to a relationship to the heights of relationship seriousness—making it Facebook official—but it's not easy. Students have to be willing to express emotional attachment to a person in a culture that punishes people that do so, and they have to be capable of responding positively to that kind of vulnerable confession, too. Not everyone can do it.

◆　　◆　　◆

Farah described herself as someone who liked to "go out to parties on the prowl for boys." Her parents had emigrated from Indonesia, but she was an all-American girl raised in a mostly white neighborhood in Minnesota. Tiq, as Farah described him, was an athlete with an artistic side. They met in their "Sociology of the City" class and bonded over a shared interest in graffiti, or what their professor called "the art of civil disobedience." This made Farah feel that she had something in common with Tiq that most women at their elite school did not.

Mostly, he just made her swoon. They started hooking up at the end of November and progressed quickly to having intercourse. "Emotionless, meaningless, and no commitment" was the goal, Farah insisted, but she thought about him on and off over winter break back in Minneapolis, and when she got back and they started hooking up again, she realized that she kind of *like* liked him.

So, she said nothing. She obeyed the demotion rule, ensuring that she didn't seem desperate. "When you have a hookup buddy, you *never* admit true feelings," she wrote. "It's best to show the least amount of interest or emotions or even more so, be cold." She elaborated:

With guys I hook up with, I play the game of ignoring him and making it seem like he is not in my interest or thoughts at all. It can come across as rude but, rather than showing any emotion, I would prefer to act like I don't care.

So, that's what she did. She flat-ironed her hair, pulled on a "boob shirt," and dropped by Pritykin Hall where she knew Tiq lived. All very nonchalantly, of course. When she saw him, she proceeded feverishly to ignore him. It was just "a little reminder that I am still here," she explained. Two hours later, her phone beeped. The text read, "Hey, where you at?" "This is exactly the kind of attention I want," she said proudly. "It took me not giving a shit to get that."

One day, they and three friends got together to smoke a few joints. After about forty-five minutes, the others took off and she and Tiq were left alone in one of the quieter, more contemplative places on campus. Most of the college's grounds are carefully manicured—roses, trimmed hedges, and pristine lawns—but the spot where students most often went to smoke felt more like being in the woods: a copse of olive trees, sun-dappled bark, a breeze rattling the leaves, squirrels.

It was a lovely day and, as they passed another blunt back and forth, their guards came down. Before too long, the conversation turned to a friend that Tiq had smoked with in high school who had died in a car crash over the break. Tiq admitted that he was pretty shaken and it softened Farah's heart. "It felt good to have a conversation," she wrote later, revealing just how little they had actually talked before that day. "It was a small amount of bliss."

It was a disappointing ten days until she heard from him again, drunk and looking to hook up. "He only texts me when he wants to fuck," she sighed. And they did. Another two weeks went by and Farah began obsessing. She deleted his number from her phone so that she couldn't text him in a moment of weakness. Texting first is losing, she explained.

But then she ran into him in the cafeteria at dinner on a Wednesday and they hooked up sober. The bliss was back: "For the first time ever, we lie in bed together, kissing now and then and holding hands. We'd never done anything that personal. We spoon and snuggle."

They were breaking the rules.

At midnight, Farah pouted about having to trek all the way back to her dorm and he invited her to stay the night. She woke up at 8 a.m. for class, kissed Tiq goodbye, and left him warm in bed. "I walk out feeling confident and high-spirited," she reported. "It felt great."

Afterward, each immediately returned to their respective corners, backs turned. Farah was fuming when she ran into him at a party a few days later and she lost her cool. She asked him why he was being so "bipolar" about her and he surprised her by shooting back the same accusation:

He told me he was just showing me how much it sucks when I am so nice to him when it's just one-on-one time with us, but in public I shut him off. . . . It felt like my stomach dropped 2304234823 feet.

The next day he accused her of having what she described as "the worst feelings a girl could have." He called her "clingy." Farah retreated and nursed her wounds. She tried to put him out of her mind, but some days later her text alert chimed. The surprisingly conciliatory message read, "I am sorry we have not talked in such a long time. I'm sorry for being such a dick." He told her he'd trudge up the hill if she'd meet him behind her building.

Fifteen minutes later they were sitting with their backs up against Rostker Hall. A few feet in front of them, the land sloped gently away, tumbling down the hill on which the college is built. They looked across the bumpy cityscape and talked about something forgettable. Movies, maybe. He hesitated, then asked, "Do you *like* like me?"

Farah's face, aimed squarely at the dirt between her knees, registered no reaction. She pulled her hoodie tighter around herself and gently nudged a small rock with her toe. Her gaze shifted to look up along the side the building, past the cream-colored stucco to the sky. "No," she lied and turned to him, making eye contact: "Do *you* like like *me*?" He looked down and shook his head.

"My heart kind of stopped," Farah wrote. As they went back to talking about nonsense, a heavy feeling of regret spread from the middle of her chest. "I sat next to him on the concrete in the cold," she recalled, "and hoped the question would come again so I could say, '*Yes*, I *do* like you.'"

Fearful of being vulnerable and practiced at being hard, Farah had so perfected the art of hooking up that she couldn't stop performing it when she needed to. And the disappointment and hurt over what happened with Tiq left her even more determined to protect herself. "Fuck love," Farah wrote after her affair with Tiq felt genuinely and truly over, "it's easier not to give a damn."

Tiq tried to start something more meaningful with Farah, but she wasn't up to it and I don't blame her. The more common practice of being treated unkindly leaves many students feeling closed off. "It's a cold, cold world out there," Farah said. When sociologist Rachel Kalish asked students if they thought hookup culture was good or bad for relationships, the majority said that it was bad. They felt that it made investing in other people feel unimportant, made sex seem less special, and interfered with learning how to be a caring partner. The skills needed for managing hookup culture, they noted, are in direct contradiction to the skills needed to propose, build, and sustain committed relationships. Perhaps most of all, students recognized that seeing "feelings as negative" could make it hard to experience them as positive. "It's just a relationship killer, I think," said one of her male interviewees in his first year, noting that the women he knew seemed "numb."

That numbness can build up over time through exposure to routine hookup culture dynamics like the ones that shaped Tiq and Farah's affair. It is no doubt exacerbated, too, when students have experiences, still well within the rules, that aren't just meaningless but downright mean.

◆   ◆   ◆

Men are frequently criticized for using unsavory language to discuss women, but some of my female students were quick to use derogatory labels, too, describing a hookup partner variously as a "douche," "tool," "self-centered jerk," "total asshole," "huge player," and "the biggest loser ever." One explained: "I have no feelings for him. . . . So I do not feel bad when I think about the fact that I am actually just using him." She thought it was a double standard to insist that women weren't allowed to do so. Another simply stated, "I would have no problem just hooking up with an asshole. I don't care who they are."

In some cases, students argue that sex with people they actively and intensely dislike is ideal because it all but ensures that they won't catch feelings. The sentiment was echoed by several women enrolled at the University of Pennsylvania. "We don't really like each other sober," said one about her regular hookup. "We literally can't sit down and have coffee." That was ideal, agreed another, who said that women generally look for "a guy that we don't actually really like his personality, but we think is really attractive and hot and good in bed."

It's not difficult to imagine where students get the idea that it's acceptable, even desirable, to have sex with people that they find socially unbearable or morally repugnant. A quick tour of our insult vocabulary reveals that the cultural association of hate and sex is pervasive in language. We use the word "fuck," after all, both to describe having sex and to deliver one of our nastiest insults, alongside a range of other invectives. We also use sexual body parts as slurs. "Scumbag" is a word that originally meant condom and other sperm receptacles, such as people with vaginas and men who receive anal sex. The variations on "you suck," like "cocksucker," work as an insult by positioning the male or female receiver in the position of sexually servicing a man. We even put the words "hate" and "fuck" together in the term "hate fuck," a phrase that refers to having sex with a person you despise.

Pornographers quite clearly think that hatred and violence are hot, and no generation in recent history has had more exposure to or been more approving of pornography. Physical aggression and insults are routine in the most mainstream material, as are obvious signs of pain and distress on the part of actresses. In porn, being called a cunt and gagging on a roughly thrust penis turns women on, and men are told in no uncertain terms that they should get off on the same. And that's the tame stuff.

One doesn't have to look into the nether regions of the Internet to find this message. In pop culture, the hottest sex is often between two people who hate each other. Dozens of TV shows and movies each year include a plotline involving a conceited (but fantastically beautiful) woman and an obnoxious (but painfully attractive) man who detest each other but end up having sex, usually thanks to a particularly heated argument. They rip off each other's clothes, throw each other against the wall, and knock over lamps. Turned on to the point of violence, they go straight to intercourse. They are "fight fucking": a Hollywood phenomenon in which two people who hate each other are also inexplicably attracted to one another, causing them to transition from fighting to fucking in an instant. Desire that can overcome true loathing must be powerful indeed.

Any young person growing up today with exposure to routine media content can easily come away with the notion that hate and lust are good bedfellows. Predictably, then, the idea bubbled up in my students' journals from time to time. It was certainly part of how a girl named Sydney thought about a guy named Brad. "When I first started hooking up with him," she wrote, "I absolutely hated him. I thought he was weird and annoying and ugly and I wanted nothing to do with him." They hooked up repeatedly, over ten times in fact. Still, she insisted, "he continued to mean nothing to me." Brad wasn't the only guy to get this treatment. She preferred callousness to caring: "You only pursue the people you know mean nothing to you and you never stick around long enough to let them. You stay clearly on the easy side of the line."

One night she found herself nestled up against the guy who meant nothing to her on his twin mattress. They had left a party together at about 3 a.m., surprised to discover that the weather had turned to what passes for winter in the South—mildly cold and a bit drizzly—and hurried back to his dorm, shivering, and jumped into bed. As the rain dribbled down the windowpane, Brad moved to have intercourse.

Sydney stopped him. She'd gone off the pill over winter break and explained to Brad that sex without a condom was no longer possible. Brad wasn't in the habit of treating his sexual partners nicely either and, because he wanted to do it anyway, he pressured her to go ahead, insisting that he'd pull out. When she told him no, he called her a "bitch" for leading him on.

Sydney's bravado withered under his cruelty. She pleaded with him, promising that she'd get a condom the next day and that they could have sex then. He responded with threats. "He said he wouldn't call me tomorrow night unless I had sex with him tonight," Sydney recalled, describing the conversation:

> I tried to explain to him that I was really scared of getting pregnant and that he was being unreasonable. He told me that if I didn't have sex with him right now I was welcome to get out of his bed, walk back to my dorm in the cold, and never hear from him again.

So, Sydney complied. They had sex. He pulled out and passed out. She spent the rest of the night staring at the ceiling, terrified of getting pregnant, imagining how she would tell her parents, wondering if she could tell Brad, and worrying about the logistics and expense of an abortion. At dawn, she got up and left him sleeping. She walked home on that damp morning, alone in the cold after all. And, she reported with a sad sense of irony, "As it turns out, he didn't call me the next night. Or any night."

There's likely more than one reason why Sydney complied when Brad was cruel, but partly it's that she had no expectation that her partner would be kind to her. In hookup culture, it isn't a partner's job to be nice. Sydney had no recourse, because calling someone a bitch is technically allowed. And she knew it.

◆　　◆　　◆

All of this—the ban on warmth, the imperative to be cool, and the permission to be cold—is really hard on students. They are just human beings—ones who can be super chill, of course, but not all the time and not in the face of just anything. Suppressing their instinct to be kind and their sense of entitlement to the same was jarring and exhausting. One of my students called it "emotionally shredding."

Most were open to love, but they would have been satisfied if their hookup partners were simply respectful. "I would love to have meaningful sex with people I respect," sighed one student hopelessly. Students just wanted something, *anything* positive to come out of their hookups. "I think it could be like, you make me feel optimistic or you make me feel alive, or you make me feel safe," wrote one. "Or you inspire me." Another clarified: "Love is not as important as trust."

Trust may, indeed, be having a lull. Young people today are significantly more likely than the two generations before them to agree that "people are just looking out for themselves." A full 60 percent of millennials and 62 percent of college students say so, compared to less than half of generation X and just over a third of the boomer generation. There is "an inherent lack of trust in everyone and everything," wrote a female student. "Like most girls I want to hook up with," explained a male student about a prospect, "I don't trust her." Hookups lead to "trust issues," said three students separately. Young people today are more cynical, in general, and they're more cynical about love in particular.

In *The End of Men*, Hanna Rosin calls freedom from love relationships "feminist progress," and lots of students are inclined to agree, but my students would have liked a little compassion alongside their liberation. They want fun and freedom, and women don't want to go back to a world where being sexually active marks them as disreputable by definition, but they also want to be treated with basic courtesy and to have kind and generous sexual exchanges with others. "What I really want right now," one sighed, "is for someone to be nice to me and just want me in that way." Men wanted this, too. Students wanted to hook up with someone who they knew felt goodwill toward them and would be courteous to them, treating them at least as well as they treat total strangers. It didn't often happen.

But at least the sex is hot, right?

7

Unequal Pleasures

As Celeste's first year of college was coming to a close, her enthusiasm for hooking up was waning. She had hooked up with twelve men, proceeding to intercourse with five of them, and not a single one had given her an orgasm. "A girl's got needs, too," she complained, writing that she had started to feel like little more than a "piece of ass" used to satisfy the male hookup fantasy. She'd learned to expect nothing from men. "The guy kind of expects to get off," she wrote, "while the girl doesn't expect anything." Her resentment built and, after one especially upsetting night, she wrote, angrily, "I am not a masturbation toy."

To be fair, Celeste was having particularly bad luck, but she isn't wrong to think that women are getting shorted in hookup culture. Women in college, like American women more generally, have fewer orgasms than their male counterparts. The numbers vary but, in general, women have one or two orgasms for every three that men enjoy. The data on college students reflect this pattern. The Online College Social Life Survey results show that in hookups men are more than twice as likely as women to have an orgasm.

Myths about men's and women's bodies suggest that this gap is a biological inevitability. Men's orgasms are easy to elicit, we are told. If anything, they arrive too effortlessly. The female orgasm, in contrast, is portrayed as finicky. If women don't have orgasms, the narrative suggests, it's because the clitoris is hard to find and difficult to operate. Even when conditions are ideal, an orgasm often fails to show. It's a mystery, we shrug. We tell ourselves that women are physiologically different—not as sexual as men—and so we presume that release is less important to them anyway.

Today's college students generally buy into these ideas. When sociologist Jess Butler asked students at the University of Southern California what accounted for gender differences in rates of orgasm, "by far," she said, "the most common explanation . . . was 'it's biological.'" Her students believed that orgasm was "harder" for women and "takes longer," but "just happens" for men. Given this sense of the nature of things, she said, her students were "unfazed" by statistics demonstrating that men were getting off more often than women.

The idea that the orgasm gap is natural, though, is wrong. Some countries, such as the United States and Russia, have up to twice as large a gap as others, such as Brazil and Japan. Among Americans, lesbian women report two to three times as many orgasms as heterosexual ones—as many, in fact, as heterosexual men. In masturbation, orgasms come easily and quickly to both sexes; on average, each requires just four efficient minutes to reach climax. Even women who never have orgasms with male partners often do regularly when they're alone.

The orgasm gap is not a biological fact; it's a social one, which reflects what people choose to do in bed together. Among college students, for example, the likelihood of a woman having an orgasm in a hookup with a man varies from 15 to 63 percent, depending on whether he performs oral sex, they engage in intercourse, she self-stimulates, or they do some combination of those things. In relationships, if couples engage in all three activities, women's likelihood of having an orgasm is 92 percent. Not so finicky, it turns out.

If hookup culture has an orgasm gap—and it does—then the question isn't what might be wrong with women's bodies, but the extent to which the female orgasm is made a priority. What we should be asking is whether men and women care enough about female orgasm to give it the ol' college try.

◆　　　◆　　　◆

One day in her journal, Ashlynn recalled a sidesplitting morning recap with her friend, Izzy. The night before Izzy had performed fellatio during a hookup and was pleasantly surprised when her partner moved to return the favor. But he "licked her," Ashlynn reported, just "*once*." She looked at Izzy. "A single lick?" she asked incredulously. "We laughed until our stomachs were sore." They found it hilarious, but obnoxious, too. "His short attention span indicates something more than laziness," Ashlynn insisted, trying to imagine what it would look like for a girl to go down on a guy and lick his penis just once. It was inconceivable. "The fellatio-cunnilingus double standard really irks me," she wrote.

It wasn't always this way. For most of European American history, oral sex of any kind was considered perverse and was forbidden alongside homosexual sex and masturbation. American marriage experts only started recommending it in the early 1900s. It was a response to the emergence of the home as a respite from capitalism and a place for care, a shift that newly required that spouses be lovers as well as life partners. Marriage, in other words, was eroticized. Husbands had a new responsibility for a novel idea: making sex pleasant for their wives.

Since women had been recast as "pure," this was believed to be a somewhat arduous task. The early sex educator Margaret Sanger, for example, likened women to stone. In her 1926 relationship advice manual, *Happiness in Marriage*, she explained that a husband's job "is to bring to life the real woman of flesh and blood concealed in the statue he adores." Elaborating, she wrote:

> His first duty is the preparation of the hidden, deepest nature of his beloved to receive his love. In opening the portals of her being, or better still in persuading the woman to open these secret portals and to receive him, the young husband deepens and intensifies tenfold the love nature of his partner.

To do so, she said, he should use "all the resources he has at his command."

Cunnilingus was the trick.

The endorsement of oral sex for women would ease the way for fellatio, as experts noticed what wives had known all along: that women's bodies weren't the only ones that could sometimes use a little help. A flagging erection got the prescription of a "genital kiss," though in either case marriage experts were clear that oral sex was only to be used to facilitate coitus, not as its substitute. With that, fellatio and cunnilingus became a team, fighting the good fight for happy marriages everywhere. And then, things changed.

Now oral sex is common among sexually active people but, as Ashlynn rightly observed, there's a double standard. Teens of both sexes agree that cunnilingus is "a bigger deal" than fellatio. Reflecting this, the majority of sexually active 16- to 18-year-old girls have performed oral sex on boys, seeing it as routine, but boys do not do the same for girls. Only 6 percent say they're in favor of the practice, though some, sounding a bit like Victorian husbands, say they will do it to gain access to intercourse. As a result, among young people, fellatio occurs much more frequently than cunnilingus.

It's true in hookups, too. When guy–girl hookups proceed to oral sex, the most common scenario is for men and women to give it to each other, but if the oral sex only goes one way, it goes the guy's way more than two-thirds of the time. In that two-thirds, when oral sex occurs, the women aren't getting a lick of it.

And if Izzy's story is any indication, this data overstates the balance between fellatio and cunnilingus because asking whether oral sex occurred doesn't tell us how much time and effort was put into each activity or whether it persisted to orgasm. We do know that when students receive oral sex in a hookup, men are almost twice as likely as women to have an orgasm. The orgasm gap, in other words, is no smaller even when oral sex is involved. Likely, these numbers reflect women's greater commitment to getting men off, but also the fact that men use oral sex like Victorian husbands did once and teenage boys do now, as a precursor to another sexual activity that favors male orgasm: intercourse.

◆   ◆   ◆

"The Vaginas Are Coming," said the signs popping up around campus. They signaled the impending annual performance of the now-classic college theater event, *The Vagina Monologues*, and students involved with the production were piling on the publicity, getting creative with ways to draw attention and make their peers squirm. On the walls of the campus game room and snack bar, they had hung posters of female student volunteers holding a whiteboard that read, "Let my vagina _____." Consistent with the theme of letting individual vaginas do the talking, students filled out the end however they wished and posed to be photographed.

As Ashlynn slid into a wooden booth with her biology textbook, an uncomfortable snicker came from the display. Curious after Izzy's "single lick" story, she opened her book but kept an eye on the people walking by. In her own experience, people seemed to think that the vulva was "at least a little bit gross" and, while sex was a near-constant topic of conversation, whenever anyone brought up cunnilingus, it got brushed off or laughed off. Talking about it crossed "some invisible line," Ashlynn guessed, between sexy and not-so-sexy sexual topics.

As she suspected, people walking past the display would sometimes "laugh and grimace." A guy guffawed at one that read, "Let my vagina froth." He twisted his face into a grimace, pointed at it, and said, "That's disgusting." This elicited laugher from the girl at his side. A bit later, Ashlynn wrote, "I saw a male friend pass one that read, 'Let my vagina flow.' He said, 'Ew, that's pretty gross,'" to his companion. When a guy and a girl eyed one that read, "Let my vagina pulsate," they began to laugh hard. "'Gross,' he said. The girl shook her head."

Four of Ashlynn's friends joined her at the table just as a group of *Vagina Monologues* promoters wandered in to hand out cookies frosted to look like vulvas. When the cookies came around, Ashlynn wrote, "all four people I was sitting with immediately averted their eyes. No one touched them." She got the distinct sense that her friends thought the cookies were obscene. Had they been in the shape of penises, she thought, her friends would have happily eaten them, even mimicking blow jobs for a chuckle. There was something lighthearted about the penis, she'd noticed, but not the vulva, not at all.

In fact, many of my female students, and especially the heterosexual ones, had internalized a "general disgust" toward their genitals. Comments like the ones observed by Ashlynn exacerbated their insecurity. Women overheard men saying that "vaginas were dirty" and that women who "squirt" are "disgusting." One woman's friend announced that he would never go down on a girl "unless she was completely shaven and I saw her clean her vagina out." Another girl sat at dinner with a guy who complained that their Vietnamese spring roll appetizer tasted like "cooter." All of this was pretty hard for women to disregard, even if most men didn't feel the same.

For some lucky women, fantastic experiences with men who enjoyed performing oral sex turned the tide—"it really impresses most girls," boasted one cunnilingus-loving guy—but most women remained ambivalent, at best, about whether it was a good idea to let a guy go down on them. Even women who believed that the negative characterization of female genitals was unfair had a hard time shaking off their worries. "I tend to be more self-conscious about the way I taste or smell," wrote one, "even though I know I'm very clean and it's really his problem if he doesn't like it."

Izzy felt the same: "I think the act that has been the most touchy for me is cunnilingus, because it's considered to be so intimate and possibly unpleasant for the person doing it." She discussed overhearing people saying, "Oh, it's smelly down there, it tastes bad, it takes forever." The single lick incident didn't help. Likewise, sexually audacious Celeste, despite being experienced and adventurous, wasn't immune to these comments. Only one of the twelve guys she had hooked up with had performed oral sex, and this was maddening—but it was a relief, too. Using the term most common among my students, she admitted that "many girls are a little uncomfortable and insecure about being eaten out, including myself. We women are afraid of being judged and talked about as being smelly or whatever."

Interested in women's discomfort with cunnilingus, sociologist Laura Backstrom and her colleagues interviewed women at Stanford and Indiana University about their thoughts on receiving oral sex. Just over a quarter of the women had strongly negative views of the practice, using words like "weird," "bizarre," "dirty," and "nasty" to describe it. The rest had positive feelings about cunnilingus, but only a few felt comfortable asking for it from men, especially in hookups. Some expressed the familiar idea that cunnilingus is somehow a "bigger deal" than fellatio. "It feels like a guy going down on you is a bigger step than you going down on a guy," said one, "which is probably unfair." "I think I felt kind of guilty almost," said another woman of the men she hooked up with, "like I felt like I was kind of subjecting people to something they didn't want to do and I felt bad about it." Women seem convinced that men don't like it.

◆　　◆　　◆

Of all of the parts of the female body, though, the one that men who like women seem keenest to access is the vagina. It is the veritable Holy Grail of heterosexual male sexuality. It's "all the way." In the 1600s they called it the "chapel of ease." In the 1700s, it was "love's altar" and "the shrine of Venus." In the 1800s they described it as a "carnal mantrap," and not in a bad way. One hundred years later it was a "knick knack" and a "ring-dang-do." Today it's "home base," "happy valley," and "the promised land." And we've been calling it a "honeypot" for nearly five hundred years.

Men—at least men who are attracted to women—put extraordinary amounts of effort into getting into the vagina. Men's desire for the vagina is half of why we exist as a species. And, in real life, there are *lots* of men who love cunnilingus. This is something that my female students, and the ones at Stanford and Indiana, are wrong about. In fact, according to the National Health and Social Life Survey, one of the largest, most comprehensive, and well-designed studies of American sexuality ever completed, men like performing cunnilingus even more than women like receiving it.

So, what is this cultural disgust at women's bodies *really* about?

It's quite obviously not about whether cunnilingus is gross. It's certainly not any grosser than fellatio. I can still recall the moment that a male friend of mine first encountered the idea of receiving such a "genital kiss." We were first-year college students, he from a very conservative Mormon background, and his immediate reaction was disgust. "But you *pee* through that thing!" he said incredulously.

It's true. Men pee through that thing. And there are other reasons why someone might find fellatio unappetizing: the smell of a man's genitals after being confined in a pair of pants all day, the difficulty of getting a penis in one's mouth, pubic hairs caught in teeth, the effort to create suction that strains the muscles underneath the jaw, difficulty catching one's breath, and the taste of precum and semen. In fact, when Jess Butler asked female students at the University of Southern California whether they liked fellatio, none of the more than two dozen she talked to claimed to enjoy it. As one said, "I'd rather not have to do it ever again in my life, but I feel like I have to." "It's gross," said another. "Nobody likes it," insisted a third in response. A person can truly and emphatically enjoy giving a blow job, but one has to be in the right frame of mind. Ditto for cunnilingus.

Yet, while the potential downsides of cunnilingus are front and center in the minds of heterosexual students of both sexes, the similar downsides of fellatio are almost never discussed and are generally considered irrelevant. "No one," a student observed, "ever talks about what a penis is supposed to smell like or what 'cum' is supposed to taste like." Noting that "scented tampons and 'feminine sprays' line the aisles of drugstores," one pointed out, rightly, "Guys don't have to make sure their junk smells like jasmine." The potentially unpleasant things about fellatio are never used to suggest that women would be justified in refusing to do it. And men never seem to mention the possibility that fellatio might be "gross" as a reason to *fear* blow jobs.

If it was just about being gross, our attitudes toward cunnilingus and fellatio would still be symmetrical. They're not. So, the idea that vaginas are gross is not really about women's bodies at all. It's about what we *do* with their bodies. That is, do we use them for getting men off or getting women off? For his orgasm or for hers? Heterosexual students seem to take to the former just fine, but the latter—the privileging of female pleasure through cunnilingus—makes some uncomfortable. That's why they laugh. They're nervous.

Men have more orgasms than women in hookup culture, then, because the culture doesn't promote reciprocity. It's specifically designed for men's orgasm. Female orgasm is acceptable, even ideal, but it's not what it's about. A bisexual man I spoke to at a campus visit put this in stark perspective, observing sheepishly that he prioritized his partner's orgasm when he hooked up with men and his own when he hooked up with women. A guy at Stanford put it equally plainly: "I don't think any hookup is based on mutual orgasm, it's really just based on an orgasm for me."

This will not be a surprise to college women anywhere. "Hookup culture" really means "three years of bad sex," concluded a student at Duke who'd had just about enough. He "didn't even care," said a woman at Brown about her most recent hookup. "I don't think he tried at all." "I think very few guys really care," a student enrolled at the University of Southern California reported. Women are "literally just there to let the guy get off."

My female students sang the same tune. They talked about desire, but it was rare for them to mention orgasm, or even physical pleasure more generally, as an outcome of hooking up. They often echoed Celeste when she complained about being a "masturbation toy." "I was just a warm body being used to give a guy an orgasm," wrote one. Men "treat me like two hands and three holes," grumbled another. "Ultimately," wrote a third, "it's about allowing the male to use your body." "The idea of being 'used' for sex like a masturbatory device," observed a guy about his female friends, "is a common complaint."

A complaint perhaps, but women, too, tend to prioritize male orgasm. "Most of the time we don't ask for anything in bed," Celeste admitted, "or at least I don't." Her priority was to impress her partners. "I want to kind of blow him out of the water," she explained. "If they attempt to do the same for me, that's great, though most of the time that does not happen." Other women agreed that they focused on giving orgasms instead of seeking them. "I don't feel like I've had a sexual experience if the guy doesn't come," wrote one. Male orgasm was paramount: "I will do everything in my power," insisted another, "to get [him] off." Another said that she would "focus completely" on her partner's orgasm. Their own pleasure was beside the point. "My sexuality was filled with anxiety and my need to please the guy instead of worrying about my own pleasure," wrote one student. "Even if I was in charge," another revealed, "I did not make sure I was being pleased."

Some women feel that expecting an orgasm from a male

hookup partner is demanding or rude. The women at the University of Southern California did as well. They told Butler that women "cater to guys," "want men to be happy," and "wanna make the guy feel good about himself." Said one interviewee, "We want them to be happy with the hookup, with the orgasm or whatever, and with us. And our ability to create that for them."

If women deprioritize their own orgasm, it might be because they suspect that it's pointless to do otherwise. Some men, like the Stanford guy above, willingly admit that they're not interested in giving women pleasure. "I don't think [her orgasm] matters as much to the guy," said another. "Say they meet a girl at a party and it's a one-night thing," explained a third about guys in general, "I don't think it's gonna matter to them." When asked about the importance of female orgasm, another male student retorted, "I don't give a shit."

Importantly, men aren't *uniformly* uninterested in female orgasm; they are *specifically* disinterested in the orgasms of women they're hooking up with. The guy who didn't "give a shit" about women's orgasms, for instance, followed up to clarify that he was "all about" orgasm if the woman was his girlfriend. Differentiating between sex with girlfriends and hookups, it turns out, is common: "I think if you're in a long-term relationship," said another guy, "it's essential that she has an orgasm during sexual activity. Short-term relationships, he specified, were entirely different.

Men generally agreed that a woman's orgasm is "more important if it's in a relationship than if it's a one-night stand" or if "it's somebody I care about." Another man explained the expectation that he gives his girlfriends orgasms like this:

Now that I'm in a relationship, I think [her orgasms are] actually pretty important. More important than I think the hookup because you have more invested in that person. . . . it's more a reciprocal thing.

Invoking the ideas of care and reciprocity to differentiate hookup sex from relationship sex is consistent with Mimi Schippers's idea that students think that relationships are a site for interpersonal kindness, but hookups are not. Many men think of relationships as a meeting of equals in which they're accountable for treating the other person with respect. Another guy made it explicit: "In a relationship," he said, "there's much more expected as far as like equality-wise, like give and take sexually."

The data on orgasm reveals this dynamic clearly. Women in relationships are having almost seven times as many orgasms as women hooking up for the first time, and the orgasm gap between men and women shrinks by half. Many men want to give orgasms to their girlfriends—whom they care about, want to please, and believe should be treated as equals—but feel little need to do their hookup partners the same courtesy.

Men, then, aren't uniformly dismissive of women's pleasure, just that of the women they're hooking up with. That's because men in committed relationships aren't playing by the rules of hookup culture. The guys who are hooking up, though, often are. And while the rules of heterosexual relationships are at least a little influenced by what women want, the rules that men play by when they're just looking to hook up are made and enforced, first and foremost, by other men. In this game, women's pleasure isn't a bonus at all; it's a bargaining chip.

◆   ◆   ◆

Corey and his friends were at a late breakfast on Saturday when his friend Simon sheepishly admitted that he'd hooked up with Tegan the night before. Tegan was a bit frumpy, not a "10," and so he waited for the ridicule that he knew would come. And, sure enough, Corey admitted, "All of my friends, including myself, immediately judged him for hooking up with a girl that we all thought was unattractive." Simon took the ribbing and backpedaled. He agreed that she wasn't good-looking (although we don't really know if he thought so) and tried to change the subject.

That night they all went out again and they lost Simon in the blur of drink and noise and people. At about 1 a.m., Corey and his friends decided they'd struck out and went back to one of their rooms to post-party. Simon barged in about an hour later with "a big smile on his face." Ready to redeem himself from the night before, he announced that he'd just had sex with Tyree, a girl he was confident everyone agreed was hot. "His enthusiasm was a lot different than from the morning," Corey commented, "as he knew that he was going to get a better reaction. And a good response he got." High fives all around.

But when Simon went back to his room to crash, the guys started gossiping about whether Tyree got around and agreed she did. Given her reputation, said one of Corey's friends, "it's not worth hooking up with her." This started a debate about Simon, whether he "had game" (could talk women into sex), and if the women he had hooked up with "counted."

Simon was buffeted by two contrasting imperatives: have sex with hot, elusive women but, whatever you do, have sex. Sometimes guys get lucky with a girl who is both beautiful and selective about whom she hooks up with, but often they have to choose between hooking up with an available woman or no woman at all. Those who hook up with women who are considered ugly or easy may attract reprimands because it means that they can't successfully play a higher-status woman. "They'll tease you like that," said one male student. "Talk about her, say she's a dog." Another explained why he tried to avoid sexual contact with women his guy friends disparaged: "I'd never hear the end of it," he said.

Matthew Desmond, the Harvard professor and MacArthur "Genius" grant recipient, calls it "shit talk." Desmond studied forest firefighters, tough men with a dangerous job who spend a lot of time in all-male, or nearly all-male, groups. "There's a large amount of shit talking that goes on out here," said one of the firefighters. "There's a large amount of teasing each other and picking on each other and poking fun at each other, and it goes back and forth all the time." Crewmembers threw barbs and tossed insults as a matter of routine. They were "loud, quick, crude, and abrasive." Shit talk had winners and losers. "To be successful," Desmond wrote, "a player must be clever and mean; his comments must prick." When insulted, he has to return an insult that is at least as sharp and he must do so "swiftly and eloquently." Most important, he must never ever lose his cool.

The denigration of women, Desmond observed, was primary fodder for shit talk. Insulting men's masculinity with feminizing slurs and making crude claims about what they did to each other's moms or girlfriends was par for the course. Its other primary fodder was the skills involved in being a good firefighter. God forbid one wielded a chainsaw poorly, didn't know what a cotter pin was, or had to take a break while digging line. Ignorance, incompetence, mistakes, or lapses could attract a volley of insults.

It was fun, said one of the firefighters: "It's a fun thing to do. To upset people out here is *hilarious*. . . . When you know you're getting under somebody's skin, it's like, yes, I'm there. I love to do it, it's awesome." They claimed that it was just good joshing and generally the guys did like it. Counterintuitively, perhaps, it was a way for them to show each other that they were close. As one of

Desmond's firefighters argued, you can't shit talk just anybody. You can only be humorously horrible to people you really love. "Like family," he said, "you can make fun of each other and they're not gonna get mad at you."

This phenomenon is not unique to firefighters, nor even to all-male groups. When two people are getting to know each other, there is often a first tease. An opportunity to crack a joke arises, and a person may wonder, "If I poke him in a place we both know is sensitive, will he trust that I am doing it in a friendly way?" If she decides to try it out and gets a laugh in response, the friendship has just leveled up. Teasing brings people closer because it's a way of saying, "I know you well enough to know where your buttons are and how hard I can push them without actually hurting you. And you know me well enough to know that I mean no harm."

Shit talk is teasing, but on steroids. "Shit talk," Desmond explains, "through a strange admixture of fraternity and antagonism, conveys both affection and belonging. It is a secret handshake, a hug and a wink, and it functions as a means of passage into the ranks of the firecrew." But, since shit talk has winners and losers, it also serves to arrange the firefighters into a hierarchy. They're brothers, but some are tougher and quicker and meaner than others, and those guys are on top.

So, when Corey and his friends gave Simon shit for hooking up with Tegan, it was a way of bonding and stratifying their band of brothers. Just like the firefighters, they used shit talk to mark Simon as part of the group, but also to grapple for position within it. This talk was often misogynistic, as it was among the firecrew, and, while masculinity was at stake for both groups, for men on campus the object of their skill set wasn't fire, but the very bodies of their female peers.

Some of Desmond's firefighters were more comfortable with

shit talk than others, and the same is true among college men. Simon seemed interested in playing the game, but wasn't quick or mean enough to do it well. If he had been a better shit talker, he would have brought up a woman that one of his guy friends had slept with that everyone agreed was uglier than Tegan or easier than Tyree. That would have turned the negative attention away from him and to someone else who could be brought down a peg. But Simon wasn't a good shit talker, at least not yet.

As for Corey, it made him nervous. He called it a "hostile environment," noting that if his friends were willing to make fun of Simon to his face and talk shit behind his back, there was no reason they wouldn't do that to him as well. "You have no idea what is going to be said about you," he wrote. It was an uneasiness that he had talked about with his closest friend. "I don't want our reputations to be hurt or judged" after a hookup with the "wrong girl," he protested.

If men are going to play this game, they need a strategy, a way to manage the contradictory imperatives to hook up only with women that count, but always hook up. The answer is to make a preemptive strike. I learned this from Brian Sweeney, a sociologist who interviewed a group of white middle- and upper-class fraternity men. These are the men who, on average, are the most enthusiastic about hooking up and most likely to endorse the sexual double standard. They are representative of the type of guy who adheres to a competitive "player masculinity" in which "men play and women get played."

There are men like this on any campus. "I mean, why do you think it's called 'scoring'?" asked a Dartmouth student rhetorically. "It's like you're scoring with the women, yeah, but you're like scoring *on* the other guys." It's "more about the social cachet it buys," said a New York University alum about hooking up. "It's a way to prove our masculinity." Men are impressed when their buddies hook up, said a student at Stanford, because "if a guy hooks up with a girl, he sort of broke down her wall of protection."

As Simon's story suggests, though, the game isn't just about getting girls, it's about getting the *right* girls. A real player can "score" with a "good" girl that other men agree "counts" as "worth" getting. The most respected fraternity brother, said one of Sweeney's interviewees, "gets the girls all the guys are after. He's the man." But guys hook up with the bad girls, too. "No man, that's nasty," said Kevin when asked if he would hook up with women who seem to hook up a lot. But then he reconsidered: "Well, all right. Yeah. I'll give you that. Guys'll be interested. They're always interested."

The preemptive strike when hooking up with a "bad girl" is to treat her badly. The frat guys told Sweeney that when they had sex with lower-status women they would be crude: "rough, lewd and overly self-gratifying." Kevin, the one who conceded that guys will pursue women even if they're low-status, said that in those cases men try to make sure that they "get something . . . without giving in return." These women got "fucked" and "balled." "Ugly girls can get hosed," said another of Sweeney's fraternity men, "guys don't really like 'em, so they get hosed." Being single-minded about sex, sexually rough, and unconcerned with her pleasure are all ways of indicating that a woman is not valued.

In trying to save face and earn points with their buddies, some college men might push a woman to go farther than she wants to go, get sexual favors but not give them in return, and act aggressively or contemptuously in bed—and talk loudly about it the next day. These are ways that they protect their place in the hierarchy of men. Men's disrespect of women is the bargaining chip. It's a way of saying, "Yeah, I hooked up with someone you don't respect, but I don't respect her either. I gave her what she had coming on behalf of both of us." To put it crudely, if the best a guy can do at the end of the night is fuck a "house rat," he's gonna fuck a house rat, but he'll make sure his guy friends know that he knows she's shit.

This is what was behind the chant that stunned the Internet in 2010, and what made it especially chilling. It came from a group of Delta Kappa Epsilon members at Yale who flung "No means yes! Yes means anal!" loudly toward a dormitory filled with women. The first half of the chant is just your typical pro-rape sentiment, the idea that women don't have the right to say no. But the second half of the chant is about what happens if she says yes. "If women say 'yes,'" writes the masculinities scholar Michael Kimmel about the chant, "where's the conquest, where's the chase, where's the pleasure? And where's the feeling that your victory is her defeat?" "Yes means anal" is a counter-move that puts the sexual encounter back into the realm of a zero-sum game. "Back to something," Kimmel explains, "that is assumed could not possibly be pleasurable for her." "Yes means anal" is a preemptive strike.

We don't know how Simon treated Tegan; he did talk shit about her after the fact, agreeing that she was ugly before changing the subject. If he didn't treat her badly during the act, he could at least save some face by sharing in his guy friends' derision for her later. As he gets better at this game, if he accepts the challenge, he'll likely get better at dehumanizing women he hooks up with and do so with more enthusiasm. Simon might learn to do more than talk shit; he might learn to *treat* some women like shit, and he'll feel justified in doing so if he decides the woman he's with is worthless. He'll also learn to protect his own reputation relative to his friends' by ridiculing *them* for the women they hook up with. As men try to protect their own status within the group by bringing their buddies down, women—who are really just innocent bystanders in this game—get smeared right along with the men.

◆   ◆   ◆

So, yeah, there's an orgasm gap on college campuses. It favors heterosexual men, and there's nothing natural about it. It reflects a privileging of male sexual pleasure, a focus on his orgasm on the part of men and women alike, and a narrative that justifies an aversion to giving women pleasure, one that many women internalize. That would be enough, but there are also men out there like the ones interviewed by Sweeney. Women who are unlucky enough to encounter those men may find that they actively take pleasure instead of giving it because using and exploiting the women they sleep with is the point.

It should be no surprise that more than half of the women who completed the Online College Social Life Survey felt disrespected by at least one guy they'd hooked up with. Some of this may just be anxiety about what men think of women who have casual sexual encounters—because they know that some men call women "nasty"—but much of it is also likely attributable to how they were treated. They notice when men are brusque or bullying. They notice when they are selfish, when they pay no attention, when they don't ask. They notice when they get treated like shit. And they notice when they don't have orgasms. We know that because, when they do have an orgasm, they're six times as likely as women who didn't to say that they enjoyed their last hookup "very much."

"Good sex is so hard to come by," complained a student named Veronica about women's experience in hookup culture, "that we can be sure sexual satisfaction is not the primary motivation for girls engaging in hooking up." She didn't understand why so many women, herself included, continued to actively seek out men to hook up with, writing:

> I can think of several examples of my friends repeatedly hooking up with the same guys, unable to provide an explanation for why. Beautiful, interesting, seemingly self-respecting girls . . . It's not the sex and it's certainly not the emotional connection they're pursuing.

Veronica is right to notice that women actively pursue opportunities to hook up with men, and probably not primarily for pleasure or emotional satisfaction, but she'd likely be surprised to discover that the majority say they enjoy their experiences. Of the women who filled out the Online College Social Life Survey, for example, 84 percent reported that they enjoyed their last hookup at least "somewhat."

In fact, when I've asked women around the country what they are getting out of hookups, they string together a long list of pleasures. Alongside the occasional orgasm, women enjoy the simple pleasure of being turned on, the exhilaration of firsts, and the satisfaction that comes with honing sexual skills. They describe the uneasy thrill of exploring a sexual identity tentatively and the joy of embracing it wholeheartedly. And, since they never know if a hookup will turn into romance, some experienced the pleasure of hope and anticipation, too.

Veronica herself would recognize some of these. Elsewhere she described hooking up as an "adrenaline rush." "Being young and having this sexual appetite and being horny and knowing that you're getting closer to scratching that itch by being physical with boys," she wrote, was intoxicating. It was, she said, "a desperately sexually frustrating time," but it felt good, too. There is pleasure to be had for women even in the face of hookup culture's deficiencies, to be sure.

Yet, in my discussions with students and in the pages of their journals, one type of pleasure stood out as especially common and strongly motivating for women. It was a real pleasure, but a troubled one—maybe, even, a dangerous one—and one that harmed not only women's relationships with men, but their relationships with each other. It was the pleasure of being chosen.

8

Wanting to Be Wanted

Brooke wasn't sure she believed in bisexuality. "I am so skeptical," she wrote, admitting that she was embarrassed to say so. She knew two women who claimed the label, but had a hard time taking either one of them seriously. One, she thought, was just trying to be sexy, while the other seemed to adopt it more as a political identity: "I thought it was just part of her 'look,'" she wrote. She wanted to be open-minded—"Who am I to say what their sexuality is?"—but she couldn't shake the idea that it couldn't be real.

She herself identified as heterosexual even though she'd kissed several women. These experiences had been at parties and she didn't think they had any relevance to her sexual identity. "I never want to actually make out with a girl when I'm sober," Brooke explained near the middle of the year, "but when I get drunk I always think it'd be fun with my girlfriends." She felt comfortable doing so because she was confident that neither she nor they had any real feelings for women. "I know what kind of person they are, and we both don't expect anything to happen afterwards," she wrote. "We can look back on it and say, oh haha, that was fun."

She was, though, sometimes distracted by women's beauty—"I find the softness of some women's bodies very appealing," she confessed—and she wrote that she found "the idea of two women giving each other pleasure empowering and exciting." But, she shrugged, "I don't have the real urge."

Brooke would look back at these comments soon and chuckle, but she was not alone in thinking that women who kiss other women at parties are just doing it for fun. She's echoing what sociologists Leila Rupp and Verta Taylor describe as the "reigning assumption about girls kissing girls in the party scene": that they're doing it as a gag or to please male onlookers, not because they have any "real urge" to be sexual with other women.

Could it be true that, all across America, women are kissing each other without a flicker of desire? Rupp and Taylor didn't think that was likely. So, they and their colleagues sought to prove it. They interviewed women at UC Santa Barbara who were or thought they might be attracted to other women and asked them if they'd ever kissed other women at parties and why. Their research design was a tongue-twister: If some girls who like girls kiss girls in public, then some girls who kiss girls in public like girls.

Their suspicions turned out to be correct. Many of the women being cheered on by men at parties aren't actually doing it for fun or male attention. "It was more of just my own desire to be with, like to try that with a woman," explained one. Another said that she started off kissing a female friend of hers when she was drunk and, then, "soon enough," she said, "we realized, okay, we're not drunk and we're making out." Eventually they became girlfriend and girlfriend and, she said happily, "I never looked back." For women who stayed in the closet, kissing girls in public was a way of hiding in plain sight. Everyone assumed they were doing it for the attention of men, so they could try it without anyone knowing they liked it, not even the women they were kissing. Though some lesbian, bisexual, and questioning women avoid college parties because they're unfriendly to sexual minorities, others find that the assumption of heterosexuality is excellent cover for same-sex eroticism.

And Brooke? She learned that she liked kissing women, too. One day in her journal she gushed about a student named Adisa in a stream-of-consciousness, single-space paragraph that went on for over a page and a half. Suffice it to say, Adisa had awoken an unrelenting and undeniable urge in Brooke. "She's honestly beautiful," she wrote. "She has big, curly hair, and big curly lips, too. . . . I don't think I've crushed so hard on someone in my entire life."

When Adisa showed sexual interest in return, suddenly Brooke's curiosity about women was no longer just theoretical, it was fully embodied.

When I see her, my heart pounds, and I get nervous. When I think about kissing her, I get this feeling in my body. I've had it before, it's hard to explain. But it's like a wave of electricity goes from my head to my stomach. Like, this full-body turn-on.

That's *desire*.

In contrast to the reigning assumption, women who kiss other women at college parties are sometimes exploring or indulging same-sex attraction. This seems pretty obvious. The interesting question, then, is why so many people have such a hard time seeing it.

◆   ◆   ◆

In an interview with *Rolling Stone* just before her sex tape hit the Internet, socialite Paris Hilton admitted something fairly profound. "My boyfriends always tell me I'm not sexual," she said. "Sexy, but not sexual." The words represent the push and pull of our sexuality. To be sexual is to experience desire; to be sexy is to inspire it. To be sexual is to be acutely aware of one's body as the source of an ancient urge: raw, undeniable. As Brooke might say, electrifying. To be sexy is to spark or stir those feelings, to be the object of desire.

To be both sexy and sexual—to be urgently attracted to someone who desires you in return—is one of the great pleasures in life. But during the Industrial Revolution this beautiful symmetry was torn apart. Men got sex and, with it, the feeling of lust. We decided that men were sexual. Women got the indistinct privilege of being the object of men's desire. We declared them sexy. Ever since, we have been told that this is one important way that men and women are different: men want, while women want to be wanted. Hence Paris Hilton: an iconic sex symbol who can seem oddly asexual.

Many of us heartily reject this gendered way of thinking about sexuality, but it likely influences our experiences of others and ourselves at least a little. And, insofar as it does, it threatens to estrange us from the part of our sexuality that has been made taboo for us. From men it takes away the pleasure of feeling sexy, of basking in another's desire. On women it puts the heavy burden of attracting and pleasing men, while refusing to acknowledge that women have sexual desires independent of men.

This is why gay women in college can hide in plain sight. If women want to be wanted, then girl-on-girl kissing must be for male attention. Their kisses *have* to be a performance because they want only to please, not be pleased. In contrast, if men were to kiss each other in full view of onlookers at a college party, it would be seen by most as overtly homosexual. In fact, while some students have a tendency to think that bisexual women are just heterosexual women who are pretending to like women, as Brooke once did, they often think that men who claim bisexuality are just homosexuals in denial. When men kiss men, we see lust, which might be why gay men inspire a more virulent strain of homophobia than gay women.

The fact that girl-on-girl kissing is so widely and so oddly believed to be a strictly *hetero*sexual activity suggests that this gendered way of thinking about sexuality—the idea that men want and women want to be wanted—has at least some purchase on college campuses. One of my male students, Lorenzo, thought so. He observed that men's language seemed to be "geared exclusively towards pursuing." "Guys tend to use language like, 'I would definitely hook up with her,'" he wrote, language that explicitly refers to men's sexual desires.

Among women, it was different. "Women discuss how much they want to look good in order to be pursued," Lorenzo reflected. "I occasionally hear blatant remarks like 'I just wish he wanted me' or 'What can I do to make him want me?'" Other times, he wrote, the language was more subtle, including comments like "My hair looks great right now, we should go to a party." He noticed that these statements implied that it was women's job to attract, to hope that the guy she liked would find her alluring enough to approach. It disturbed him to know that so many women had accepted their status as sexual objects.

◆　　◆　　◆

Then again, being a sexual object can feel quite good. There really is nothing quite like knowing that someone wants us. We are told to love ourselves, to love our bodies, but this is no substitute. The pleasure of being desired has to come from the desire of someone else. And there's no doubt that it can feel amazing.

Cynthia knew this feeling. One night after playing drinking games, she and a guy named Dustin ended up in his dorm room. She was new to hooking up and she paused in anticipation, taking in the bare walls and the unmade bed before he led her past a pile of dirty clothes on the floor, spun his desk chair around, and pulled her into his lap. "He was the *worst* kisser!" she recalled with obvious delight.

Dustin was one of the hot guys on campus, an athlete and a known player. Cynthia had no illusions about his intentions. "I could already sense that he was the party-hard, hook-up-with-as-many-girls-as-I-possibly-can-in-college type," she wrote. This didn't bother her at all, but she lost interest in pursuing the hookup when she realized how bad he was with his mouth.

Still on his lap, she pulled back, made earnest eye contact with her wide brown eyes, and told Dustin explicitly not to take off her shirt and bra. He looked right back at her, reached around her torso, and *snap*. She pretended to chastise him: "Dustin, I told you that wasn't coming off." He responded, cheekily, "Well you didn't seem to stop me." This, she admitted, was true. He dislodged her shirt and bra and turned his unpleasant attention to her breasts, then threw her onto the lower bunk and climbed on top of her.

Cynthia, unfazed, interrupted him again, making an excuse that she had to be up early the next day. Dustin made a last-ditch effort to save the hookup; he tried a pickup artist tactic called "negging." This is a sexual compliance strategy that involves insulting women in order to undermine their confidence, leading them to seek reassurance. If it works, when a man tells a woman she's not particularly sexually attractive, she'll want to have sex with him to prove to herself that she is.

Dustin negged. He told Cynthia that she wasn't special to him and that she should feel lucky he picked her. He could have any girl, he said, implying that she could easily be replaced. She rolled her eyes and got up to leave. He cried blue balls, complained that it "wasn't fair," and gave her three options:

Option A: We fuck, which I think is a long shot. Option B: You give me a blow job, which I also think is a long shot, but it's possible. Option C: You leave, but I reserve the right to resent you.

Dustin's last-ditch effort only made Cynthia more pleased with herself. "I just kept saying, 'I don't know' and smiling," she wrote. I could almost see the glimmer in her eye.

◆　　◆　　◆

It feels good to be wanted, and even someone's bad behavior can feel good if it's accompanied by that feeling. Many of my female students experienced it. Alondra, for example, the student who told us about hooking up at the bar called Murphy's, talked about how at least ten football players followed her on Instagram within a couple months of getting to campus. It takes about three minutes, she reported, between accepting a follow request from a guy and having all of the photos of her liked. At minute four, she gets a compliment with emojis. That week she had taken the bait and given one particularly well-known athlete her phone number. He sent "tons of texts" complimenting her appearance and telling her how attractive he found her, then asked her if she wanted to hook up. When she said no, he countered by asking, "How long do I have to wait?"

Though Alondra didn't usually take men's interest in her

very seriously, she certainly enjoyed it. "After a long night out," she wrote about the fun of parties, "you always feel more confident." To her, the texts she got the next day were proof that men wanted her. She liked that they often had to remind her who they were because she wasn't able to keep track of them all. "The more attention we get," she surmised, "the more pretty we feel."

Many of my female students relished being desired by men, but if this sometimes boosted confidence, it at least as often crushed it. More than a third wrote at length of their fear that their bodies weren't acceptable to their male peers. In contrast, men spent little time writing about whether they were fit enough, handsome enough, or well-dressed enough to be worthy of a woman's approval. When men in my sample did express concern about their bodies, they were invariably non-heterosexual or non-white.

For women, the pressure could be intense. Some felt that any physical imperfection was failure. "If a girl does not have the perfect body," wrote one, dismayed, "she is instantly not even considered." "I thought that having a body like [a model] was the only way men would want to have sex with me," confessed another. Men's opinion of women's bodies symbolized more than just rejection; it was an existential threat: "It left me feeling," wrote one student who worried about being unattractive, "like I was nothing."

As the feminist Naomi Wolf once observed, "A culture fixated on female thinness is not an obsession about female beauty, but an obsession about female obedience." Wolf argues that when women perform for the hypothetical male gaze in exchange for validation, they're not showing men that they're beautiful, they're showing them that they care what men think of them, that they'll defer to men's opinion, that they'll follow men's rules, that they'll submit.

Cynthia, that girl who so enjoyed Dustin's bad-boy behavior, was not immune to insecurity. Sometime before hooking up with him, she discussed her fear that men wouldn't find her attractive. "We feel that if we have any flaws," she wrote anxiously, "they will consider us ugly. Women need to be absolutely perfect physically, perfect hair, skin, weight, height, and so on." It made her feel insecure and it caused her to obsessively monitor her appearance. "I constantly look at myself in the mirror," she reported, "facing the side to see how much my stomach is extending out, or how big my butt looks, or how fat my arms are."

When Dustin begged her to stay, it felt good, but it was also a relief, a respite, a break from the constant worry that she wasn't pretty enough. "[It] makes me feel attractive when he notices me," she wrote, "it makes me feel like I am hot, someone who he would want to hook up with." Dustin's attention was a reprieve from the frightening possibility that men didn't find her sexy.

Because Cynthia was heterosexual, she'd learned to think of compliments from women as relatively worthless. Only men could ease her fears. "When a guy compliments me," she explained, "it means a whole lot more to me than when I hear the same compliment from a girl. It means that the guy is noticing me . . . It boosts my self-esteem." Instead of being a source of comfort, other women were another source of anxiety. "I walk around comparing myself to the other women I see," she wrote, suggesting that she saw herself in a competition with them for men's approval. Other women were a threat.

If Cynthia were to be transported back to a big city in the 1920s, she would recognize this dynamic. This was the decade, if you recall, in which Americans began living in cities in large numbers and entrepreneurs began devising ways to entertain the masses. It was when courtship left the home and took to the streets, where men instead of women had control. That was the decade in which makeup became a woman's best friend and fat became her worst enemy. It was the decade in which women began, in throngs, to try to be sexy for men.

It was competitive then, but the "male shortage" caused by the brutality of World War II brought competition among women to a whole new level. That was when the *New York Times* warned that hundreds of thousands of women would die alone. The fear was enough to transform a society's mating strategy, and going steady was born. On college campuses, the numbers worked in women's favor, though. Since only a quarter of undergraduates at the time were female, if a girl wanted a boyfriend she could have her pick.

Not anymore. On any given campus today, women comprise almost 60 percent of undergraduates. For every two women who can attract a man's attention, however briefly, there is one left with no attention at all. It is as if on college campuses we have recreated off-campus postwar conditions. Men are in short supply and women who want or need their validation might have to work hard, even fight, to get it.

The idea that women's bodies are on trial, though, isn't simply an accident of demographics. Nor is it just something that women absorb from a lifetime of television, movies, and web series; books, magazines, and newspapers; advertisements, billboards, and commercials; Internet surfing, video games, music, and more—though it is. Women's body confidence isn't simply already low, it's being actively torn down by the people around them.

My female students received daily reminders that their male peers were judging their bodies. Men flipped through magazines and casually commented. They posted sexy photographs of women on their Facebook walls, eliciting virtual drooling. "Thoughts about girls' attractiveness are constantly thrown around in [men's] conversations," one of my male students admitted. Men criticized some of the most beautiful women in the world, going after models and actresses whose appearance had earned them millions. Women noticed. No one was safe.

Working in the computer lab, one of my female students listened to two guys evaluate the appearance of a woman online. "Dude, look at how hot this girl is?" said one, but the other replied with disgust in his voice, "But, look . . . oh my god." Distracted, she found herself wondering what exactly was so unacceptable: "I assume maybe she was in an accident, or got a tan, or gained weight, or cut her hair, or changed her style. There are so many things a girl can do that sabotage her beauty."

One of my female students was told, "Your boobs aren't big enough." Another overheard a guy say that a woman's "tits are way too big." One student's male friend routinely complained about "his frustration with 'ugly' girls" being in his line of sight. Another reported that her male friends would point to women's Facebook profiles and make comments. "They're usually quick," she reported, "to add phrases like, 'She's kind of ugly,' 'Damn look at that ass,' 'She's hot right?' or 'What do you think about the way she looks?'" She expressed concern that these men talked about her this way when she wasn't around. It didn't matter if the comments were positive or negative; the fact that they were being evaluated was enough to make women uncomfortable. "I know the guy will be judging me," wrote one female student nervously.

For women on campus, it can feel like negging from all sides. Being constantly reminded that men are or might be criticizing them is upsetting, and some women struggle mightily with maintaining self-worth in the face of such tough critics. Under these circumstances, many *are* motivated to seek reassurance from men, maybe even especially the most judgmental men, just to regain some confidence. Some, like Dustin, exploit this, but men don't have to. All the negging gives men the key to women's self-esteem whether they want it or not and, in return, many women are a little more compliant than they might otherwise have been. "A quietly mad population," wrote Naomi Wolf shrewdly, "is a tractable one."

◆　　◆　　◆

"Guys are so fucking harsh!" complained one of my students, but the women on campus could be harsh, too. Women were sometimes complicit in the draining of their female peers' body confidence, mocking or criticizing how they looked and dressed. One of my female students said that, thanks to two particularly aggressive women, walking into one class was like being pelted by rotten tomatoes. "I usually brace myself for a searing evaluation of my clothing," she wrote, "I have been told that I look like 'Jane Goodall on her day off,' asked, 'Just back from the nunnery?' and told that no matter what my outfit I always manage 'to bring it back to kindergarten.'" On the first hot day of spring she wore shorts and heard them whispering in disgust. "Did you see her legs?" She noted that whether she dressed like a nun or not, she would be criticized.

Another of my students listed all the things that other women had told her to change about herself:

> I have been told that I need a new wardrobe, to let my hair
> grow out and dye it, and to shape my eyebrows. Oh, and I need
> a manicure. . . . I have been called "butch" more times than
> I can count. I have also been told that I dress like a homeless
> person and that I need a proper haircut.

These comments were meant to help, she thought, but she resented them nonetheless. No one had "seemed bothered" by what she looked like back home and, in any case, if she had to choose between being fashionable and paying tuition, she'd pick the latter every time. But she couldn't help but be thrown by the comments. "Maybe I need to learn how to dress?" she wrote, adding a question mark to the statement. "I have never cared about this issue until people pointed it out to me."

"Mean girls" are a trope these days, an iteration of the stereotype that women are especially critical of and competitive with one another. We describe them as "catty," drawing on an equally unfair stereotype of cats that suggests they are prone to hissing and spitting at one another. But human conflict is almost always over rank or resources. We fight when we feel we need to, when we fear what might happen if we do not. When women act catty toward one another, it isn't a sign of their essential nature, it's a clue as to where the power is.

The reality television show *Battle of the Bods*, mercifully now off the air, can help us see this. In each episode, five men or five women, already selected for their attractiveness, line up in their underwear to have each of their body parts separately ranked from the "hottest to the nottest" by an invisible, unnamed panel of the opposite sex. The group being evaluated is instructed by the host to guess how the panel ranked them. If they are able to rank themselves "correctly"—that is, as the panel did—they win a cash prize. So, the typical show includes a sometimes brutal conversation between contestants about one another's flaws with the aim of somehow coming to an agreement as to which of them is the most beautiful and which the most ugly.

The format is completely artificial and designed to produce as much rancor as possible, but the dynamic nonetheless perfectly distills a very real feature of everyday life for women in college: their bodies are on trial, there are winners and losers, and only men's opinions matter. In one episode, the five women ordered themselves according to how they'd been ranked by the hidden panelists and the camera panned greedily to the woman ranked last. She looked dejected. "Don't worry," said the host cruelly, "I think you've got a great *face*." The woman bolted backstage in response, sobbing, and two of the other contestants followed her to try to console her. "Do you have any idea how many girls auditioned?" one asked, trying to remind her that she had already been judged to be gorgeous. "You got on the show! You're beautiful!" the other said encouragingly.

But the other women's opinions didn't matter to Number Five, so female solidarity didn't make her feel any better. Instead, she lashed out against the two girls left on stage: Number Three and Number Four. "Those girls are *hideous!*" she insisted, punching up at her closest rivals and emphasizing the word. "The one has that huge *mole* on her side!" "It's not my fault she has low self-esteem," said Number Three, the girl with the mole, her voice full of disdain. And when Number Five shouted that she'd "rather have nobody win any money than be humiliated," the woman with the mole yelled back, "I got number five twice! Do you see me sitting here boo-hooing and crying?" Number Five responded with a racial slur, hollering, "Sorry I'm not a tough-ass East LA chola!" It had devolved into what could fairly be called a catfight.

If women accept that men's opinion of their appearance is a measure of their worth, then other women pose a threat, since they may be evaluated as "better than" by the ones granted the power to evaluate. Some women, in this scenario, will be willing to fight for men's attention, but it isn't because women are naturally this way. Maybe some will fight because they're viciously competitive and want to be on top, but some just fear being Number Five; they're fighting in the hope of not coming in last.

When women channel the male gaze, then, what they are really doing is trying to reassure themselves that when it is aimed at them they'll be evaluated positively. It's a phenomenon intended to divide and conquer women. And it does. The women on the reality show could just get together, call bullshit, walk off, and feel beautiful without men, but they don't. Many women on campuses in America have even less freedom to walk away. Their institution is total and it includes unforgiving and unending rounds of critique.

◆   ◆   ◆

The women who won on *Battle of the Bods* had the satisfaction of knowing that at least some men found them more attractive than other women, but they also got cash prizes. The rewards for women on college campuses are more than just psychological, too. Some who play the game are seeking not just reprieve from the worry that they're unattractive, but the opportunity to share in the experiences that men generally control. That is, the off-campus party locations and alcohol, the "whole college experience." Men host the parties and women's beauty, flirtatiousness, and potential sexual availability is the price of admission.

Oftentimes it's almost exactly like an episode of *Battle of the Bods*. Hosts pick themes explicitly designed to encourage women to dress sexily, but women understand that they are expected to do so regardless, to choose their outfit exclusively, as one University of Southern California student put it, from the "whore side" of their closet. A neon-themed party described by my students attracted women wearing "the tightest and skimpiest neon and bright-colored clothing." A beach-themed party brought out women dressed as mermaids, in miniskirts and bikini tops. This happens even in winter. On any given night, wrote one student, there are "a lot of girls in little outfits being like, 'I'm cold.'"

Sexy costume themes reward women for revealing and provocative clothes, stratify them and put them into competition, all while reminding them that it's their job to make parties sexy. In contrast, men are rarely, if ever, expected to dress in ways that present their bodies to women for evaluation. To the neon party, men just wore the most colorful T-shirts they owned. They wore "normal streetwear clothing" to the beach party. Amazingly, men even wore clothes to the Anything But Clothes party. There is nothing remarkable about men's non-participation in costuming. Instead, as Owen learned when he fruitlessly googled "burlesque," it's widely understood that the imperative to dress sexily only applies to women.

Some party themes make the power dynamic explicit, placing men and women into unequal relationships, like "CEOs and office hoes" (employer and employee), the racist "colonial bros and Nava-hoes" (colonizer and colonized) and, simply, "pimps and hoes" (there's a theme to the themes). One student described a frat party as pedophilia-themed. The men who attended, she wrote, "were encouraged to dress up as sexual predators." Women were supposed to come looking underage. Her roommate had gone shopping for clothes that would give off a "prepubescent girl" look: a "glittery XL Hello Kitty brand T-shirt" from the children's section, "a short jean-skirt," and some fat scrunchies that she planned to use to give herself "dramatic, bubble-gum pigtails." My student described it as an obvious attempt "to solidify men's role of domination and female subordination."

In some cases, women can't even get into parties if they don't dress up. Many fraternity parties station a brother at the door who decides who may enter. It's his job to pick partygoers out of the crowd, choosing the mostly conventionally attractive, provocatively dressed women, who appear willing to play their part. Once inside, women are overrepresented by design, even more than they already are on campus. Men make sure they're the minority so that women are forced to compete for their attention and the guys can have their pick.

"Those that possess the alcohol have the power," was how Jill Russett put it. For her PhD in education, she interviewed women about their experiences at such parties. They explained that alcohol, or the "good" alcohol, is sometimes kept upstairs in men's bedrooms or otherwise away from the main socializing and dancing area. To get invited into these more private parts of the house for drinks, looking "better" than other women was imperative. As one of her interviewees said:

> If I showed up in this sweatshirt, a guy's not going to be like, "Here's a shot," so you wear as minimal clothing as you can, and the power is all in their hands, like they are like, "Oh you're not pretty . . . so I'm not going to give you alcohol because that is just wasting my time."

Another of her interviewees commented, "It's definitely not a gender neutral party setting . . . the girls on campus don't really get to make a lot of the decisions." A Dartmouth woman agreed: "When men run the scene, they feel entitled to their space, they feel entitled to their actions. I think there is a subconscious feeling of dominance."

When women *are* in charge of parties, events feel more gender-egalitarian. A comparison between Princeton and Harvard is illustrative. Both severed any official relationship with fraternities in the 1800s, but all-male "eating clubs" (at the former) and "final clubs" (at the latter) emerged in their place. In 1990, Princeton required that their eating clubs integrate, a move that significantly changed the nature of these groups. By 2015, four of the eleven eating clubs elected female presidents, the largest proportion since they went coed. That year Eliza Mott, then president of the oldest and most prestigious club on campus, argued that full integration shifted the balance of power. "Women have greater authority over the party environment," she said, "and thus greater access to security for themselves and others in danger."

In contrast, Harvard's final clubs have mostly resisted pressure to integrate, and cause the same problems as the most notorious of fraternities. A report released by the college in 2016 characterized the dynamics of the clubs as "men in positions of power engaging with women on unequal and too often on very sexual terms." Almost half of the women surveyed who had participated in final club activities had been sexually assaulted by their senior year. Entering a male-dominated final club was, to put it starkly, a Harvard woman's single greatest risk factor for sexual assault.

Women are aware that being the object of male desire is a double-edged sword. "We simultaneously are grossed out by men's objectification of women," wrote one, "but also crave it." Another was both relieved and sad, writing, "Guys don't look at me like they look at other girls." Alondra noted that her desire for male approval left her feeling the "need to go out night after night." When she did, she admitted that she tried to show "more skin" than her friends to guarantee that she wouldn't be the one girl "dancing alone," the loser ranked last, a Number Five. "It's a constant search for a validation," said a student at Boston University, "that never really comes."

The pleasure of being desired is a double-edged sword, too, because the psychological reward likely inhibits women's physical pleasure. Students can come to "self-objectify," think of themselves from another's perspective, as objects of someone else's gaze. When a person becomes preoccupied with how people outside of their body experience it and forget to just be in it, they are self-objectifying.

Cynthia would certainly recognize the phenomenon. "Women . . . look at themselves through the eyes of men," she wrote one day, reflecting on her hookup with Dustin. "This is exactly what I am doing."

I still remember the day I learned to do it. It was sixth grade, I was wearing shorts, and I had just slid into one of those school chairs with the built-in desk. Someone I had a crush on was sitting a couple rows to my right and just a little bit behind. I looked down at my legs, suddenly self-conscious, and I made them look skinny to myself by pressing my toes into the ground and raising my knees. As my legs rose a bit off the chair, the flesh of my thighs was pulled by gravity and it filled in the space underneath them. It was as if I was looking at the spine of a book.

But if you look at the book face on, it takes on another shape entirely. If I mushed my legs flat against the seat, the flesh spread out right and left so that, from my point of view, my thighs looked fat. I suddenly realized that, if I wanted my legs to look skinny to a person two rows to my right, they needed to look fat to me. That double awareness—the awareness, first, of my own body as an object to be looked at and, second, that I could take the perspective of someone else and manipulate my body to try to please another's gaze—is self-objectification.

In sexual encounters, women who self-objectify learn to focus on how they look instead of how they feel. They engage in a practice called "spectatoring," in which a woman takes on the perspective of her partner. A woman who is overly concerned with how she looks might try to stay in sexual positions that she thinks are flattering, arrange her body and limbs to make herself look thinner or curvier, try to keep her face looking pretty, and ensure she doesn't make any embarrassing noises. She may even avoid orgasm because climaxing means losing control of these things.

One student recognized this behavior in herself, describing it this way:

> Because I'm so self-conscious, I always think about the way I look during sex. This stops me from doing a number of things during sexual encounters; for example, I hate having sex with the lights on because I'm embarrassed about my naked body; I don't like to be in sexual positions where my stomach is squished or my butt is exposed because I'm self-conscious of those body parts; and I used to never allow my male partners to perform oral sex on me because I was self-conscious about the way my vagina looked or smelled. I would constantly be trying to see myself how my partner was seeing me.

For women who do this, sexual encounters can become, in one student's words, "out-of-body" experiences, and that inhibits their physical pleasure. Psychologists have found that objectifying one's own body is associated with faking orgasm, a sense of helplessness, lack of communication with one's partner, difficulty with sexual arousal, and other forms of sexual dysfunction. In short, no matter how attractive a woman actually is, the more she worries about how she looks, the less likely she'll experience sexual desire, pleasure, and orgasm.

◆ / ◆ ◆

It can seem as if men and women are at odds in hookup culture. In many ways, they are. Men hooking up with women are often unkind, assuming that they have to make their lack of interest in anything "meaningful" painfully clear, and women often respond by treating men equally dismissively. The majority of orgasms go to men, reflecting a culture in which women who hook up with men give pleasure more often than they receive it, and sometimes men are purposefully exploitative and derogatory. Some men are also harshly judgmental of women's bodies, actively undermining their efforts to feel good about themselves, or just not caring if what they're doing is damaging. Some use that insecurity to manipulate women into doing things they're not sure they want to do. And, as the next chapter will show most horrifically, hookup culture enables sexual violence, and overwhelmingly it is men who victimize women.

If you pull back far enough, though, if you look not at the interactions between men and women but at hookup culture's incentives and punishments, then its treatment of men and women looks very much the same. Men and women are in conflict, ironically, because hookup culture bears down on all students equally with the same perverted imperatives.

It's helpful to look back at the story of Corey and Simon. Simon was the guy who got razzed by his buddies for hooking up with women they decided didn't "count." He and his friends were always jostling for rank. If he didn't hook up with women they approved of often enough, he lost esteem in their eyes. The shit talk could get harsh and the guys sometimes lashed out at one another. Corey called it a "hostile environment." He wasn't a social climber, but he feared being ranked last. He didn't want to be a Number Five either.

Trying to ensure that they have at least some social capital on campus, many men learn to manage the contradictory rules of hookup culture—that is, hook up constantly, but do so only with beautiful, elusive women—by treating women their friends think are worthless badly, which includes the withholding of orgasm. In this way, some men's sexual choices are in part a performance for other men, a way to earn their approval and be judged positively. Treating their hookup partners nicely isn't a strategically viable option because neither they nor their buddies care, theoretically anyway, about women's opinions.

Women who are interested in men are similarly placed into competition with one another. The cost of losing is high and the rewards of winning are real. Sometimes they're willing to take down the women around them to ensure that they come out on top. Sometimes they're just fighting to avoid the existential fear that they are "nothing." Sometimes they're just trying to have the college experience they've been promised.

Hookup culture puts men and women who are hooking up with each other at odds, that's for sure, but it also forces them into competition with other members of the same sex. Men and women alike look to men for approval and devalue the opinions of women. So, men always get to decide who comes out on top. In this battle, both men and women can get mean. And the reason that women have fewer orgasms in hookups is because *both* men and women are performing sexually, in part, for a male audience.

All of this jostling for position is anxiety-producing, uncomfortable, and sometimes painful. It certainly doesn't often make for good sex. But bad sex, as unpleasant as it sounds, is by no means the worst thing that can happen to a person in hookup culture.

9

Flirting with Danger

He was one of Natalie's best friends and, years later, they would still be close. "I care for him in a strangely maternal way," she wrote in her first year, trying to describe their relationship, "because he's really immature, but really honest, and a genuinely good soul." She saw the positive in him, though she acknowledged the bad, calling him "stubborn" and "uncompromising." As an example, she talked about how he once forbade her to go to a regular grocery store "because there was too much packaging," making her go to two stores instead of one to get everything she wanted. He just found it difficult to "understand other people's points of view," she wrote. She liked him anyway.

One night they found themselves in bed together. He lived just a few doors down, so it wasn't unusual for him to pop in for a platonic snuggle. That night she lay with her back to him on her twin mattress; he on top of her blankets and she underneath. He was propped up on his elbow behind her, reading a copy of *Portnoy's Complaint* that he rested on her shoulder, when suddenly his body

became tense and she felt him press against her. Natalie opened
her eyes, contemplated the scrap of orange fabric tossed haphaz-
ardly over the bedside lamp, then turned around and kissed him.
"I find him really sexy," she admitted, "despite his personality
shortcomings."

Twenty-five steamy minutes later she paused. There were limits
to what she felt comfortable doing in a hookup and so she told him,
"We're not going to have sex because I know neither of us actually like each other." He responded by asking for a blow job, which
"shocked" her. She didn't consider herself the kind of girl who just
sexually serviced men at their request, and that was no mystery to
him. She told him no.

His response was, in her view, simply pigheaded. Instead of letting it drop, he argued and pushed and complained. "I would initiate that if I wanted to," she explained to him again sternly, but it
made no dent in his pro-blow job position. She looked at the orange
lamp and deliberated:

> He still wants it, and it's sort of awkward at this standstill, but
> mostly it just feels like every other time he's being stubborn, I
> don't really mind, he's my friend; it's a simple pleasure, okay
> fine. And I'm not thinking about it at all in the terms of sexual
> coercion, I'm thinking of it in terms of him getting his way and
> making me shop at two different grocery stores.

So, she did it. She climbed under the bedspread and got him
off. "Annoying," she recalled, "but not a big deal." He didn't return
the favor.

The next day he treated her like every other girl he'd hooked
up with that year. He ignored her. This was too much for Natalie,
and when she finally got his attention again, she accused him

of sidelining female pleasure and feeling entitled to an orgasm. "And he's listening," she reported to me later, "and he's trying to say things like, 'To me, oral sex is really intimate,'" referring to cunnilingus but not fellatio, "and, 'I'm sorry, you know I can be pushy.'" It wasn't a satisfying conversation but he seemed to listen or, at least, Natalie said, "I felt like he heard me. And I really don't remember it being a big thing."

Then, later in the semester, a girl on campus reported that he had raped her. Natalie reeled. She wasn't sure she trusted the woman who named him, but based on her own experience, she also had no trouble believing that he would act coercively. And how coercive do people get to be, she wondered, before their behavior counts as criminal?

She asked him, point blank, "How could you have gotten off on making her do something she didn't want to do?" He was mute, slumped in his desk chair, his eyes turned sideways behind his mop of brown hair. She talked at him, torn between begging for an explanation and delivering a lecture. His response, finally, was, "I get what you're saying. But she seemed like she wanted it."

Natalie was crestfallen. "This kind of incident makes me really feel like we're fucked," she wrote. "If moans of protest are dirty talk and the whole point is to fuck someone senseless, there is no such thing as rape." They weren't friends again for quite some time.

◆   ◆   ◆

Among all but the most obstinate, there is no longer any debate as to the seriousness of the problem of sexual assault on campus. Our best estimate is that at least one in five women in college, and one in sixteen men, will be a victim of sexual assault. Among the women who responded to the Online College Social

Life Survey, 10 percent reported being physically forced to have intercourse, 15 percent said that someone tried to force them but failed, and 11 percent said they had been victimized while passed out, asleep, drugged, or otherwise incapacitated. All told, one in four had been victimized, some more than once.

Excluding the eleven instances of sexual abuse and assault that my students suffered before arriving on campus, eight of my students wrote in their journals of being sexually assaulted in their first year, and ten additional cases were described secondhand. Of those eighteen cases, sixteen were victimizations of women by men and two of men by women. There were certainly more. One student, who described two cases in one entry, disclosed that those were "only the ones I feel are extremely relevant to what I'm observing this week—there are countless others," she wrote, "that I could list from last semester as well as this one."

Most campus assaults occur at or after a party, so the term that best captures what happens in college these days is "party rape." There are two theories for its prevalence. One holds that rape is a crime committed by dangerous psychopaths: a small percentage of men who deliberately and routinely exploit and abuse women and other men. These men strategically choose their victims, carefully plot their crimes, lie in wait, and rape with glee. These are serial rapists; they will do it again and again as long as they can.

The other theory holds that rape is situational, that there are people who will not rape until and unless they find themselves in an environment that elicits sexual assault. For these individuals, being in a rape-prone place among rape-supportive people can incite predatory behavior, even compel it. According to this theory, even otherwise good people may become sexually aggressive in circumstances that allow and reward that behavior.

Both theories are supported by evidence. Some students who

perpetrate sexual crimes are unrepentant rapists. They have raped before and will again. Other students who do so are prompted by an environment that elicits sexual aggression. Hookup culture is implicated—in the first case as camouflage and in the second as a catalyst—because it's a rape culture, a set of ideas and practices that naturalize, justify, and glorify sexual pressure, coercion, and violence.

◆ ◆ ◆

The feminist legal scholar Catharine MacKinnon once argued that rape was not prohibited, but regulated. She was writing in 1989, four years before it became illegal to rape one's spouse in all fifty states. At the time, rape was quite clearly regulated: you could rape your wife, just not anyone else. MacKinnon, though, wasn't just talking about the law; she was talking about what happened outside the law, too. She was saying something far more provocative: that no matter the law, certain strategies for gaining sexual compliance are sometimes allowed.

In fact, behaviors that are illegal—such as harassment and unwanted sexual touching—are not only tolerated, they're the norm in places like bars, clubs, and parties. People can get away with things in drinking establishments that they can't get away with almost anywhere else. This applies to everyone, but because the sexual pursuit of women is a core tenant of masculinity, men are more likely than women to initiate these encounters.

In one survey of over 250 men at twenty-two colleges, over 90 percent of men who frequented drinking establishments admitted to engaging in non-consensual behaviors: pressing up against women from behind, grabbing their bodies, and brushing up against them intentionally to get contact. Heterosexual men who are young, invested in masculinity, and antagonistic toward women are especially likely to do these things. As a result, most women who go to bars, clubs, and parties have learned to live with this kind of sexual contact. Generally, they rationalize away men's bad behavior as "typical drunk guy behavior," the college version of "boys will be boys." Regulation, not prohibition.

It's important to acknowledge that this is what many people want: a regulated environment in which to enjoy the rush of touching and being touched. Most college parties are exactly this kind of setting, and students attend with full knowledge that this is the case. One woman, referring to the likelihood that "hands find their way up your shirt or down your pants," asked:

> Does going to a dance mean that you're consenting to touching as well? Honestly, I think yes or at least it gives an invitation until you decline or reject such behaviors. . . . It's just SO widely understood that THAT's what's going to be happening at a dance that most people already know that going in.

Another student confirmed, "the scene at dances is one of presumed consent." Men have implicit permission to touch and women have the right to accept or end men's advances.

This dynamic has been widely criticized, and for good reason, but it is also a well-understood cultural routine that facilitates wanted sexual contact in a way that can be safe. In theory, students escalate sexual contact along an agreed-upon trajectory and at a reasonable pace. Insofar as women can slow down or stop the interaction before it has gone very far past their comfort level, it's functional and non-victimizing. It's a pragmatic, if gendered, way to negotiate boundaries, short of asking questions like, "And may I now move my hand an inch to the right? No? How 'bout now?"

In reality, there are those who operate within this system responsibly and those who do not. Students encounter peers who are cautious, even overly so, ones who violently push past their boundaries, and everything in between: awkward incompetence, drunken belligerence, and straight-up manipulation. As a result, even women who attend parties specifically for the prospect of being touched report very mixed experiences. Most have one or two stories about a time when someone quite obviously crossed the line.

Of all the parties described in my students' journals, a dance called "Traffic Jam" best encapsulated the appeal of these settings, how they elicit sexually aggressive behavior, and the danger they pose. The costume theme was "stoplight": students were instructed to wear green if they were "down to fuck," red if they were in a relationship, and yellow if they weren't sure what they wanted. It was one of the more anticipated events of the semester.

Consistent with the theme, the dance took place on campus in a grey-toned underground parking garage. It was a vast, vertically squished space with dozens of widely spaced pillars and a low ceiling crisscrossed by concrete beams. On any other night, students might have walked through it alone, eyed the flickering lights, listened to their lone footsteps, and got the heebie-jeebies.

This night, though, the parking garage was pulsing. The fluorescents didn't flicker; they were dark. A DJ pumped out deafening, distorted music that ricocheted through the structure. His green and blue laser beams pierced through the party fog, sped across the uneven ceiling, and bounced off pillars, while his flashing strobe lights made it impossible for eyes to adjust to the darkness.

It was "an entire shit show," recalled one onlooker. A mass of sweaty bodies wearing yellow, red, and green undulated to the noise. Some students wore green on top to indicate "go," red underneath to indicate "stop." Sometimes yellow undies peeked out cheekily from beneath red shorts. "Couples were everywhere heavily making out and grinding," wrote a student who wore red, "up against walls, butts out, and possibly fingers in vaginas." Outside of the dense nucleus of sexual activity were women winding their bodies invitingly and couples flirting with a hookup. A smattering of men lurked at the rim.

"They looked like lions circling a herd of antelope," wrote Jonah. He was standing with his back to one of the pillars that held up the ceiling and, at six foot four, he had a better view than most. He was gay and a few of his female friends had asked him to "make sure no 'creepers' made unwanted advances." It was so dark, though, the music was so loud, and people were so drunk. Women were kissing "just whoever came at them," he noticed. Between the deep black corners, the flashing lights, and the thick concrete, Jonah couldn't keep track of everyone. "It was heinous," he reflected later, "literally a nightmare from any kind of sexual assault viewpoint."

The week before the party, several of my students expressed concern about the expectation that they wear red, yellow, or green to indicate their sexual availability. One of Jonah's friends, Danica, explained that she was "really turned off" by it. "Wearing green," she wrote uneasily, "is an invitation for anything to be done to you." The idea that a color could be interpreted as consent to being touched or kissed was no different, she argued, than saying that a woman in a miniskirt is asking for it. Like some other women who attended, Danica opted to wear red even though she wasn't averse to hooking up. She feared that wearing green would incite "uninvited touching."

One student wrote that the theme seemed to give "guys the idea that they were allowed to do whatever they want." She wore red, but still felt like an "open target." A student who wore yellow thought it no different from a typical dance. Basically, it was a "low-key orgy."

She always felt the need to be careful: "With alcohol and horniness and the need to be cool," she wrote, "you get 'bad nights.'"

Recalling the conversations that happened the week after Traffic Jam, Jonah reported that he "heard numerous reports of attempted sexual coercion; mainly things like 'I couldn't get him to stop following me' or 'He kept grabbing my butt even after I moved his hands.'" Mason, who attended with his girlfriend, noticed similar aggressive pushing of boundaries: "Girls were clearly being grinded up on without their consent," he reported. He and a friend spent the night strategically coming between their female friends and "predatory guys." It was a "hot mess," he recalled.

Traffic Jam may have been a particularly intense night, but my students' stories affirm that these sorts of experiences are part and parcel of going to college parties. "Disrespectful" was a word that came up frequently, alongside the idea that men disregard women's "boundaries." "I guess dance parties are a 'good' excuse to touch people and get away with it," a student remarked.

If this is how some men behave in public, how do they behave behind closed doors?

◆　　◆　　◆

"A man who hesitates, masturbates," is how a guy enrolled at the University of Florida put it. Some men act instead of asking, counting on women to acquiesce or object after the fact. Because if "just being" at a college party opens a woman up to being fondled or touched without her permission, "just going" to his room might suggest to some men that equally sneaky, manipulative, or coercive measures are allowed.

"Men don't always listen," observed one of my female students, "even when it's important." One Harvard student said that when she hooked up with men she often had the feeling that she didn't "matter." "A lot of sex feels like this," she wrote. Even when women say yes, she said, "we fear . . . that if we did say no, or if we don't like the pressure on our necks or the way they touch us, it wouldn't matter. It wouldn't count, because we don't count."

It isn't just sexual predators who think or act this way; being sexually persuasive is a basic tenet of American masculinity, even an imperative. "If you're a guy," says masculinities scholar Michael Kimmel, "you have an 'endless loop' playing in your head: 'Gotta get laid, you're not a man unless you try for it, keep going, what's wrong with you?'" If it's men's right to try for sexual contact, if it is the very definition of a real man, then the question isn't *whether* he should try to overcome her resistance, but *how*. In certain circumstances, when women seem uninterested it's not a rejection, it's a challenge.

When Natalie told her friend she didn't want to give him a blow job, did he see her rejection as a challenge? Did he find other women challenging as well? We'll never know. Natalie insists that he was and is a very nice person—and I believe her—but that doesn't mean he didn't assault someone. There's a lot of leeway in the system and men have varying tolerances for taking advantage. Do nice guys and good men sometimes cross the line? You bet they do. Four out of five college men who commit rape before graduating college do so only one time. Who knows why, but it's possible that they had the opportunity, along with a lapse of judgment, and went for it.

The near ubiquitous presence of alcohol at college parties makes these lapses all the more likely. In facilitating women's compliance or incapacitation, alcohol is the rapist's greatest weapon. While "roofies" have become a cultural touchstone, liquor is the drug of choice. We only need to pay attention to the seemingly constant stream of leaked fraternity correspondence to know this. "Get the bitches in the right state of intoxication," instructs an email from American University's Epsilon Iota that was meant to stay between brothers. Another from the University of Southern California describes the joy of "taking down" an "easy target" who is drunk. A member of the Phi Kappa Tau fraternity at Georgia Tech sent out a guide called "Luring Your Rapebait" that included the tip "If anything ever fails, go get more alcohol" in all capital letters.

Men are three times as likely to assault a woman who has been drinking as one who has not. In some cases, women are pushed by men to drink more than they want, or tricked into doing so. Over the course of one rough morning, Danica learned that a guy who'd been trying to hook up with her the night before had also been pouring her doubles without her knowledge. "The person who gave me alcohol was also the one who seemed to want to dance with me the most," she recalled, grateful that nothing terrible had happened.

Fraternities and other all-male social clubs deserve special attention because of their privileged institutional position, their attractiveness to party-oriented first-year students, and their outsized role in sexual violence. Studies routinely find that fraternity men are second only to male athletes in their endorsement of the sexual double standard. They are also more likely than non-fraternity men to promote homophobia, hypermasculinity, and male dominance; to tolerate violent and sexist jokes, attitudes, and behaviors; and to endorse false beliefs about rape. They are more likely than the average student to be found responsible for sexual assault. When repeat offenders are identified on campus, they belong to fraternities almost a quarter of the time.

Some fraternities have cultivated cultures that resist the sexual objectification and exploitation of women. Others are purely academic; some are social but of a different ilk from the mainline fraternities. Men in African American fraternities, for example, have more egalitarian attitudes toward women. But the fraternity historian Nicholas Syrett is firm that "fraternity men, as a group, [have] been the most organized and vocal in creating a hostile climate for female students on campuses." And since they have essentially complete control over what happens at their houses, their parties are specifically designed to be an uneven field of play that gives men the upper hand in getting what they want from women.

◆　　◆　　◆

In these environments, true predators thrive. For the small percentage of men who are inclined to be sexually aggressive, hookup culture is camouflage. The coercive behaviors that they engage in—plying women with alcohol, being sexually insistent, hooking up with women who are exceptionally drunk, and pulling them into secluded parts of a party—blend into the behaviors of their peers.

In one study, 4 percent of college men admitted to more than one act of sexual violence, for an average of six rapes each. In a similar study of navy enlistees, 9 percent admitted to multiple assaults. DNA testing is uncovering repeat offenders, too. When Detroit started to process the backlog of evidence collected from the bodies of victims, they discovered 110 serial rapists in the first 1,600 DNA samples they tested. An effort in Cleveland had a similar result. Repeat offenders are a part of the problem.

At the campuses I studied, my students named names and I was able to patch their stories together, so I know there were specific men displaying predatory behavior. There were two separate accounts, for example, describing a particular student as sexually aggressive. In one instance, he backed a woman into a corner and kissed her against her will, stiffly grabbing her chin and straightening her face when she repeatedly turned away and said no. There was another man who was described by several students as "creepy" or "stalkerish." One night his come-ons "gradually grew more and more threatening" toward a woman who was refusing his advances. Two of my students told of keeping track of a hall mate that they believed would rape if he had the chance. They rescued at least one woman from his dorm room door as he fumbled for his keys. She was drunk to the point of near oblivion. Another male student had "quite the reputation" for "practically carrying" women back to his room for hookups. At least twice the women he brought home were so intoxicated that they urinated in his bed after passing out.

Late one night, a man like this came home drunk from the nearby bar that first-year students liked to make a second home and found Seong in the dorm common room. He hassled her to play ping pong and she reluctantly agreed. After he scored his first point, he hollered, "That's a hand job!" and announced that they were playing for sexual favors. After a second point, he said, "Aww, you want to blow me now." And after the fifth point, "You're fucked. There's nowhere to go. You only have three holes." He then pointed to her mouth, her crotch, and her behind and commented, "You just want to get it in the ass, don't you, you freaky girl?" Mimicking anal intercourse, he scrunched his face, thrust his groin back and forth, and pushed the end of the ping pong paddle in and out of his clenched fist.

Another night when she was playing the latest *Resident Evil*, he came in, sat next to her on the couch, and began to grope her torso and breasts. He slipped his hand under her shirt and tugged at her bra, trying to dislodge it. "What are you doing?" Seong exclaimed, squirming out of his grasp, and he responded, "I just want to take a look. See what your tits are like. You're so hot. I just want to fuck you." He paused. "Are you uncomfortable," he inter-

jected with a sadistic smile. She replied yes and he relented, grabbing a console and joining her in the video game, but when it was
over he started up again. "What the fuck!" she interjected. And
he replied, "You haven't opposed *this* yet." Only at this moment,
as she began cursing and yelling, did the friend sitting right next
to her intervene.

◆　　　◆　　　◆

Intervention by bystanders is one of the most effective ways we
know to stop sexual assaults from happening, but many students
don't recognize harassment or assault when they see it or are reluctant to get involved. In fact, now that every tween, teen, and college
student has a cell phone with a recording device, it's not uncommon
to see photographic and video evidence of sexual violence that was
originally collected for its entertainment value instead of its value
in a court of law. This material is often doubly disturbing because,
in addition to seeing a person victimized on tape, we listen to the
observers cheer on the rapist, eagerly suggest further depravities,
and insult and humiliate the often unconscious victim.

Journalist Peggy Orenstein noted how often the men in these
videos seem to think that what they are doing is great fun. "Track-
ing those incidents," she wrote for *Girls and Sex*:

> it struck me how often the word *funny* or, more commonly,
> *hilarious* came up among boys recounting stories of women's
> sexual degradation. . . . "Hilarious" offers distance, allowing
> them to look without feeling, to subvert a more compassion-
> ate response that might be read as weak, overly sensitive, and
> unmasculine. "Hilarious" is particularly disturbing as a safe
> haven for bystanders.

216 / AMERICAN HOOKUP

"To upset people out here is hilarious," the firefighter had said about the fun of violently misogynistic shit talk. "It was probably just 'boys having fun,'" the campus security officer had said to un-fun Clare Hollowell. Orenstein is right that we all too often dismiss men's harassment and abuse as harmless, even funny, and this is dangerous. In particular, it reduces the likelihood that a bystander will intervene. "If assault is 'hilarious,'" she concludes, "they don't have to take it seriously, they don't have to respond: there is no problem."

In a culture where aggressive sexual behavior is sometimes allowed, and being unkind is expected, it can be difficult to know when a sexual encounter is going from hot to heated, callous to criminal, or even whether the observer should think it's horrifying or hilarious. More than half of students who recall witnessing sexual violence or harassment say they did nothing, mostly because they weren't sure what to do. Students worry—way too much—about getting it wrong.

So, it takes work to get students to intervene and, if they don't get the right training, they generally won't. Jonah, the student who tried to keep his female friends safe at Traffic Jam, argued that his male friends did little to reduce the amount of sexually aggressive treatment women received:

> I don't see any culture of men "calling out" their male peers who are violating the rights of women. I don't know if this is because men don't know when their friends are being too aggressive or if they are too afraid to say something to them.

When men are popular or influential on campus—when they are class officers, fraternity presidents, or otherwise well-liked by peers or supported by the institution—it's especially difficult for a student to intervene in an assault or report one after the fact, particularly if the victim doesn't have equal standing on campus. Part of rape being regulated, argues MacKinnon, is that there are some people who have the power to rape with relative impunity.

On the national stage this sometimes plays out for all to see. Bill Cosby is one such case. Thirty-five years would go by between his first alleged assault in 1965 and the first police report in 2000; another fifteen years would pass before he would face more than passing public scrutiny. When Arnold Schwarzenegger announced his candidacy for the governorship of California in 2003, at least nine women came forward with stories of sexual harassment and uninvited sexual touching. He apologized publicly for his behavior and then roundly won the election. No charges were filed. In 1977, film director Roman Polanski pleaded guilty to "unlawful sexual intercourse with a minor" but fled to France to avoid serving time.

Polanski's victim was a thirteen-year-old girl. He was a prominent forty-six-year-old man who fed her champagne and Quaaludes. But when he was tried, and again when he was nearly extradited in 2009, media industry people came rushing to his defense. In *Asking For It*, Kate Harding collected the excuses: *The View* host Whoopi Goldberg wondered if it was "rape-rape" (that is, *real* rape); a CBS correspondent contended that the child was pushed by her mother to "seduce" him (implying that Polanski was the victim); and a *Washington Post* columnist suggested that he simply couldn't have known she was under eighteen (and shouldn't be held responsible for failing to be sure). At least 138 Hollywood figures signed a petition to void Polanski's sentence. Powerful people were on his side.

Whether colleges provide similar protection to their athletes is the subject of controversy. In 2016, Florida State University settled a lawsuit brought by Erica Kinsman for $950,000. She alleged that, after being sexually assaulted by Jameis Winston, the college covered up her allegations and thwarted the investigation. Winston was a quarterback who would lead FSU through two undefeated seasons, win them a national championship, and take home the Heisman Trophy. The college denies wrongdoing, as does Winston. In the 2015 NFL draft, he was the first overall pick. He is now a quarterback for the Tampa Bay Buccaneers.

In the last five years, we've seen similar questions as to whether administrations responded properly to reports of assaults by athletes at Baylor, Columbia, Notre Dame, Vanderbilt, Hobart and William Smith, Boston University, Niagara University, and the Universities of Connecticut, Delaware, Kansas, Michigan, Missouri, Montana, New Mexico, Richmond, Tennessee, and Tulsa. And that's just a non-exhaustive list I put together after a bit of googling.

In an article for *Time*, Kareem Abdul-Jabbar, a six-time NBA champion and Most Valuable Player, implored colleges to stop protecting athletes who commit sexual assault. "As a former college athlete," he wrote, "I'm especially aware of the culture of entitlement that some athletes feel as they strut around campus with the belief that they can do no wrong." Colleges tie their reputation and fundraising capacity to these men and then defend them as if finding them responsible for sexual assault was self-harm. Perhaps it is, which makes for a perverse incentive. When men and women are assaulted by these high-status students, they know that getting the institution to hold them accountable will be even more difficult, and that, in the meantime, they'll be subject to the wrath of those who liken athletes to gods.

◆　　　◆　　　◆

If hookup culture is designed to facilitate men's sexual access to women and if both men and women tend to embrace this, if there are powerful men on campus and women that students agree are worthless, then only in the most extreme case with just the right conditions will men be held responsible for gaining that access. Otherwise, the blame is squarely placed on the victim's shoulders, if it ever comes to light at all.

This is what likely would have happened if Evelyn had reported her assault. Evelyn was violently raped by a man who shared a name with, and is likely the same person as, the belligerent student who harassed and groped Seong. One night, as he and Evelyn were dropping by to pick something up on their way from one party to another, he pushed her into her dorm room and closed the door behind them. "I don't really remember how my clothes got off anymore," she wrote, trying to recall the incident through a memory blurred by intoxication and trauma. "The next thing I remember was that we were on my bed and he started to have sex with me. He didn't ask me if it was okay and he wasn't wearing a condom."

"This was it," she remembered thinking and, despite the fact that he was six foot one and she five foot even, she fought back. She chocked him, pushing his head back hard enough to knock it into the wall. He reacted violently in return:

> He pinned my head down on the bed. I wasn't able to move since he had so much leverage on me. I couldn't breathe and I was struggling to get free. I pulled at his hands and arms and tried to pull my face away, but he didn't respond.

Evelyn kept fighting and she was able to interrupt her assault. Research has shown that yelling, punching, or fleeing reduces the likelihood of a completed rape by 81 percent without increasing the severity of injuries sustained by victims. For Evelyn, fighting back worked. "I managed to break free," she wrote, "and I told him if he did it again I'd beat the shit out of him."

She started pulling on her clothes, hiding her body from the man who had just violated it, but she had second thoughts. Her mind turned to the party across campus and she pictured one of her friends, a "tiny, very thin, sweet" girl named Faith who she knew was still at the dance. "I thought that if I let [him] go," she told me later, "he would go back to the dance and find someone weaker than me to take advantage of."

She looked across the room at her rapist. If she let him have sex with her after all, she decided, at least it would be one night he wouldn't rape anyone else. So, she turned back to him and consented to sex with a condom. "Everything he did felt terrible," she recalled. "I tried not to be there." In the morning, she discovered a two-inch long laceration at the entrance to her vagina.

The wound took a month to heal, but Evelyn didn't heal with it. When I caught up with her years later, she was still struggling to recover from her assault. "I feel like he ate my brain, chewed it up and put it back in my skull," she said, "and now I'm trying to unchew it."

Evelyn's story is incredible. In the midst of a horrific life event, she sacrificed herself to try and protect those who she worried were more vulnerable. *Incredible.* But many people would argue that her story is also un-credible. How would the fact that she consented retroactively have played in a courtroom? You can almost hear the defense attorney asking the questions: "Why would she consent to sex with her rapist? How traumatized could she have been if she decided to do it anyway? If she wanted to protect other women, why didn't she report the assault right then and there? Doesn't this sound like reasonable doubt to you?"

In a rape culture, doubt is the default setting and victimhood is granted only in the most unlikely of circumstances, when there is a perfect victim. This imaginary victim is a woman who has lived a perfect life and was having a perfect day on the day she was raped. At the time of the assault, she will have been doing perfectly respectable things in a perfectly respectable place wearing a perfectly respectable outfit. To the perfect victim, the rapist will be a stranger with a weapon and she will say the perfect thing and fight back just the perfect amount. Afterward, the perfect victim will immediately call the police, leaving the crime scene—her body—just perfectly as it was. At the police station, the perfect victim will be just perfectly destroyed. The nurse will gently ask to photograph the bruises emerging on her arms and inner thighs. "They are the perfect evidence," she will say.

There are no perfect victims. There *are* typical ones, though. And Evelyn is typical. The typical victim is also female, but her life has been decidedly imperfect and so are the circumstances of her assault. The typical victim's memory is warped by trauma such that she forgets, misremembers, or tells inconsistent stories. The typical victim is familiar with her rapist and often makes decisions after the offense that seem friendly or romantic in retrospect. The typical victim doesn't tell any authority—80 percent of assaults of college students go unreported—and, if she does tell, she may laugh or seem unperturbed or wait as long as a year to do so. That's typical.

There are no perfect victims; there are only real ones. As Richard Morgan said in the *Washington Post*, detailing his own rape, "Rape contains multitudes" and we will not understand it until we "get much more imaginative about it." But the idea that only a perfect person can be raped is one of our most persuasive rape myths. Even women often blame the victim, in part because it's one of the only ways for them to feel safe in a situation that they know deep down is dangerous.

Even victims often blame themselves. Jonah's friend Danica happened upon a girl crying on a curb late one Friday night. She didn't know her, but sat down to see what was wrong. "Please leave me alone," the girl said. "I just want to feel like shit by myself." Danica asked if she could just sit quietly next to her and she agreed and, after a few minutes, the crying girl told her that she and her boyfriend had broken up because she'd had sex with another guy.

She said that she'd been flirtatious and that they'd kissed a few times before, but that the night they had sex she was "blackout drunk." It was her own fault, she said, "her fault for flirting," "her fault for drinking, and her fault for cheating." She was sure that no one would believe that she didn't intend to have sex with him. "It's my fault. I know it's my fault," she said repeatedly, in tears. What the girl on the curb didn't know was that the guy who had sex with her while she was blacked out had the same name as the man who tormented Seong and raped Evelyn. If she *had* known, she might not have been so quick to place the blame entirely on her own shoulders, but that's what she did.

◆   ◆   ◆

In the last days of 2015, the mega-celebrity Bill Cosby was finally arraigned on felony charges of indecent assault. As he was guided into a police department to be fingerprinted and photographed, he passed a bank of news cameras and a small crowd. One of the demonstrators could be heard yelling, "You're a monster!" over the collective shouting.

In the garish light of today, after more than fifty women have come forward with chillingly similar stories, it is easy to see Cosby as a monster. It took fifteen years of accusations going back five decades, though, and several civil suits before America seemed ready to consider the possibility that Cosby was a bad man. It was too painful, maybe, because we had come to think of him as synonymous with Cliff Huxtable, his character on *The Cosby Show*, perhaps the most lovable father ever to grace American TV screens.

Now we say that Bill Cosby is no Cliff Huxtable; Bill Cosby is a monster, Cliff Huxtable the very model of the good man. But we shouldn't be so confident that Dr. Huxtable is not a rapist, too. Good people rape when their judgment is perverted and the circumstances are just right. Upstanding people rape: leaders of our communities, husbands, doctors. Most of them rape, maybe, only once. "We will never know," sociologist Allan Johnson insists, if a young "Cliff Huxtable—in college, perhaps, or during his medical training—ever got a woman drunk or stoned or otherwise unable to say no to having sex with him." Men that seem good, men that *are* good, sometimes rape.

Hookup culture is dangerous because it's the ideal environment for the serial rapist. But it is dangerous, too, because it seduces too many students into thinking that in certain situations sexual aggression is allowed. We need to fear it because it puts students at risk of being victimized, but also because it puts them at risk of committing a crime, even if just once, because hookup culture says that they can and they should.

Moving On

Esther grew up "really out there." Her mother was Moroccan and had emigrated from Israel before meeting and marrying her dad, so she grew up as a member of a religious minority with an ethnically ambiguous look. She'd also been raised to express her sexuality and gender identity as she wished and she became an enthusiast early. She had her first experience with consensual sex at age fourteen and enjoyed hookups throughout high school and college. Eventually she would come to see herself as just a little queer.

She was transformed by a class on Eastern philosophy. "To everyone else it was just a textbook," she recalled, "but to me it was an existential crisis." After freshman year, she became involved with a diverse group of students fighting for progressive change on campus. When I talked to her after graduation, she was embarking on a career devoted to bringing mindful practices to the lives and work of activists. She left college with a stronger sense of who she was and a clear idea of what she wanted to contribute to the world.

Along the way, her relationship to sexuality changed, too. She came to have much higher standards for the level of communication that she shared with her partners and she required a different level of trust. Instead of "meaningless sex," she aimed for sexual encounters that were "deeply spiritual." But she was still an enthusiast. Being able to be sexually active early with many partners, she told me, had been like therapy. She had been sexually assaulted at thirteen and positive, freely chosen, pleasurable sexual experiences were the first stage of her recovery.

Like Esther, a little over half of the students in this book who started out as enthusiasts were still excited about hooking up at the end of our time together. Another three had joined their ranks. Hookup enthusiasts may be a minority on college campuses, but they're not a trivial one and their experiences show that casual sex can be fulfilling and affirming both in college and beyond.

Most of my abstainers also felt confident about their choice not to engage with hookup culture. They were the most stable group of students. Of them, more than three-quarters would remain abstainers throughout the year. Another dozen students would later decide that opting out was best for them, too. A few of these decided against hooking up after having singularly terrible moments that irrevocably harmed their ability to enjoy the opportunity for casual encounters; many simply decided that, on balance, it wasn't worth it; others just lost interest.

Among the dabblers, a third defected and a handful joined, with most of the movement being between dabbling and abstaining. Though the dabblers in my study were by definition unsure of their motivations, ambivalent about hooking up, or doing so primarily in the hope of forming a relationship, most who participated were glad they did. When I caught up with Ashlynn, for example, the student who so astutely observed her peers' discomfort with cunnilingus, she recalled her dad telling her in high school that she

226 / AMERICAN HOOKUP

should have "a good idea of what sex means" for her. At the time, she had felt that sex should mean love, so she planned on ensuring that all of her sexual experiences would be "special."

In college, though, this felt too constraining. She eventually did have other kinds of sexual experiences: hookups that were just for pleasure, some good, some awkward, and some bad. She also took on the difficult task of being present for several friends who had been sexually assaulted. As the years progressed, she said, "I just felt like I heard fewer and fewer stories of fun hookups and more and more of people being raped." She became skeptical of the idea that sex could always be special. It could be meaningful and good, she decided, but it could also involve a "whole spectrum of negative experiences." She described this realization as "a loss of innocence," but one that was strangely comforting. "I felt better equipped to accept things," she said, setting aside the possibility of sexual assault, but embracing the imperfect, awkward, and not-so-special. "There is some peace in knowing that things may not go exactly how you want them to every time."

Many of my students felt similarly, saying that hooking up made them smarter about sex, helped them to develop more sophisticated sexual philosophies, and left them more prepared to handle whatever came their way. This was true, too, for Riley, the girl who loosened up. She hooked up with Craig several times, despite his "sloppy tongue" and clumsy hands. She never came to like him very much, even in a friendly way, and the last time they hooked up it was "slightly scary." She made an abrupt move to end it. At first he tried to ignore her—"his whole attitude was forceful," she said— and when she made it clear that she couldn't be easily bullied into sex, he acted resentful. It was an altogether uncomfortable experience that left Riley shaken. The thing she had most feared about hooking up had happened: it got "gross."

But the next day, she was fine. "This is hard to explain," she said. "I was so afraid that I wouldn't be able to handle it, so hooking up with someone I didn't know that well, and stopping when I wanted, and feeling okay about it the next day . . . made me feel strong." Things had got "gross," she'd had the strength to stop the encounter, and it hadn't wrecked her. Quite the opposite, in fact; it made her feel more capable of taking care of herself than ever.

Deep down, she realized, she'd been worried that one misstep, one bad choice in partners, would irrevocably harm her. This was a distressing thing to believe and she realized that her rule to have sex only when in love wasn't just a moral principle, it was an effort to protect a self that she worried could be easily destroyed. "I was so afraid," she said, "that I'd feel ruined, dirty, broken." But her experiences with Craig taught her that her sexuality was robust and resilient. It was not, as she had feared, something that a little disrespect could damage. She wasn't "ruined after one encounter," after all. "I wouldn't do it again," she concluded, "but I'm glad I did it."

Celeste was glad, too. She was the student who complained of feeling like a "masturbation toy" after hooking up with twelve men who seemed to have no interest in her pleasure. Then she met Minjun. Their hookup didn't start at a party; it started in the library. They were studying for an "Introduction to Philosophy" class they shared and, after summarizing Pascal's wager, their conversation turned to their own attempts to find meaning in their lives, struggles with their families, worries about their future, and the meaning of life.

Their first kiss was brimming with the vulnerability that comes with contemplating cosmic uncertainty, and it only got hotter from there. It was a "mingling of souls," Celeste reported happily. "Both of us have never had sex that was so incredibly satisfying on so many levels." And, this time, she had an orgasm. She hadn't known that sex like that was possible, but she did now. "This man," she said, "is someone who I can say had changed me indefinitely." Celeste was grateful that hookup culture brought her Min, but she didn't regret her other experiences. "Whether the hookups were good or bad," she said, "it was always a learning experience. I would not be who I am today without them."

Lots of students told stories like Ashlynn's, Riley's, and Celeste's, but not all of them did. Neither Roslyn nor Evelyn, for example, were able to look back at their first year with the same optimistic attitude. Roslyn was still struggling to find peace with her strong, tall, biracial body. She graduated from striver to dabbler in her sophomore year, hooking up with mixed results. After college, though, she focused on becoming comfortable with herself, putting a temporary moratorium on romantic and sexual interactions with men to focus on "self-care, mental health, and well-being." She had gained the strength to resist succumbing to the need for men's attention, but it was still there simmering.

Evelyn was still suffering from the night she was assaulted. "I thought I was strong enough to deal with rape as it was happening to me," she said, "and I was right, because I survived." Afterward, though, she retreated from the hookup scene and began to avoid most men. She had flashbacks and uncontrollable moments of panic. She feared that she would be forever "broken and unwanted," unlovable because of her trauma. But she did eventually seek out and find kindness in men and solace in their arms. When I talked to her, her body had healed and her heart had started to recover, but her psyche was still wounded. "I did not know how to defend myself against the mind-fuck," she said. She now allowed herself a certain level of fragility. "My rape has made me realize that there are many ways to be strong," she surmised, "and admitting that you can be weakened sometimes can be one of them."

◆   ◆   ◆

Hookup culture was particularly cruel to Evelyn and Roslyn. For most students, it was just a heavy dose of realism. Some, like Ashlynn, knew that they had gotten lucky, escaping without any serious, lasting harm. And, in the end, the sexual culture on campus was just one dimension of their collegiate experience and didn't define all of their time there.

The first big change happened in sophomore year, when most of the students I followed up with made true friends. Burke said that his friendships were "one of the beautiful things about [college]." He remained relationship-oriented, and his friends came to feel like family. Wren, the pansexual student who almost transferred after her first year, found a whole allotment of fabulously queer women when she joined the intramural softball team. Mara eventually stopped girl flirting and dropped out of her sorority. "I was a terrible sorority girl," she admitted with a laugh. Instead she became part of a close-knit group of friends outside of the Greek system and felt "fulfilled by the people around me," she said, "and so loved." She still partied and hooked up, but "not the kind of stuff that makes parents want to gouge their eyes out."

Even shy, sexually frustrated Xavier made friends. Eager to escape the striver category, he decided to try to break his dry spell by befriending a girl he wanted to hook up with, but it turned out that pretending to be her friend was a lot like *being* her friend. He came to care about her in a genuine way and never did hook up with her, for which he was glad. By sophomore year his two very best friends were women. "Luckily, I was able to mature," he said in retrospect.

In their sophomore and junior years, many students also

became engrossed in their education. Ashlynn discovered a passion for working in drug addiction prevention. She joined a team of educators and spent a lot of time at local middle and high schools. It was "fulfilling and fascinating," she said happily. After his first kiss, Omar declared a "time-consuming" major. He never did have an orgy; at least, he hasn't yet. The romantic, Emory, joined a literary club and directed his emotional energy toward writing screenplays. Jonah, the gay guy who watched over his girlfriends at Traffic Jam, tacked a minor in child development onto his already demanding academic schedule.

Some students settled into committed relationships, mostly monogamous. Emory and Brooke, the girl who didn't believe in bisexuality, had girlfriends. Brooke eventually did kiss Adisa, the woman with the "curly lips," and they had a fling that lasted through the summer after her first year. "It was my first full-out queer experience and it was great," she reminisced. She believes in bisexuality now and identifies as "fluid." Looking back, she said, "I can see it was always that way."

Jonah, Mara, and Marisol all had boyfriends in their sophomore or junior years. So did Luke, the doleful gay virgin who came out in college only to discover that his virginity did not magically disappear. When I caught up with him a few years later, he said, "Everything has changed! I don't feel terrible about everything anymore!" His freshman year, he said, had been a difficult transitional one in which he had to relearn how to be himself. "I'd spent so much time hiding," he said, "that I didn't know how to be who I was." Being in the closet, he said, "is like losing yourself in an undercover identity. Stopping was surprisingly difficult."

In between his mortifying confessions and heart-crushing infatuations, he had long talks with new friends and, slowly, he emerged. He toned down the drama a bit, realizing that his life wasn't "abjectly terrible," just "mediocre." He became a bit less awkward and started to recognize that he was generally well-liked. As freshman year turned into sophomore year, he said, "I became more competent at being a person."

He had his first sexual experience at nineteen with a boy he met on a dating site. It was his first date, his first kiss, and his first sexual experience. He then embarked on what he called a "four-month slutty phase" during which he hooked up with five or six people: one guy he met at a gay club and the others through websites or apps. He never hooked up with any of the other gay men on campus.

Before the end of his sophomore year, he met Lance at an off-campus party. Lance was Luke's opposite: lackadaisical where Luke was detail-oriented, playful where he was serious, forthright where he was conciliatory. It was an instant connection. They hooked up that night and the next morning, Lance turned to Luke and said, "Let's go on an adventure!" They've been together ever since.

Violet, one of the eight students who was in a monogamous relationship her entire first year, was still with her boyfriend. She was one of the women who didn't party or hook up, leaving her feeling isolated and possibly contributing to her depression. Now graduated, she and her boyfriend were thinking of buying a house together. She was happy.

If abstainers weren't already in a relationship when they started college, the ones I followed up with didn't get into one while they were there. Laura didn't. She was the girl who mocked the grinding at parties. It seemed to her that there were only two kinds of women in college: "casual sex girls" and "conservative girls." Where, exactly, did a sociable but slightly prudish feminist fit in? In her first year, this question inspired her to write, forebodingly, "I cannot envision a happy relationship trajectory for myself."

When I read her this line after graduation, she was shocked. "Wow," she said. The summer after her senior year, she did end up in a relationship, a short but happy one. It softened her heart a little. "I felt . . . you know," she said sheepishly, "*clichés*." They were kind to each other. Her boyfriend, she remembered warmly, was "better," better for her than the person she would have made up for herself. Though they broke up, each to pursue their own separate lives, the experience was affirming. "I think of putting myself out there now," she said, reflecting on what she wrote years before. "I can envision it now."

◆   ◆   ◆

For *Vanity Fair*, journalist Nancy Jo Sales profiled a handful of highly educated, mostly white millennials who congregated in the bars of Manhattan, and concluded that we are at the "dawn of the 'dating apocalypse.'" In her story, young people in bars looked at Tinder instead of each other, finding a partner was akin to online shopping, and sex was "easy." "Too easy," the men she talked to said. "You can meet somebody and fuck them in twenty minutes," explained one. "I've gotten numbers on Tinder just by sending emojis," said another.

People didn't get to know one another in Sales's dystopia. They just got on their respective devices, picked someone hot, sent each other erotic emojis, met up for sex, and never contacted each other again. The date—that intentional romantic evening designed to allow people to find out if they like each other before getting naked—seemed dead, and commitment was going with it to the grave. But if people who actively participate in hookup culture are more likely to be young, heterosexual, white, and wealthy, then interviewing twenty-somethings in New York is a surefire way to draw that conclusion.

We can call off the funeral. The little we do know about post-college experiences suggests that most grads do transition to something that looks at least a little more like dating. For *Hooking Up*, which was published in 2008, sociologist Kathleen Bogle interviewed people about how their lives had changed since leaving college; "across the board," she said, they described a different lifestyle. They started full-time jobs, moved to new cities where they didn't know anyone, and found that apartment buildings weren't anything like residence halls. They spent more time alone. They got up early and went to bed on time. Women were surprised to find that they were asked out to dinner.

For Bogle's interviewees, dating had almost entirely replaced hooking up. They were no longer surrounded by peers in whom they placed an implicit (if unadvisable) trust. If they did meet someone they were interested in hooking up with, they probably weren't neighbors. Women, especially, but some men, too, were reluctant to get into a car and drive to someone else's turf. There were also fewer Saturday and Sunday morning recaps, and casual sex was an inappropriate topic around the water cooler at work.

Bogle's interviewees also suggested that the time for hooking up had passed. College was for going wild, but after graduation, Bogle explained, "a new 'definition of the situation' [took] hold." Even fraternity men, she noted, were leaving their hard-partying, womanizing ways behind. Everyone seemed to be looking for something a little more subdued. One of her male interviewees described the change in himself this way:

> I don't know, you are looking for more [of a] relationship. I know this person, I can trust them, I can share things. If I have a bad day, they will listen to me, those kinds of concepts. Meeting someone in a bar, buying them drinks, getting them

drunk and hooking up in your car, there is not quality there at all. You don't even know if that is their real name they gave you . . . As you get older, you . . . want something more solid.

So, Bogle's grads dated, quite traditionally in fact, with men proposing outings, paying, opening car doors, and the like. "Men seemed to interact with the opposite sex as one might expect their grandfathers would have done," Bogle said, seeming surprised. Though they may have hooked up with abandon in their college years, everyone seemed to transition quite seamlessly to dating once college was over.

Like Bogle's interviewees, most of my grads were not hooking up, certainly not regularly, and their lives had changed in similar ways. They had to work harder to find people they were attracted to now that the organized group activities that had facilitated hooking up in college were behind them. Burke, for example, had moved to rural Vermont to work on an organic farm. After about a month there were no new people to meet and it was a sixty-mile drive to the nearest big city. Emory and Roslyn had moved back home to live with their parents, which wasn't conducive to casual sexual encounters. Roslyn was also working fifty to seventy-five hours a week as a youth advocate. She was tired at the end of the day. When my grads did go out drinking, there was rarely any-where nearby to get horizontal. Driving to somebody's house was a deterrent in itself and having to drive at all usually kept the level of inebriation at an all-too-reasonable, non-hookup-inducing level.

Sometimes, if the situation was just right, hookups happened. One of Bogle's interviewees said that hooking up was still in full swing at "the shore," a beach vacation spot that brought together many young single people for drinking and sunbathing. Likewise, a few of my students had found themselves hooking up at the occasional house party, but the raucous blowouts didn't happen with nearly the same frequency.

None of my students continued to feel like they were "inside" a hookup culture, except Omar. When I called him to reminisce about his first kiss with that shy brunette, I discovered that he didn't kiss women at all anymore. After college, he came out as gay and moved to New York. In the Manhattan neighborhood of Chelsea, surrounded by gay men and living directly across the street from a gay bar, there was plenty of hooking up to be had. His hookups led to a relationship, as they often do, and he was living with his boy-friend when we talked. A recent report found that a third of new marriages could be traced to a hookup. That seems high to me, but maybe Omar will be among them.

Of the students I followed up with, only Esther and Petra were still enthusiastic about hooking up. After college, Petra enrolled in a master's program, and she still preferred hookups to getting involved. She met guys she was attracted to, she said, but it didn't occur to her to think about dating them. "It's weird when people are date-y," she laughed. She had her career to contend with and had no intention of making any "big compromises" for anyone any-time soon, so something serious was off the table. Hooking up still worked for her.

There was one way, though, that my grads were very unlike Bogle's. Almost all of the single students I followed up with were struggling with the transition to dating—going on dates, that is, *before* hooking up. They used words like "weird" and "miserable" to describe it. My first reaction was to think, "Yes, that sounds about right. Welcome to dating, kids! It's a thing grownups do that is weird and miserable." But I eventually came around to the idea that there is something uniquely byzantine going on for new col-lege grads.

Laura called it "hard." She felt that hookup culture and dating culture were blurred post-grad. It was as if both sets of rules applied simultaneously and a person could change course at any time. If she was standoffish, would it be read as rude (new rules)? Or if she was warm, would be it be seen as clingy (old rules)? Should she text him back when he texts her (new rules)? Or should she wait so as to seem nonchalant (old rules)? "There's no ground beneath your feet," she said. Everything seemed to be in flux.

Laura might be right that hookup culture and dating culture coexist among new college grads. Alternatively, hookup culture may have infiltrated dating for all adults, shaping dating culture for all of us. That could very well be confusing.

"People have completely forgotten how to date," was how Burke put it. He was always more interested in dating than hooking up, but it was difficult in college because he had no car and almost no money. As a man with a decent-paying job, it's easier. He's able to suggest activities, take the wheel, literally and figuratively, and even pay for things. Women aren't used to it, he observed, but they like it.

Since dating culture still gives men the right to take charge, it may be easier for guys who want to date after college to do so. Women who are equally forthright can be seen as aggressive, so they may be stuck hoping that the guy knows what he's doing—and there may not be many young men who do. Burke, as he always was, might still be in the minority. He certainly had the sense that he is.

Only one student described a seamless transition to dating. After coming to identify as a survivor instead of a victim of sexual molestation, thanks to the friends she made in her first year, Marisol began dreaming of starting a nonprofit organization dedicated to helping children. Business school was the first step. She was accepted to a competitive program in a big city, where people were aggressive. Her fellow business students, she said, didn't hesitate to ask her out. Maybe it takes a certain kind of person to brashly forge ahead into a new sexual culture with confidence.

It may be that dating culture isn't as strong as it was almost a decade ago. Things may really be changing quickly. We know they sometimes do. At the colleges where I've lectured, seniors sometimes pull me aside anxiously and ask how they are supposed to behave once they graduate. For quite some time, I thought they were exaggerating their confusion, but I've come to think that they mean it seriously. Some seem to find dating as mysterious as they would a VHS tape or a rotary phone. When the subject of dating came up, they would frequently inquire, "Like, dinner and a movie?" The phrase "dinner and a movie" came to stand in for this thing they had heard of called a "date," but they didn't really have any idea what it was or how to do it.

At Boston College, a philosophy professor named Kerry Cronin similarly discovered that her students didn't seem to know what dating involved. She decided to make asking someone on a date a required activity in one of her classes, but her students were so stumped as to how to do it that she had to develop an elaborate set of instructions: A date must involve only two people; there has to be genuine romantic interest; the date has to be an activity that allows for a conversation (no dance clubs and no dark movie theaters); it has to be over before 10 p.m.; and it can end in a kiss, but that's it. Cronin specified, too, how a person initiates a second date if they want one or communicates that they do not. I think some of my grads would be grateful for such clear instructions.

Open communication in general seemed strange and new to some of my students. Dating felt weird to them in part because it required that they be at least a little honest about their intentions.

"[Because] you have to arrange a meet-up," Mara explained, it was impossible to make it seem careless and meaningless. When a guy she went on a couple of dates with was "earnest" and "transparent" with her, she said it was "almost comical" compared to what she was used to. Some grads are stumped, too, by how to express interest in nonsexual ways. If they don't try to have sex with you, one asked, how can you tell if they're attracted to you?

Some of my students were still learning how to be nice to one another. Sydney learned by example. She was the student who hooked up with men she distinctly disliked, only to go through that terrible night when Brad called her a "bitch" for not wanting to have sex without a condom. Eventually, she met a man who showed her that it didn't have to be that way.

"The best description of Wes that I can give," she said affectionately,

> is that he's the kind of guy you already know would be a great father. He's really smart, sincerely friendly, patient, and almost always has a smile on his face. He's not exactly the type of guy you scope out at a party—I mean he's sort of a nerd—but he's just *Wes*.

Sydney met him in college at a typical hookup-inducing party. Normally, she explained, she wouldn't have "given Wes a second thought," but it was 3 a.m. and she was "plastered." It was one of those "inevitable" hookups, the kind that just happen because it's late and everyone's drunk and hooking up is what people do. She shrugged and they went back to his place. They kissed, but he surprised her by deciding that she was too drunk to go further.

The next morning, he "shattered" everything she thought she knew about men. At first her intention was to flee—"I remember waking up next to him in the morning," she said, "wondering why I was even there"—but there was something in his voice. He acted nonchalant about whether she stayed or went, as the rules of hookup culture required, but Sydney heard a "hint of pleading." So, she decided to take a chance. Reflecting, she said:

> I knew that I felt safe with him—drunk, sober, as a friend, and in bed. I wanted to let him know he was safe with me too. So I got back in bed, and I told him that I would stay as long as I was welcome to.

They stayed together for quite some time.

Farah hadn't been so lucky. She was still trying to melt down the cold shell that she'd built around herself to survive hookup culture. I caught up with her after graduation and we reflected on what happened when Tiq had asked her if she *like* liked him. "I wasn't honest," she said. "I lied to him." She explained that she'd simply been too scared to tell him the truth. It was a painful experience, and he would be the last person she hooked up with in college. She was hurt, she said, not by Tiq so much as by the culture itself.

In any case, she got busy with school and internships. Junior and senior years were "all science," she said. She traveled a lot and went abroad to learn more about rainforest conservation. When I talked to her, she had her dream job fighting deforestation not too far from where her parents were born in Indonesia.

Career-wise, she was thriving, but she was still working on learning how to open up, still fearful of being vulnerable. She continued to worry about seeming "too clingy," as she did in her freshman year, and got anxious about crafting just the right text. She'd recently considered asking someone to go to a museum with her, but wondered if that sounded desperate. "I don't want to seem as if I need anyone," she said a bit sadly. That summer, though, she'd met a man who had been quite nice to her and he'd given her hope. "I'm ready to explore more sexual and romantic relationships now," she said tentatively, "and to not be so afraid of holding hands. Because it's not scary and it actually feels wonderful."

CONCLUSION

Changing the Culture

Hookup culture is now part of American history, the newest way that young people have come to initiate sexual encounters and form romantic relationships. In some ways, it is a mashup of the best things about the sexual cultures of the last one hundred years. Like the gay men of the 1970s, students in hookup culture are inspired by a joyous sense of liberation and the belief that they have the right to indulge their desires and no reason to feel shame. Like the middle-class youth of the 1950s, today's college students get to explore the whole range of sexual options if they want to and, thanks to effective, accessible birth control, they get to do so with much fewer unintended pregnancies and early marriages. Like the young working people who took advantage of the dazzling new nightlife in the cities of the 1920s, students relish novelty and the opportunity to be at least a little unruly. And, like men and women throughout history, and perhaps against all odds, students fall in love. Young people break the rules, as they always have, and out of hookups come committed, lasting, emotionally supportive relationships.

But hookup culture also carries with it some of the worst things about the last hundred years. It is still gripped, for example, by the limiting gender stereotypes that emerged during the Industrial Revolution, that fissuring of love and sex that left us thinking that women's hearts are weak and men's hearts are hard, that men's desires are ablaze and women's barely flicker.

Thanks to these stereotypes, when men pursue sex on campus today it is interpreted as a sign of a healthy, red-blooded masculinity, but we still don't acknowledge a healthy, red-blooded femininity. When women of color are sexual, it's seen as a racial trait; when poor and working-class women are sexual, it's read as "trashy"; and when middle-class white women are sexual, it's interpreted, all too often, as just a proxy for relational yearning. And, since hookup culture demands that students seem uninterested in romance lest they seem desperate, this stereotype ensures that women usually lose the competition over who can care less, if only by default.

These stereotypes also warp what seems possible, making it difficult to advocate for sex that is both casual and kind. As a result, when women express a desire for a caring partner, it's almost always interpreted as desperation for a boyfriend rather than a request to be treated well. And when men stiff-arm their hookup partners after the fact, they are assumed to do so because they want to keep things casual, not because we've decided that it's okay for them to refuse to do the emotional labor that is essential to all respectful interactions.

Hookup culture also continues to uphold the particular strain of gender inequality that took hold in the 1920s, giving men the power to control both love and sex and making women into rivals for male attention. In fact, on campus things may have gotten worse. Competition among women can be especially fierce thanks to the fact that they attend college in higher numbers than men.

College today is oddly like postwar America, those years after so many men were killed in World War II, when the idea that women are greedy for boyfriends took hold.

A woman's sexiness is still held up as a measure of her worth, and men continue to be the arbiters of whether women are sufficiently sexy. It's not altogether unenjoyable for women, but it is often intimidating and emotionally harmful as well. Meanwhile, men are competing for men's approval, too. Some men seek their own orgasms to impress other men and deny them to women for the same reason, while women focus on being hot enough to get guys off in ways that undermine their own pleasure.

Hookup culture has also failed to integrate the best things about gay liberation: people and practices that are wonderfully queer. Instead, it remains hostile or indifferent to non-heterosexual desire, sometimes but rarely setting up environments in which heterosexuality isn't assumed, catered to, and celebrated.

Being sexually active on campus is still dangerous, too. When the young men and women of the 1950s abandoned public dates for private intimacy, students became more vulnerable to sexual predation. Research published in 1957—to my knowledge, the earliest study of sexual assault on campus—found that 21 percent of college women claimed to have been victims of an attempted or completed sexual assault, the same number we find today. Hookup culture continues this ominous tradition by catalyzing sexual aggression among otherwise non-aggressive men and offering camouflage to genuine predators. With pleasure comes danger, and we have yet to fully figure out how to reduce the latter without inhibiting the former.

Feminists tried to change many of these things, to ensure that women and men could engage with one another sexually as equals, but they were only successful in fixing half the problem. They opened doors for women, giving them the opportunity to embrace the part of life that had been given to men during urbanization: the right to work, to pursue male-dominated occupations, to be unabashedly ambitious, and to seek out sex just for fun. And they tried to open doors for men, too—to give them the right to pursue female-dominated occupations or to focus on the home, the right to prioritize nurturance and care and to hold sex close to their hearts—but Americans resisted the latter change more than they have the former. We are still waiting for men to embrace the part of life that was once given exclusively to women, and for the society around them to reward them for doing so.

In hookup culture, we see these dynamics play out clearly. Since the ideal that is held up is a stereotypically masculine way of engaging sexually, both men and women aim to have "meaningless sex." Expressing emotions is seen as weak. Hookup culture, strongly masculinized, demands carelessness, rewards callousness, and punishes kindness. In this scenario, both men and women have the opportunity to have sex, but neither is entirely free to love.

◆　　◆　　◆

It should be no surprise that heterosexual men express greater comfort with hooking up than other students. The culture is designed to their advantage, or, more specifically, to the advantage of well-off, good-looking, white heterosexual men who feel comfortable treating sex as a game. They have little to lose by hooking up. Their behaviors are consistent with our ideas of what men will or should do; they face no special consequences due to their race; their sexual preference is centered; the demographics are in their favor; and with wealthy families back home, there are few penalties for the mediocre academic performance that can accompany hard partying. These men like hookup culture the most and they often have the power to shape campus life. They are socially attractive, occupy important roles on campus, cost the institution little in the form of scholarships or investment, and over their lifetimes donate more money than other kinds of students.

If hookups didn't so consistently benefit men, your average female college student might be more interested in pursuing casual sex. In a classic study from the 1980s, men and women enrolled at Florida State University were randomly approached on campus and offered casual, heterosexual sex. Seventy percent of the men said yes, but not a single one of the women did the same.

In 2010, University of Michigan psychologist Terri Conley thought to ask why. She found that a substantial portion of the difference could be attributed to the fact that women didn't trust the men approaching them and expected that they would be self-ish in bed. If women were guaranteed that the man would be kind and sexually skilled, they were significantly more likely to say yes. Young heterosexual women on campus may be less inclined than their male counterparts to have casual sex because they know that to do so is to risk victimization, while the hookups they do have aren't particularly pleasurable for them. Some decide that the potential reward doesn't outweigh the risk.

But to focus on heterosexual women's dissatisfaction with casual sex is to miss the big picture. The majority of students would prefer more meaningful connections with others. They want an easier path toward forming committed, loving relationships. Most would also be glad if their casual relationships were a little less competitive and lot kinder. And while heterosexual men have more orgasms than women, it is at the expense of a full range of sexual expression. Alienated from the pleasure that can come with being desired, and told that it's unmanly and pathetic to seek emotional connection with their sexual partners, men suffer in hookup culture, too.

Students wish they had more options. Some pine for the going-steady lifestyle of the 1950s. Many mourn the antiracist, feminist utopia that their grandparents envisioned but never saw fully realized. Quite a few would like things to be a lot more queer. Some want a hookup culture that is warmer: where students aren't just poly—hooking up with multiple partners—but poly*amorous*—hooking up with multiple partners who are loving toward them. There are certainly some who would quite like something more akin to college in the 1700s: a lot more studying and whole lot less "fun."

I think in this is a hint as to what we might hope to see in the coming decades: a diversification of what is possible. We need a more complex and rich cultural life on campus, not just a different one. Students want the opportunity to choose monogamy or not; the right to be treated kindly always; freedom from the rigid constraints on what it means to be a man or woman, including whom we're allowed to desire and whether we want to be male or female at all; and the option to decide whether being sexy—or even sexual—is something one wants in the first place. We need to chip away at hookup culture's dominance and force it to compete with other, more humane sexual cultures that we can envision, and many more that we haven't envisioned yet.

We must transform hookup culture, too, because some students will always prefer hookups. We need to say yes to the opportunity for casual sexual encounters, but no to the absence of care, unfair distribution of pleasure, unrelenting pressure to be hot, and risk of sexual violence. We need to flush out and end racism, sexism, ableism, classism, and other biases. We need a new culture of hooking up, one that keeps the good and roundly rejects the bad.

A campus with lots of healthy, competing sexual cultures is full of opportunity. It requires students to really think about what they want for themselves and from one another. It also requires them to talk to one another instead of assuming (often erroneously) that they know what their peers want. Competing cultures would encourage thoughtfulness, communication, tolerance, and introspection, and all of those things are great for sex.

I do think it's possible. The historian Stephanie Coontz argues that never in the history of humanity have so many different ways of loving been allowed. In her essay "The World Historical Transformation of Marriage," she writes:

> Almost any separate way of organizing caregiving, childrearing, residential arrangements, sexual interactions, or interpersonal redistribution of resources has been tried by some society at some point in time. But the coexistence in *one* society of so many alternative ways of doing all of these different things— and the comparative legitimacy accorded to many of them— has never been seen before.

Love has diversified.

Sex can, too. Diversifying the way we love, marry, and raise children wasn't easy, and protecting greater freedom requires constant vigilance. But people fought to make it so and they succeeded in creating a reality unimaginable even a generation ago. Perhaps now it's time to fight on behalf of sex. College campuses are an excellent place to start. Today's young people are more open, permissive, earnest, hopeful for the future, and welcoming of diversity than any other generation in memory.

Seeing what's happening on campus as a culture—recognizing that it's not the hookup itself, but hookup culture that is the problem—is the first step to changing it. Because culture is a type of shared consciousness, change has to happen collectively. And it can. Especially because so many colleges qualify as total institutions, because of the sheer togetherness of the student body, a campus can transform, and faster than you might suspect.

But students need everyone else to change, too. We are all in the fog. We face an onslaught of sexualized messaging designed to make us worry that our sex lives are inadequate. There is an erotic marketplace off campus, too, and it is distorted by prejudice, a fixation on wealth, and a shallow worship of youth and beauty. For certain, there is an orgasm gap between men and women outside of college, and the practices that enhance sexual encounters—communication, creativity, tolerance, confidence, and knowledge—are scarcer than they should be. We all tend to look to men for approval while valuing women's opinions too little. Sexual violence is epidemic everywhere, and unfortunately anyone, male or female, can be cold and cruel.

The corrosive elements of hookup culture are in all of our lives: in our workplaces, in our politics and the media, within our families and friendships, and, yes, in bars and bedrooms. They're even in our marriages. It makes no sense, then, to shake our fingers at college students. They are us. If we want to fix hookup culture, we have to fix American culture. When we do, we can nurture sexualities that are kinder and safer, more pleasurable and authentic, more fun and truly free.

Acknowledgments

It was in my first year of college that I enrolled in the human sexuality class that would alter the course of my life. My instructors, John and Janice Baldwin, plucked me out of the crowd and made me part of their team. They gave a frightened first-generation college student the confidence to pursue sexuality studies. With added oomph from Matt Mutchler's extraordinary "Sociology of AIDS" class, I was launched into a master's program led by Ron Moglia who once told me, when I said dismissively that I wasn't "interested in feminist theory," that I'd be the equivalent of a fool to fail to learn it. He knew just what to say.

When I turned to sociology, it was John DeLamater who set me on my path. Just how instrumental he was in getting me admitted to my PhD program I'll never know, but I am endlessly grateful. I discovered that Ron Moglia was beyond right when I met Myra Marx Ferree. I toiled in graduate school under the high bar she set and, thanks to her boundless guidance, was chosen by Dolores

Trevizo, Jan Lin, and Lance Hannon to join them as faculty. They protected me as a junior faculty member, gave me responsibilities that have helped me grow as a tenured professor, and, along with the other members of my department and the dean, graciously gave me the time to write this book.

I would not be here without each and every one of them. To my teachers, mentors, and guides, thank you.

My identity as a writer is thanks to Gwen Sharp and Myra Marx Ferree, both of whom, in their own ways, set me on this path. My gratitude to Michael Kimmel, who encouraged me; to Nathaniel Jacks, who decided I could do this; and to Alane Salierno Mason, who was the perfect editor for me: brilliant, exacting, and without mercy. I thank Paula England and her collaborators, who have so generously shared their quantitative research, and all of the other scholars who have laid the groundwork for our understanding of hookup culture; and Caroline Heldman, who was instrumental in conceptualizing this research project and was my partner in collecting some of the raw qualitative data.

My heartfelt thanks to Sasha Levitt. She blends her excellent criticism with endless enthusiasm and propped me up through the harder days. Thanks also to my best friend, Gwen Sharp, who has been pushing me to be the best version of myself for almost twenty years. She is the very model of integrity and intellectual honesty; it's always a good idea to have at least one person like her in your corner. They were my rocks in this process.

Thank you to the many family, friends, acquaintances, and colleagues who read and responded to early drafts of this manuscript: Dana Berkowitz, Kelli Gowan, Mike McHale, Julie Hernandez, Carole Johnson, Erin Kinchen, Tim Leonard, Tom Megginson, Heather Ostrom, Dmitriy Pritykin, Mimi Schippers, Whitney Simon, Monica Snowden, Kay West, Brett Wheeler, Sally Kenney, and the Tulane Sexual Assault Reading Group. Thank you also to those of you who have offered patience, support, and advice, especially Annie Clark, D'Lane Compton, Amy Denissen, Danielle Dirks, Carey Faulkner, Jessie Ford, Amanda Hanson Gates, Jorge Gonzalez, Lance Hannon, Doug Hartmann, Sharon Hays, Jay Livingston, David Landsberg, Heather Lukes, Tristen Kade, Marcus Kondar, Keith Marzalek, Patty Miccichi, Peggy Orenstein, Dolores Ramos, Ari Ratner, Michael Rostker, Brigid Schulte, Peg Streep, Brian Sweeney, Chris Uggen, and my family, especially my grandmother, and the whole crew at The Grotto, including the cat.

And, of course, bottomless thanks to the students to whom this book is dedicated. You made me laugh, broke my heart, and made me believe in humanity, one kindness, one insight, and one revelation at a time. I was moved, captivated, and inspired to learn how you coped with this dizzying time in your lives. I believe everyone else will be, too.

Notes

INTRODUCTION: THE NEW CULTURE OF SEX

15   **depressed, anxious, and overwhelmed:** Eagan et al. (2014); Twenge (2000, 2006).

15   **Half of first-year students:** Eagan et al. (2014).

15   **One in three students:** American College Health Association (2013).

15   **a persistent malaise:** Bersamin et al. (2013), Bogle (2008), England et al. (2008), Epstein et al. (2009), Eshbaugh and Gute (2008), Fisher et al. (2012), Flack et al. (2007), Hamilton and Armstrong (2009), Freitas (2008, 2013), Glenn and Marquardt (2001), Grello et al. (2006), Katz et al. (2012), Lewis et al. (2012), Paul and Hayes (2002), Lewis et al. (2000), Smith et al. (2011), Smith et al. (2008), Wade and Heldman (2012).

16   **Kathleen Bogle:** Bogle (2008).

16   **"guys' sex":** Kimmel (2008).

16   **Jon Birger:** Birger (2015).

16   **Hanna Rosin and Kate Taylor:** Rosin (2012), Taylor (2013).

16   **the "Mrs. Degree":** Holland and Eisenhart (1992).

16   **women with economically stable families:** Armstrong and Hamilton (2013).

16   ***Rolling Stone* and *New York*:** Morris (2014); "Sex on Campus: The Politics of Hookups, Genders, 'Yes,'" *New York*, October 19–November 1, 2015.

16   **At *Elle*:** Sciortino (2015).

17   **students guessed:** Bogle (2008).

17   **young men figured that 80 percent:** Kimmel (2008).

17   **report slightly fewer sexual partners:** Monto and Carey (2014). See also Twenge et al. (2015).

17   **The average graduating senior:** Ford et al. (2015). See also Hoffman and Berntson (2014).

18   **Studies looking specifically at the sexual cultures:** Abercrombie and Mays (2013), Foxhall (2010), Grello et al. (2006), Katz et al. (2012), Knox and Zusman (2009), Najmabadi (2012), Uecker et al. (2015).

18   **Almost a third of students:** Ford et al. (2015).

19   **a representative of the American South:** Usyk (2007).

19   **a woman at the University of Georgia:** Abercrombie and Mays (2013).

19   **A woman at Tulane:** Manzone (2015).

19   **a student at Cornell:** Kimmel (2008).

19   **a student at Yale:** Foxhall (2010).

19   **at Connecticut College:** Yacos (2014).

19   **at Arizona State:** Kimmel (2008).

20   **at Chico State:** Karp (2014).

20   **at Whitman:** Vandervilt (2012).

20   **The average student:** Jessie Ford and Paula England, personal communication.

20   **highest risk of sexual assault:** Cranney (2015).

21   **sexual attitudes and behavior:** Friedland and Gardinali (2013), Freitas (2008), Owen et al. (2010).

23   **I've traveled to speak:** The full list of institutions includes Boise State University, California State University at Northridge, Carlton College, Citrus College (three times), Dartmouth University, Franklin and Marshall College, Harvard University (twice), Indiana State University, Louisiana State University at Baton Rouge, Loyola University at New Orleans, Macalester College, Marshall University, Occidental College, Pacific Lutheran University, Pomona College, Queens University of Kingston, Shawnee State University, Tulane University, University of Illinois at Urbana-Champaign, University of Missouri at Columbia, University of Wisconsin at River Falls, Westminster College, Wichita State University, and Yale University.

24   **over 24,000 students:** Colleges and universities whose students contributed to the OCSLS dataset include Beloit College, Carroll College, The Evergreen State College, Framingham State College, Harvard University, Indiana University, Ithaca College, Middle Tennessee State University, Ohio University, Radford University, Stanford University, Stony

Brook University, the University of Arizona, the University of Massachusetts, the University of California at Merced, the University of California at Riverside, the University of California at Santa Barbara, the
University of Illinois at Chicago, the University of Pennsylvania, the
University of Washington, and Whitman College.

CHAPTER 1: HOOKING UP, A HOW-TO

29 **"intoxicated self":** Vander Ven (2011).
29 **"drunkworld":** Ibid.
30 **study of non-drinking students:** Herman-Kinney and Kinney (2013).
31 **a student at UC Santa Barbara:** Quoted in Mainardi (2014).
32 **a female student at Davidson College:** Kostoryz (2014).
33 **At Stanford University:** Ronen (2010).
33 **University of Pennsylvania student:** Taylor (2013).
34 **"cute":** Armstrong and Hamilton (2013), Sweeney (2014a).
35 **University of Wisconsin student:** Kimmel (2008).
35 **University of Northern Iowa, a guy:** Ibid.
35 **Bowdoin student:** Kinstler (2012).
36 **woman at Duke:** Reitman (2006).
36 **Using indicators like hotness:** Sweeney (2014a).
36 **In her focus groups:** Butler (2013).
38 **A Stanford student:** Ronen (2010).
38 **student at the University of Kansas:** Page (2011).
40 **in 40 percent of hookups:** Ford et al. (2015).
40 **Danielle Currier:** Currier (2013).
40 **a student at Tufts University:** Dee Dee and Deb (2011).
40 **Students at Radford, Tulane, and Southern Methodist:** Kimmel
     (2008), Lack (2010), Manzone (2015).
40 **student at the University of Southern California:** Butler (2013).
40 **Bowdoin student:** Kinstler (2012).
40 **"yada yada yada of sex":** Kimmel (2008).
42 **"making love":** Smith (1872).
43 **University of Michigan guy:** Epstein et al. (2009).
43 **most casual sex:** Ford et al. (2015).
43 **student at Marist College:** Nosal (2015).
43 **University of Florida, Gainesville student:** Moskovitz (2015).
44 **student at Lehigh:** "Hook-up Culture Dominates Lehigh Social Scene,"
     Lehigh Valley Live, February 11, 2013.
46 **we know that most people:** Ford et al. (2015).

46 **woman enrolled at Tufts:** Dee Dee and Deb (2011).

46 **student at Bellarmine University:** Sales (2015).

46 **three-quarters of seniors:** Armstrong (2012).

47 **student at Bowdoin:** Kinstler (2012).

49 **The hookup is not in itself new:** D'Emilio and Friedman (1988), Peril (2006), Reay (2014), Syrett (2009).

49 **"Casual sex was happening before":** Quoted in Freitas (2008).

CHAPTER 2: HOW SEX BECAME FUN

50 **"I am not, and have never been, a fun person":** Hollowell (2010).

50 **student enrolled at Duke:** Reitman (2006).

55 **"One of the worst labels":** Cheston (2013).

55 **"Fun and freedom":** De Grazia (1962).

56 **According to the social rules:** Kimmel (2008).

56 **20 percent of the American population:** United States Summary (2012).

57 **That loaded phrase:** Google Ngrams. Retrieved February 10, 2016 (books.google.com/ngrams).

58 **They were reimagined:** Freeman (1982), Seidman (1990).

58 **New York City was home to:** Acton (1870), Coontz (2012).

59 **As far as courtship goes:** Bailey (1989).

60 **It was the beginning:** Stearns (2002).

60 **Some of the biggest names:** Piess (2011).

60 **Sales of cosmetics:** D'Emilio,and Freedman (1988).

60 **"A culture fixated on female thinness":** Wolf (1991).

60 *New York Times* **reported:** Greenbaum (1945).

60 *Good Housekeeping*: Discussed in Bailey (1989).

60 *Esquire* **added fuel:** Discussed in Pitzulo (2011).

60 **In 1938, the newspaper for the all-female:** Discussed in Bailey (1989).

61 **In 1957, the president of Amherst:** Heidel (1957).

61 **"During my first two weeks at Smith":** Johnson (1957).

61 **They mostly thought it sounded boring:** Bailey (1989).

61 **"Does going-steady spoil dance fun?":** Jarrett (1957).

61 **At Vassar:** Derr et al. (1959).

61 **Half of women had premarital sex:** Kinsey (1948).

62 **Premarital sex was strongly condemned:** Coontz (1992).

62 **Suburban housewives:** Friedan (1963).

62 **Hugh Hefner:** Ehrenreich (1987).

62 **"Something is happening":** Gilbert (1966).

63 **Emily Kane:** Kane (2006).
65 **"Well-behaved women":** Ulrich (1976).
66 **women's personalities were measuring:** Twenge (1997).
67 **woman at the University of Florida:** Usyk (2008).
67 **woman at Syracuse:** Morris (2014).
67 **student at the University of Pennsylvania:** Taylor (2013).
67 **Hookups are described:** Armstrong and Hamilton (2013), Bay-Cheng and Goodkind (2015).
67 **As recently as the 1980s, college women:** Holland and Eisenhart (1992).
68 **28 percent of women:** Friedland and Gardinali (2013).
68 **female student at Princeton:** Kimmel (2008).
68 **Wesleyan University alum:** Grossman (2012).
68 **female senior at Northwestern:** Traister (2016).
68 **This is Hanna Rosin's argument:** Rosin (2012).
69 **Rosin is certainly not wrong:** Aubrey and Smith (2013).
69 **The sexual double standard:** Allison and Risman (2013); Crawford and Popp (2003).

CHAPTER 3: SEX IN DRUNKWORLD

74 **In pop culture, lust looms large:** Conklin (2008), Reynolds (2014).
75 **two Mount Allison University psychologists:** Wasylikiw and Currie (2012).
76 **A more systematic analysis:** Hartley and Morphew (2008).
76 **Caitlin Flanagan:** Flanagan (2014).
77 **"veritable straitjacket":** Brubacher and Rudy (1997).
77 **Between visits to the chapel:** Syrett (2009).
77 **Student performance:** Thelin (2004).
77 **higher education became a battleground:** Brubacher and Rudy (1997).
78 **University of Virginia students:** Bowman (2015), Creighton (2015), Wagoner, Jr. (1986).
78 **Kappa Alpha:** Syrett (2009).
79 **They rejected the religious values:** Rudolph (1962 [1990]).
79 **They used their clubs:** Thelin (2004).
79 **"I am an aristocrat":** Quoted in ibid.
79 **"I would incomparably rather resign":** Hitchcock (1863).
79 **In 1863, the third president of Amherst:** Ibid.
80 **299 chapters:** Syrett (2009).
80 **"I did get one of the nicest pieces of ass":** Quoted in ibid.

81   **"The question of family":** Gauss (1931).

81   **In the newly popular college-themed novel:** Hevel (2014).

81   **dean of men at the University of Wisconsin:** Radio address quoted in Schwartz (2010).

81   **Frat culture had become:** Ibid.

82   **Chafing under the restrictions:** Peril (2006).

82   **"I imagine that one of the biggest troubles":** X and Haley (1965).

82   **"it's naturally part of college life":** Quoted in Sperber (2000).

83   **College drinking didn't slow down:** Moffett (1989), Vander Ven (2011), Wechsler and Wuethrich (2002).

83   **The National Panhellenic Conference forbids:** National Panhellenic Council (2015).

83   **men of Greek row are able to corner:** Armstrong and Hamilton (2013), Boswell and Spade (1996), Russett (2008).

84   **Raising the legal drinking age:** Moffett (1989).

84   **"Tonight's forecast":** Twitter.com. Retrieved February 10, 2016 (https:// twitter.com/ReggiesBR/status/607980395154391040).

84   **LSU student:** Eddy (2015).

85   **"The clubs have a monopoly":** Sopher (2014).

85   **Their lifestyle has become:** Moffett (1989).

85   **"dramatic drunkenness":** Vander Ven (2011).

86   **A Duke student:** Reitman (2006).

86   **students from Bowdoin, the University of Pennsylvania, and the University of Illinois:** Allison and Risman (2014), Kinstler (2012), Pardes (2013). See also Baker et al., (2013–14), Bogle (2008), Freitas (2008).

86   **At the University of Pennsylvania:** Pardes (2013).

86   **At Princeton:** Chen (2012).

86   **student at Yale:** Foxhall (2010).

89   **"total institutions":** Goffman (1961).

CHAPTER 4: OPTING OUT

92   **men and women are equally likely:** Ford et al. (2015).

93   **at the University of Houston:** Schafler (2015).

93   **guy at UC Santa Cruz:** Ayers (2006).

93   **at the University of Florida:** Nieves (2013).

93   **at the University of Georgia:** Abercrombie and Mays (2013).

93   **hierarchy of sexual desirability:** Jacobs and Labov (2002), Lin and Lundquist (2013), Rosenfeld and Thomas (2012), Rudder (2009), Qian and Lichter (2007, 2011), U.S. Census Bureau (2010).

94   **black women hook up less often:** Paula England, personal communication; data based on the OCSLS. See also Allison and Risman (2014), Brimeyer and Smith (2014), Butler and Hays (n.d.), Kimmel (2008), Knox and Zusman (2009), Owen et al. (2010).

94   **"You can be anybody":** Hunt et al. (2005).

94   **An Asian male enrolled at Occidental College:** Yoo (2014).

94   **Compared to white students:** Ahrold and Meston (2008), Eagan et al. (2014), Jackson et al. (2011), *Journal of Blacks in Higher Education* (2000), Kennedy and Gorzalka (2002), Knox and Zusman (2009), Penhollow et al. (2007), Stombler and Padavic (1997), Stombler and Martin (1994), Wechsler and Kuo (2003).

95   **black man enrolled at the University of Southern California:** Butler (2013).

95   **Black men at Middlebury College and Ohio State:** Kimmel (2008).

95   **Students of color are also more likely:** Allison and Risman (2014), Armstrong and Hamilton (2013), Brimeyer and Smith (2014), Hamilton and Armstrong (2009), Owen et al. (2010), Weitzman and England (2014).

95   **Low-income teenagers:** Guttmacher Institute (2015), Office of Juvenile Justice and Delinquency Prevention (2012), Patrick et al. (2012), Reiman (2012).

96   **Working-class students:** Allison and Risman (2014).

96   **Religious students:** Brimeyer and Smith (2014), Fielder and Carey (2010), Owen et al. (2010), Owen et al. (2011), Penhollow et al. (2007).

97   **men who attend church:** Brimeyer and Smith (2014), Burdette et al. (2009), Freitas (2008), Kuperberg and Padgett (2015), Mir (2014).

97   **Recent profiles of sex on campus:** "Sex on Campus: The Politics of Hookups, Genders, 'Yes,'" *New York*, October 19–November 1, 2015; Morris (2014).

98   **"just screams so much like":** Hamilton (2007).

98   **UC Santa Barbara student:** Rupp and Taylor (2013).

99   **women who participate in girl-on-girl kissing:** Hamilton (2007).

99   **"outsider within":** Collins (1986).

104   **"morning debrief":** Butler (2013).

104   **Sunday morning at Tulane and Connecticut College:** Manzone (2015), Yacos (2014).

104   **woman enrolled at Whitman:** Vandervilt (2012).

108   **Abstainers were at risk:** Pugh (2009).

109   **Elizabeth Armstrong and Laura Hamilton:** Armstrong and Hamilton (2013).

111   **since *Life* conflated:** Discussed in Schwartz (2010).

CHAPTER 5: OPTING IN

113 **"The scene became explosive":** Truscott IV (1969).

113 **They set the place on fire:** Smith (1969).

114 **"was very liberating":** Lovett (2005).

115 **"emerging adulthood":** Arnett (2006).

115 **Compared to their parents:** Taylor (2014).

115 **More than half of full-time:** Saad (2014).

116 **Partly because of these demands:** U.S. Census Bureau (n.d.).

116 **student enrolled at the University of Illinois:** Coyle (2014).

117 **It was one of the fastest:** Brandt (1987).

117 **not at much risk:** East et al. (2007), Fehr et al. (2015), Hickey and Cleland (2013), Lewis et al. (2009), O'Sullivan et al. (2010), Roberts (2006).

117 **Students are significantly more concerned:** Garside et al. (2001), O'Sullivan et al. (2010).

118 **If students think they're protected:** Renner et al. (2012), Spiller et al. (2012).

119 **In the 1990s, half of:** Carpenter (2005).

119 **A third of students:** Garcia and Reiber (2008), Orenstein (2016).

119 **In the *New York Times*:** Taylor (2013).

121 **surveyed over five hundred students:** Uecker et al. (2015).

121 **student at George Washington University:** Kimmel (2008).

121 **utilitarian at Stanford:** Media Education Foundation (2013).

127 **A study at Cornell:** Vrangalova and Ong (2014).

130 **A combination of others' discomfort:** Robillard and Fichten (1983), Neufeld et al. (2002).

130 **"difficult things to do":** Wade (2014).

130 **There has been no research:** Beemyn et al. (2005), Pusch (2003), Rankin (2003).

CHAPTER 6: CARELESS AND CAREFREE

135 **two College of New Jersey psychologists:** Paul and Hayes (2002).

136 **holding hands:** Bazelon (2014).

138 **Susan Bordo:** Bordo (1997).

139 **Alana Massey:** Massey (2015).

140 **a female student at Boston College:** Sales (2015).

140 **It's true that women report:** Friedland and Gardinali (2013), Hyde (2005), Oliver and Hyde (1993).

143 **Mimi Schippers:** Schippers (n.d.). See also Lovejoy (2015).

144 **"Lehigh look-away":** "Hook-up Culture Dominates Lehigh Social Scene," *Lehigh Valley Live*, February 11. 2013.

144 **Women at other colleges:** Dee Dee and Deb (2011), Hitchings (2015), Kostoryz (2014), Nosal (2015), Rowens (2014).

145 **Students, then, are given:** Schippers (n.d.).

145 **The irony is:** Kuperberg and Padgett (forthcoming).

145 **Rachel Kalish:** Kalish (2014).

146 **student at Dartmouth:** Van Syckle (2015).

147 **A University of Kansas woman:** Page (2011).

152 **at the University of Pennsylvania:** Taylor (2013).

153 **Pornographers quite clearly think:** Dines (2011), Jensen (2007).

153 **no generation in recent history:** Carroll et al. (2008).

156 **"people are just looking out":** "Millennials in Adulthood," Pew Research Center: Social and Demographic Trends, March 7, 2014; Zukin and Szeltner (2012).

CHAPTER 7: UNEQUAL PLEASURES

158 **women have one or two orgasms:** Herbenick et al. (2010), Kinsey et al. (1953), Laumann et al. (1994).

159 **in hookups men are more than twice:** England et al. (2008).

159 **"the most common explanation":** Butler (2013).

159 **Some countries, such as the United States:** Beauchamp (2015).

159 **Among Americans, lesbian women:** Coleman et al. (1983), Friedland and Gardinali (2013), Garcia et al. (2014), Harvey et al. (2004), Hite (1977), Tilos (2014).

159 **In masturbation, orgasms come:** Douglass and Douglass (1997), Kinsey et al. (1953), Thompson (1989).

159 **Even women who never have orgasms:** Wade et al. (2005).

160 **the likelihood of a woman having an orgasm:** Armstrong et al. (2015).

160 **For most of European American history:** Hunt and Curtis (2006).

161 **In her 1926 relationship advice manual:** Sanger (1926).

161 **Teens of both sexes agree:** Orenstein (2016). Lewis and Marston (2014).

162 **Among young people, fellatio occurs:** Bay-Cheng et al. (2009).

162 **When guy–girl hookups proceed to oral sex:** Ford et al. (2015).

162 **when students receive oral sex:** Ibid.

165 **Interested in women's discomfort with cunnilingus:** Backstrom et al. (2012).

165 **"chapel of ease":** Timeline of Slang Terms for the Vagina. Retrieved February 13, 2016 (http://timeglider.com/timeline/07f47d6b843da763).

166   **National Health and Social Life Survey:** Laumann et al. (1994).

166   **Jess Butler:** Butler (2013).

167   **A guy at Stanford:** Media Education Foundation (2013).

168   **student at Duke:** Reed (2013).

168   **woman at Brown:** Kitroeff (2013).

168   **at the University of Southern California:** Butler (2013).

170   **"In a relationship":** Armstrong et al. (2012).

170   **Women in relationships:** Ford et al. (2015).

171   **"They'll tease you":** Sweeney (2014a).

172   **Desmond studied forest firefighters:** Desmond (2007).

174   **Brian Sweeney:** Sweeney (2014a).

174   **Dartmouth student:** Kimmel (2008).

174   **New York University alum:** Delistraty (2013).

175   **student at Stanford:** Kimmel (2008).

176   **But the second half of the chant:** Kimmel (2010).

177   **It should be no surprise:** Ford et al. (2015).

177   **We know that because:** Ibid.

178   **84 percent reported:** Ibid.

CHAPTER 8: WANTING TO BE WANTED

181   **She's echoing:** Rupp and Taylor (2010).

181   **So, they and their colleagues sought:** Rupp et al. (2014).

183   *Rolling Stone:* Grigoria (2003).

184   **some students have a tendency:** Yost and Thomas (2012).

189   *New York Times:* Greenbaum (1945).

189   **a quarter of undergraduates:** Astin and Lindholm (2002).

189   **women comprise:** National Center for Education Statistics (n.d.).

189   **For every two women:** Birger (2015).

194   **University of Southern California student:** Butler (2013).

196   **"Those that possess the alcohol":** Russett (2008).

196   **A Dartmouth woman:** Van Syckle (2015).

197   **"Women have greater authority":** Parts (2015).

197   **Harvard's final clubs:** Kahn (2015), Suslovic and Weiers (2015).

197   **A report released by the college:** Harvard University Task Force on the Prevention of Sexual Assault (2016).

197   **student at Boston University:** Mintz (2014).

199   **Psychologists have found:** Erchull and Liss (2014), Hirschman et al. (2006), Lustig (2012), Sanchez and Kiefer (2007).

CHAPTER 9: FLIRTING WITH DANGER

204 **Our best estimate:** Armstrong and Budnick (2015), Cantor et al. (2015), Fisher et al. (2000), Kilpatrick et al. (2007), Krebs et al. (2007), Sinozich and Langton (2014), White House Task Force to Protect Students from Sexual Assault (2014).

204 **Among the women who responded:** Ford and England (2015).

205 **Most campus assaults:** Armstrong et al. (2006), Sampson (2002).

206 **Catharine MacKinnon:** MacKinnon (1989).

206 **survey of over 250 men:** Thompson and Cracco (2008). See also Becker and Tinkler (2015), Kavanaugh (2013), Parks and Miller (1997).

210 **guy enrolled at the University of Florida:** Perrone and Harnish (2010).

210 **One Harvard student:** Gattuso (2015).

211 **"If you're a guy":** Kimmel (2008).

211 **Four out of five college men:** Swartout et al. (2015).

212 **"Get the bitches":** Ryan (2014).

212 **A member of the Phi Kappa Tau:** Torres (2013).

212 **Another from the University of Southern California:** Hartmann (2011).

212 **Men are three times as likely:** Mohler-Kuo et al. (2004).

212 **Fraternities and other all-male:** Abbey et al. (2001), Boyle (2015), Humphrey and Kahn (2000), McMahon (2010), Mohler-Kuo et al. (2004), Murnen and Kohlman (2007), Schwartz and Nogrady (1996), United Educators (2015).

212 **Some fraternities have cultivated cultures:** Anderson (2008).

213 **Men in African American fraternities:** Ray and Rosow (2010).

213 **Nicholas Syrett:** Syrett (2009).

213 **4 percent of college men:** Lisak and Miller (2002).

213 **study of navy enlistees:** McWhorter et al. (2009).

213 **DNA testing:** Delmore (2014), Eckholm (2014).

215 **Peggy Orenstein:** Orenstein (2016).

216 **More than half of students:** Cantor et al. (2015).

217 **Bill Cosby:** Kim and Littlefield (2015).

217 **Arnold Schwarzenegger:** "Sex Scandal Draws Arnie Apology," BBC News, October 3, 2003.

217 **Roman Polanski:** "The Slow-Burning Polanski Saga," BBC News, September 28, 2009.

217 **In *Asking For It*:** Harding (2015).

217 **In 2016, Florida State University:** Tracy (2016).

218 **In the last five years:** Adler (2016), Axon (2014), Bogdanich (2014), Eaton-Robb (2013), Kingkade (2013, 2014), Krakauer (2015), Lavigne

(2016), New (2016), North (2010, 2012), Palmer (2014), Prohaska (2016), Ranker (2016), Wadhwani (2016); "Lawsuit Claims New Mexico Violated Title IX in Alleged Gang Rape," *Sports Illustrated*, February 23, 2015; "Delaware Sued for Mishandling Athlete Rape Allegation," *Inside Higher Ed*, January 3, 2014.

218   **In an article for *Time*:** Abdul-Jabbar (2015).
219   **Research has shown that yelling:** Hollander (2009).
221   **The typical victim:** Sinozich and Langton (2014), United Educators (2015).
221   **Richard Morgan:** Morgan (2014).
221   **Even women often blame the victim:** Armstrong and Hamilton (2013).
222   **One of the demonstrators:** Ember and Bowley (2015).
223   **"We will never know":** Johnson (2015).

CHAPTER 10: MOVING ON

232   **For *Vanity Fair*:** Sales (2015).
233   **The little we do know:** Bogle (2008).
235   **A recent report:** Rhoades and Stanley (2014).
237   **At Boston College:** Cicchese (2014).

CONCLUSION: CHANGING THE CULTURE

243   **Research published in 1957:** Kirkpatrick and Kanin (1957).
245   **In a classic study from the 1980s:** Clark and Hatfield (1989).
245   **University of Michigan psychologist:** Conley (2010).
247   **Stephanie Coontz:** Coontz (2004).

Sources

Abbey, Antonia, Pam McAuslan, Tina Zawacki, A. Monique Clinton, and
Philip Buck. 2001. Attitudinal, Experiential and Situational Predictors
of Sexual Assault Perpetration. *Journal of Interpersonal Violence* 16, 8:
784–807.

Abdul-Jabbar, Kareem. 2015. Colleges Should Stop Protecting Sexual Predators. *Time*, January 30.

Abercrombie, Chelsey, and Stephen Mays. 2013. Let's Talk about Sex: The
Truth Behind the Myth of Hook-up Culture at the University of Georgia.
The Red and Black, October 31.

Acton, William. 1870. *Prostitution, Considered in its Moral, Social, and Sanitary
Aspects*. London: John Churchill and Sons.

Adler, Lindsey. 2016. Lawsuit: University of Arkansas Tried to Wait to Expel
Olympic Athlete Until He'd Graduated. *Deadspin*, August 30.

Ahrold, Tierney, and Cindy Meston. 2008. Ethnic Differences in Sexual Attitudes of U.S. College Students: Gender, Acculturation, and Religiosity
Factors. *Archives of Sexual Behavior* 39, 1: 190–202.

Allison, Rachel, and Barbara J. Risman. 2013. A Double Standard for "Hooking Up": How Far Have We Come toward Gender Equality? *Social Science
Research* 42, 5: 1191–1206.

———. 2014. "It Goes Hand in Hand with the Parties": Race, Class, and
Residence in College Student Negotiations in Hooking Up. *Sociological
Perspectives* 57, 1: 102–23.

American College Health Association. 2013. *American College Health Association–National College Health Assessment II: Reference Group Executive Summary Spring 2013*. Hanover, MD: American College Health Association.

Retrieved December 5, 2015 (http://www.acha-ncha.org/docs/ACHA-NCHA-II_ReferenceGroup_ExecutiveSUmmary_Spring2013.pdf).

Anderson, Eric. 2008. Inclusive Masculinity in a Fraternal Setting. *Men and Masculinities* 10, 5: 604–20.

Armstrong, Elizabeth A., and Jamie Budnick. 2015. Sexual Assault on Campus. Council on Contemporary Families, April 20. Retrieved February 15, 2016 (https://contemporaryfamilies.org/assault-on-campus-brief-report/).

Armstrong, Elizabeth A., Paula England, and Alison C. K. Fogarty. 2012. Accounting for Women's Orgasm and Sexual Enjoyment in College Hookups and Relationships. *American Sociological Review* 77, 3: 435–62.

———. 2015. Orgasm in College Hookups and Relationships. In Barbara Risman and Virginia Rutter (eds.), *Families as They Really Are* (2nd ed.). New York: W. W. Norton.

Armstrong, Elizabeth A., and Laura Hamilton. 2013. *Paying for the Party: How College Maintains Inequality.* Cambridge, MA: Harvard University Press.

Armstrong, Elizabeth A., Laura Hamilton, and Brian Sweeney. 2006. Sexual Assault on Campus: A Multilevel, Integrative Approach to Party Rape. *Social Problems* 53, 4: 483–99.

Arnett, Jeffrey. 2006. *Emerging Adulthood: The Winding Road from the Late Teens through the Twenties.* Oxford: Oxford University Press.

Astin, Helen, and Jennifer Lindholm. 2002. Academic Aspiration and Degree Attainment of Women. In Judith Worell (ed.), *Encyclopedia of Women and Gender: Sex Similarities and Differences and the Impact of Society on Gender,* vol. 1. Cambridge, UK: Academic Press.

Aubrey, Jennifer, and Siobhan Smith. 2013. Development and Validation of the Endorsement of the Hookup Culture Index. *Journal of Sex Research* 50, 5: 435–48.

Axon, Rachel. 2014. Patrick Swilling Jr. Responds to Lawsuit in Open Letter. *USA Today,* August 21.

Ayers, Kate. 2006. The State of the Union: Sex and Dating at UC Santa Cruz. *City on a Hill Press,* November 16.

Backstrom, Laura, Elizabeth Armstrong, and Jennifer Puentes. 2012. Women's Negotiation of Cunnilingus in College Hookups and Relationships. *Journal of Sex Research* 49, 1: 1–12.

Bailey, Beth. 1989. *From Front Porch to Back Seat: Courtship in Twentieth-Century America.* Baltimore and London: Johns Hopkins University Press.

Baker, Phyllis, B. Keith Crew, and Kevin Leicht. 2013–14. The Gendered Way of Hooking Up among College Students. *Universitas* 9.

Bay-Cheng, Laina, and Sara Goodkind. 2015. Sex and the Single (Neoliberal) Girl: Perspectives on Being Single Among Socioeconomically Diverse Young Women. *Sex Roles* 73, 11/12: n. p. Retrieved February

29, 2016 (https://www.springerprofessional.de/journal-11199-onlinefirst
-articles/5748366).

————, Adjoa Robinson, and Alyssa Zucker. 2009. Behavioral and Relational
Contexts of Adolescent Desire, Wanting, and Pleasure: Undergraduate
Women's Retrospective Accounts. *Journal of Sex Research* 46, 6: 511–24.

Bazelon, Emily. 2014. Hooking Up at an Affirmative-Consent Campus? It's
Complicated. *New York Times Magazine*, October 21.

Beauchamp, Zack. 2015. 6 Maps and Charts that Explain Sex around the
World. *Vox*, May 26.

Becker, Sarah, and Justine Tinkler. 2015. "Me Getting Plastered and Her
Provoking My Eyes": Young People's Attribute of Blame for Sexual
Aggression in Public Drinking Spaces. *Feminist Criminology* 10, 3:
235–58.

Beemyn, Brett, Billy Curtis, Masen Davis, and Nancy Jean Tubbs. 2005.
Transgender Issues on College Campuses. *New Directions for Student Services* 111: 49–60.

Bersamin, Merlina, B. L. Zamboanga, S. J. Schwartz, M. B. Donnnellan, M.
Hudson, R. S. Weisskirch, S. Y. Kim, V. B. Agocha, S. K. Whitebourne,
and S. J. Caraway. 2013. Risky Business: Is There an Association between
Casual Sex and Mental Health among Emerging Adults? *Journal of Sex
Research* 51, 1: 43–51.

Birger, Jon. 2015. *Date-onomics: How Dating Became a Lopsided Numbers Game.*
New York: Workman.

Bogdanich, Walt. 2014. Reporting Rape, and Wishing She Hadn't. *New York
Times*, July 12.

Bogle, Kathleen. 2008. *Hooking Up: Sex, Dating, and Relationships on Campus.*
New York: New York University Press.

Bordo, Susan. 1997. *Twilight Zones: The Hidden Life of Cultural Images from
Plato to O. J.* Berkeley: University of California Press.

Boswell, A. Ayres, and Joan Spade. 1996. Fraternities and Collegiate Rape
Culture: Why Are Some Fraternities More Dangerous Places for Women?
Gender and Society 10, 2: 133–47.

Bowman, Rex. 2015. *Rot, Riot, and Rebellion: Mr. Jefferson's Struggle to Save
the University that Changed America.* Charlottesville: University of Virginia
Press.

Boyle, Kaitlin. 2015. Social Psychological Processes that Facilitate Sexual
Assault within the Fraternity Party Subculture. *Sociology Compass* 9, 5:
386–99.

Brandt, Allan. 1987. *No Magic Bullet: A Social History of Venereal Disease in the
United States Since 1880.* Oxford: Oxford University Press.

Brimeyer, Ted, and William Smith. 2014. Religion, Race, Social Class, and

Gender Differences in Dating and Hooking Up among College Students. *Sociological Spectrum* 32, 5: 462–73.

Brubacher, John Seiler, and Willis Rudy. 1997. *Higher Education in Transition: A History of American Colleges and Universities*. Piscataway, NJ: Transaction.

Burdette, Amy, Christopher Ellison, Terrence Hill, and Norval Glenn. 2009. "Hooking Up" at College: Does Religion Make a Difference? *Journal for the Scientific Study of Religion* 48, 3: 535–51.

Butler, Jess. 2013. "Sexual Subjects: Hooking Up in the Age of Postfeminism." PhD dissertation, Department of Sociology, University of Southern California, Los Angeles, CA.

———, and Sharon Hays. n.d. Hooking Up as a Shared Cultural Narrative. Unpublished manuscript.

Cantor, David, Bonnie Fisher, Susan Chibnall, Reanne Townsend, Hyunshik Lee, Carol Bruce, and Gail Thomas. 2015. Report on the AAU Campus Climate Survey on Sexual Assault and Sexual Misconduct. Association of American Universities. Retrieved February 15, 2016 (https://www.aau .edu/registration/public/PAdocs/Survey_Communication_9-18/Final_ Report_9-18-15.pdf).

Carpenter, Laura. 2005. *Virginity Lost: An Intimate Portrait of First Sexual Experiences*. New York: New York University Press.

Carroll, Jason, Laura Padilla-Walker, Larry Nelson, Chad Olson, Carolyn Barry, and Stephanie Madsen. 2008. Generation XXX: Pornography Acceptance and Use among Emerging Adults. *Journal of Adolescent Research* 23, 1: 6–30.

Chen, Vivienne. 2012. In Defense of Hookups, Not Hookup Culture. *Daily Princetonian*, November 7.

Cheston, Duke. 2013. The Cruelty of Hook-Up Culture. John William Pope Center for Higher Education Policy. Retrieved March 3, 2016 (http:// www.popecenter.org/commentaries/article.html?id=2816).

Cicchese, Heather. 2014. College Class Tries to Revive the Lost Art of Dating. *Boston Globe*, May 16.

Clark, Russell, and Elaine Hatfield. 1989. Gender Differences in Receptivity to Sexual Offers. *Journal of Psychology and Human Sexuality* 2, 1: 39–55.

Coleman, Emily, Peter Hoon, and Emily Hoon. 1983. Arousability and Sexual Satisfaction in Lesbian and Heterosexual Women. *Journal of Sex Research* 19, 1: 58–73.

Collins, Patricia Hill. 1986. Learning from the Outsider Within: The Sociological Significance of Black Feminist Thought. *Social Problems* 33, 6: S14–S32.

Conklin, John. 2008. *Campus Life in the Movies: A Critical Survey from the Silent Era to the Present.* Jefferson, NC: McFarland.

Conley, Terri. 2010. Perceived Proposer Personality Characteristics and Gender Differences in Acceptance of Casual Sex Offers. *Journal of Personality and Social Psychology* 100, 2: 309–29.

Coontz, Stephanie. 1992. *The Way We Never Were: American Families and the Nostalgia Trap.* New York: Basic Books.

———. 2004. The World Historical Transformation of Marriage. *Journal of Marriage and Family* 66, 4: 974–79.

———. 2012. Blame Affairs on Evolution of Sex Roles. CNN, November 18.

Coyle, Katie. 2014. Another Article about the Hookup Culture. *Odyssey*, November 24.

Cranney, Stephen. 2015. The Relationship Between Sexual Victimization and Year in School in U.S. Colleges: Investigating the Parameters of the "Red Zone." *Journal of Interpersonal Violence* 30, 17: 3133–45.

Crawford, Mary, and Danielle Popp. 2003. Sexual Double Standards: A Review and Methodological Critique of Two Decades of Research. *Journal of Sex Research* 40, 1: 13–26.

Creighton, Catherine. 2015. Pavilion X: A Brief History (1820–1895). Jefferson's University Early Life Project, June 18.

Currier, Danielle. 2013. Strategic Ambiguity: Protecting Emphasized Femininity and Hegemonic Masculinity in the Hookup Culture. *Gender and Society* 27, 5: 704–27.

Dee Dee and Deb. 2011. College Hookup Culture Part I: She Says. *Huffington Post*, November 29.

De Grazia, Sebastian. 1962. *Of Time, Work and Leisure.* New York: Twentieth Century Fund.

Delistraty, Cody. 2013. The Truth about Men and Hook-Up Culture. *Thought Catalog*, September 25.

Delmore, Erin. 2014. 100 Serial Rapists ID'd from Detroit Kit Backlog. MSNBC, March 17.

D'Emilio, John, and Estelle Friedman. 1988. *Intimate Matters: A History of Sexuality in America.* New York: Harper and Row.

Derr, P. B., William Asher, and Frederick Olds. 1959. Naval Stagliner's Association Crusade Urgently Seeks VC's Active Support. *Vassar Chronicle* XVI, 13.

Desmond, Matthew. 2007. *On the Fireline: Living and Dying with Wildland Firefighters.* Chicago: University of Chicago Press.

Dines, Gail. 2011. *Pornland: How Porn Has Hijacked Our Sexuality.* New York: Beacon Press.

Douglass, Marcia, and Lisa Douglass. 1997. *Are We Having Fun Yet?* New York: Hyperion.

Eagan, Kevin, Ellen Stolzenberg, Joseph Ramirez, Melissa Aragon, Maria Ramirez Suchard, and Sylvia Hurtado. 2014. *The American Freshman: National Norms Fall 2014.* Los Angeles: Higher Education Research Institute, UCLA.

East, Leah, Debra Jackson, Louise O'Brien, and Kathleen Peters. 2007. Use of the Male Condom by Heterosexual Adolescents and Young People: Literature Review. *Journal of Advanced Nursing* 59, 2: 103–10.

Eaton-Robb, Pat. 2013. UConn Disputes Coach's Claim that He Didn't Know Player Was Accused of Sexual Assault. *Huffington Post*, November 6.

Eckholm, Erik. 2014. No Longer Ignored, Evidence Solves Rape Cases Years Later. *New York Times*, August 2.

Eddy, Kate. 2015. The Definitive Ranking of Bars in Tigerland. *Odyssey*, April 6.

Ehrenreich, Barbara. 1987. *The Hearts of Men: American Dreams and the Flight from Commitment.* New York: Anchor Books.

Ember, Sydney, and Graham Bowley. 2015. Bill Cosby Charged in Sexual Assault Case. *New York Times*, December 30.

England, Paula, Emily Shafer, and Alison Fogarty. 2008. Hooking Up and Forming Relationships on Today's College Campuses. In Michael Kimmel and Amy Aronson (eds.), *The Gendered Society Reader*, 3rd edition, 531–47. New York: Oxford University Press.

Epstein, Marina, Jerel Calzo, Andrew Smiler, and L. Monique Ward. 2009. "Anything from Making Out to Having Sex": Men's Negotiations of Hooking Up and Friends with Benefits Scripts. *Journal of Sex Research* 46, 5: 414–24.

Erchull, Mindy, and Miriam Liss. 2014. The Object of One's Desire: How Perceived Sexual Empowerment Through Objectification is Related to Sexual Outcomes. *Sexuality and Culture* 18, 4: 773–88.

Eshbaugh, Elaine, and Gary Gute. 2008. Hookups and Sexual Regret among College Women. *Journal of Social Psychology* 148, 1: 77–89.

Fehr, Sara, Rebecca Vidourek, and Keith King. 2015. Intra- and Inter-personal Barriers to Condom Use among College Students: A Review of the Literature. *Sexuality and Culture* 19, 1: 103–21.

Fielder, Robyn, and Michael Carey. 2010. Predictors and Consequences of Sexual "Hookups" among College Students: A Short-Term Prospective Study. *Archives of Sexual Behavior* 39, 5: 346–59.

Fisher, Bonnie, Francis Cullen, and Michael Turner. 2000. The Sexual Victimization of College Women. Washington, DC: National Institute of Justice and Bureau of Justice Statistics.

Fisher, Maryanne, Kerry Worth, Justin Garcia, and Tami Meredith. 2012. Feelings of Regret Following Uncommitted Sexual Encounters in Canadian University Students. *Culture, Health and Sexuality* 14, 1: 45–57.

Flack, William, Kimberly Daubman, Marcia Caron, Jenica Asadorian, Nicole D'Aureli, Shannon Gigliotti, Anna Hall, Sarah Kiser, and Erin Stine. 2007. Risk Factors and Consequences of Unwanted Sex among University Students—Hooking Up, Alcohol, and Stress Response. *Journal of Interpersonal Violence* 22, 2: 139–57.

Flanagan, Caitlin. 2014. The Dark Power of Fraternities. *Atlantic*, March.

Ford, Jessie, and Paula England. 2015. What Percent of College Women Are Sexually Assaulted in College? *Contexts*, January 12.

———, and Jonathan Bearak. 2015. The American College Hookup Scene: Findings from the Online College Social Life Survey. American Sociological Association Annual Meeting, Chicago, August.

Foxhall, Emily. 2010. Yalies, Under the Covers. *Yale News*, February 8.

Freeman, Estelle. 1982. Sexuality in Nineteenth-Century America: Behavior, Ideology, and Politics. *Reviews in American History* 10, 4: 196-215.

Freitas, Donna. 2008. *Sex and the Soul: Juggling Sexuality, Spirituality, Romance, and Religion on America's College Campuses.* Oxford: Oxford University Press.

———. 2013. *The End of Sex: How Hookup Culture is Leaving a Generation Unhappy, Sexually Unfulfilled, and Confused about Intimacy.* New York: Basic Books.

Friedan, Betty. 1963. *The Feminine Mystique.* New York: W. W. Norton.

Friedland, Roger, and Paolo Gardinali. 2013. Hey God, Is That You in My Underpants?: Sex, Love and Religiosity among American College Students. In Alan Frank, Patricia Clough, and Steven Seidman (eds.), *Intimacies: A New World of Relational Life.* New York: Routledge.

Garcia, Justin, Elisabeth Lloyd, Kim Wallen, and Helen Fisher. 2014. Variation in Orgasm Occurrence by Sexual Orientation in a Sample of U.S. Singles. *International Society for Sexual Medicine* 11, 11: 2645–52.

———, and Chris Reiber. 2008. Hook-up Behavior: A Biopsychosocial Perspective. *Journal of Social, Evolutionary, and Cultural Psychology* 2, 4: 192–208.

Garside, Ruth, Richard Ayres, Mike Owen, Virginia Pearson, and Judith Roizen. 2001. "They Never Tell You about the Consequences": Young People's Awareness of Sexually Transmitted Infections. *International Journal of STD & AIDS* 12, 9: 582–88.

Gattuso, Reina. 2015. Rape Culture is a Contract We Never Actually Signed. Feministing. Retrieved February 15, 2016 (http://feministing.com/2015/05/26/rape-culture-is-a-contract-we-never-actually-signed/).

Gauss, Christian Frederick. 1931. *Life in College*. Ann Arbor, MI: C. Scribner's Sons.

Gilbert, Eugene. 1966. Going-Steady Craze for Teens Could Be on the Downhill. *Lawrence Journal-World*, March 22.

Glenn, Norval, and Elizabeth Marquardt. 2001. *Hooking Up, Hanging Out, and Hoping for Mr. Right: College Women on Dating and Mating Today*. New York: An Institute for American Values Report to the Independent Women's Forum.

Goffman, Erving. 1961. *Asylums: Essays on the Social Situation of Mental Patients and Other Inmates*. New York: Doubleday & Company, Inc.

Greenbaum, Lucy. 1945. In Marriage It's a Man's Market. *New York Times Magazine*, June 17.

Grello, Catherine, Deborah Welsh, and Melinda Harper. 2006. No Strings Attached: The Nature of Casual Sex in College Students. *Journal of Sex Research* 43, 3: 255–67.

Grigoria, Vanessa. 2003. Princess Paris. *Rolling Stone*, November 19.

Grossman, Erica. 2012. Mistress of Our Own Domain: Behind the Myth of Hookup Culture. *Huffington Post*, September 14.

Guttmacher Institute. 2015. Unintended Pregnancy in the United States. Retrieved February 24, 2016 (https://www.guttmacher.org/pubs/FB -Unintended-Pregnancy-US.html).

Hamilton, Laura. 2007. Trading on Heterosexuality: College Women's Gender Strategies and Homophobia. *Gender and Society* 21, 2: 145–72.

———, and Elizabeth Armstrong. 2009. Gendered Sexuality in Young Adulthood: Double Binds and Flawed Options. *Gender and Society* 23, 5: 589–616.

Harding, Kate. 2015. *Asking For It: The Alarming Rise of Rape Culture and What We Can Do About It*. Boston: De Capo Lifelong Books.

Hartley, Matthew, and Christopher Morphew. 2008. What's Being Sold and To What End? A Content Analysis of College Viewbooks. *Journal of Higher Education* 79, 6: 671–91.

Hartmann, Margaret. 2011. Frat Email Explains Women Are "Targets," Not "Actual People." *Jezebel*, March 8.

Harvard University Task Force on the Prevention of Sexual Assault. 2016. Final Report. Retrieved March 19, 2016 (http://sexualassaulttaskforce. harvard.edu/files/taskforce/files/final_report_of_the_task_force_on_ the_prevention_of_sexual_assault_16_03_07.pdf?m=1457452164).

Harvey, John, Amy Wenzel, and Susan Sprecher. 2004. *The Handbook of Sexuality in Close Relationships*. New York: Routledge.

Heidel, Don. 1957. Coeds: Is It Too Late? *Florida Flambeau*, February 22.

Herbenick, Debby, Michael Reece, Vanessa Schick, Stephanie Sanders, Brian

Dodge, and J. Dennis Fortenberry. 2010. An Event-Level Analysis of the Sexual Characteristics and Composition among Adults Ages 18 to 59: Results from a National Probability Sample in the United States. *Journal of Sexual Medicine* 7, 5: 346–61.

Herman-Kinney, Nancy, and David Kinney. 2013. Sober as Deviant: The Stigma of Sobriety and How Some College Students "Stay Dry" on a "Wet" Campus. *Journal of Contemporary Ethnography* 42, 1: 64–103.

Hevel, Michael. 2014. Setting the Stage for Animal House: Student Drinking in College Novels, 1865–1933. *Journal of Higher Education* 85, 3: 370–401.

Hickey, Mary, and Chuck Cleland. 2013. Sexually Transmitted Infection Risk Perception among Female College Students. *Journal of the American Association of Nurse Practitioners* 25, 7: 377–84.

Hirschman, Celeste, Emily Impett, and Deborah Schooler. 2006. Dis/embodied Voices: What Late-Adolescent Girls Can Teach Us about Objectification and Sexuality. *Sexuality Research and Social Policy* 3, 4: 8–20.

Hitchcock, Edward. 1863. *Reminiscences of Amherst College: Historical Scientific, Biographical and Autobiographical.* Carlisle, MA: Applewood Books.

Hitchings, Maggie. 2015. An Open Letter to Freshman Entering the College Hookup Culture. *Odyssey,* September 8.

Hite, Shere. 1977. *The Hite Report: A Nationwide Study of Female Sexuality.* New York: Seven Stories Press.

Hoffman, Kristi, and Marit Berntson. 2014. Predicting Participation in "Friends with Benefits" Relationships. American Sociological Association Annual Meeting, San Francisco, August.

Holland, Dorothy, and Margaret Eisenhart. 1992. *Educated in Romance: Women, Achievement, and College Culture.* Chicago: University of Chicago Press.

Hollander, Jocelyn. 2009. The Roots of Resistance to Women's Self-Defense. *Violence Against Women* 15, 5: 574–94.

Hollowell, Clare. 2010. The Subject of Fun: Young Women, Freedom and Feminism. PhD dissertation, Centre for Gender and Women's Studies, Lancaster University, Lancaster, UK.

Humphrey, Stephen, and Arnold Kahn. 2000. Fraternities, Athletic Teams, and Rape. *Journal of Interpersonal Violence* 15, 12: 1313–22.

Hunt, Alan, and Bruce Curtis. 2006. A Genealogy of the Genital Kiss: Oral Sex in the Twentieth Century. *Canadian Journal of Human Sexuality* 15, 2: 69.

Hunt, Geoffrey, Kristin Evans, Eileen Wu, and Alicia Reyes. 2005. Asian American Youth, the Dance Scene, and Club Drugs. *Journal of Drug Issues* 35, 4: 695–732.

Hyde, Janet. 2005. The Gender Similarities Hypothesis. *American Psychologist* 60, 6: 581–92.

Jackson, Pamela Braboy, Sibyl Kleiner, Claudia Geist, and Kara Cebulko. 2011. Conventions of Courtship: Gender and Race Differences in the Significance of Dating. *Journal of Family Issues* 32, 5: 629–54.

Jacobs, Jerry, and Teresa Labov. 2002. Gender Differentials in Intermarriage among Sixteen Race and Ethnic Groups. *Sociological Forum* 17, 4: 621–46.

Jarrett, Nancy. 1957. Lakeland Teen-agers Split on Query, "Does Going-Steady Spoil Dance Fun?" *Lakeland Ledger*, August 18.

Jensen, Robert. 2007. Getting Off: Pornography and the End of Masculinity. Brooklyn: South End Press.

Johnson, Allan. 2015. Can a Good Man Rape? *Unraveling the Knot*, December 5.

Johnson, Nora. 1957. Sex and the College Girl. *Atlantic*, November.

Journal of Blacks in Higher Education. 2000. News and Views: Alcohol Abuse Remains High on College Campus, But Black Students Drink to Excess Far Less Often Than Whites. *Journal of Blacks in Higher Education* 28: 19–20.

Kahn, Mattie. 2015. Will Harvard's Most Exclusive All-Male Clubs Finally Admit Women? *Elle*, November 30.

Kalish, Rachel. 2014. Exclusive Relationships in the Context of Hookup Culture. American Sociological Association Annual Meeting, San Francisco, August.

Kane, Emily. 2006. "No Way My Boys Are Going To Be Like That!": Parents' Responses to Children's Gender Noncomformity. *Gender and Society* 20, 2: 149–76.

Karp, Michael. 2014. The O-Face: Handling Hookup Culture. *Orion*, February 19.

Kavanaugh, Philip. 2013. The Continuum of Sexual Violence: Women's Accounts of Victimization in Urban Nightlife. *Feminist Criminology* 8, 1: 20–39.

Katz, Jennifer, Vanessa Tirone, and Erika van der Kloet. 2012. Moving In and Hooking Up: Women's and Men's Casual Sexual Experiences During the First Two Months of College. *Electronic Journal of Human Sexuality* 15: 1.

Kennedy, Margaret, and Boris Gorzalka. 2002. Asian and Non-Asian Attitudes Toward Rape, Sexual Harassment and Sexuality. *Sex Roles* 46, 7–8: 227–38.

Kilpatrick, Dean, Heidi Resnick, Kenneth Ruggiero, Lauren Conoscenti, and Janna McCauley. 2007. Drug-Facilitated, Incapacitated, and Forcible Rape: A National Study. National Crime Victims Research and Treatment Center. Retrieved February 15, 2016 (https://www.ncjrs.gov/pdffiles1/nij/grants/219181.pdf).

Kim, Kyle, and Christina Littlefield. 2015. Bill Cosby: A 50-Year Chronicle of Accusations and Accomplishments. *Los Angeles Times*, December 30.

Kimmel, Michael. 2008. *Guyland: The Perilous World Where Boys Become Men*. New York: HarperCollins.

———. 2010. The Men, and Women, of Yale. *Ms. Magazine* blog, October 17.

Kingkade, Tyler. 2013. Amherst, Vanderbilt Accused of Botching Sexual Assault Complaints. *Huffington Post*, November 14.

———. 2014. Michigan Universities Face Federal Investigations into Sexual Assaults. *Huffington Post*, February 26.

Kinsey, Alfred. 1948. *Sexual Behavior of the Human Male*. Bloomington: Indiana University Press.

———, Wardell Pomeroy, Clyde Martin, and Paul Gebhard. 1953. *Sexual Behavior in the Human Female*. Philadelphia: Saunders.

Kinstler, Linda. 2012. "Everyone's Doing It": Defining Campus Hookup Culture. *Bowdoin Orient*, December 7.

Kirkpatrick, Clifford, and Eugene Kanin. 1957. Male Sex Aggression on a University Campus. *American Sociological Review* 22, 1: 52–58.

Kitroeff, Natalie. 2013. In Hookups, Inequality Still Reigns. *New York Times*, November 11.

Knox, David, and Marty Zusman. 2009. Sexuality in Black and White: Data from 783 Undergraduates. *Electronic Journal of Human Sexuality* 12: 1.

Kostoryz, Sarah. 2014. The Endorsement of College Hookup Culture. *Common Places* 5, Fall.

Krakauer, Jon. 2015. *Missoula: Rape and the Justice System in a College Town*. New York: Doubleday.

Krebs, Christopher, Christine Lindquist, Tara Warner, Bonnie Fischer, and Sandra Martin. 2007. The Campus Sexual Assault Study. National Institute of Justice. Retrieved February 15, 2016 (https://www.ncjrs.gov/pdffiles1/nij/grants/221153.pdf).

Kuperberg, Arielle, and Joseph Padgett. 2015. Dating and Hooking Up in College: Meeting Contexts, Sex, and Variation by Gender, Partner's Gender, and Class Standing. *Journal of Sex Research* 52, 5: 517–31.

———. Forthcoming. The Role of Culture in Explaining College Students' Selection into Hookups, Dates, and Long-Term Romantic Relationships. *Journal of Social and Personal Relationships*.

Lack, Taylor. 2010. The Hookup Culture: Party, Hookup, No Strings Attached. *Daily Campus*, April 14.

Laumann, Edward, John Gagnon, Robert Michael, and Stuart Michaels. 1994. *The Social Organization of Sexuality: Sexual Practices in the United States*. Chicago: University of Chicago Press.

Lavigne, Paula. 2016. Baylor Faces Accusations of Ignoring Sex Assault Victims. ESPN, February 2.

Lewis, John, Maria-Jose Miguez-Burbano, and Robert Malow. 2009. HIV Risk Behavior Among College Students in the United States. *College Student Journal* 43, 2: 475–91.

Lewis, Melissa, Hollie Granato, Jessica Blayney, Ty Lostutter, and Jason Kilmer. 2012. Predictors of Hooking Up Sexual Behaviors and Emotional Reactions among U.S. College Students. *Archives of Sexual Behavior* 41, 2: 1219–29.

Lewis, Ruth, and Cicely Marston. 2014. Give and Take? Reciprocity in Young People's Accounts of Oral Heterosex. American Sociological Association Annual Meeting, San Francisco, August.

Lin, Ken-Hou, and Jennifer Lundquist. 2013. Mate Selection in Cyberspace: The Intersection of Race, Gender, and Education. *American Journal of Sociology* 119, 1: 183–215.

Lisak, David, and Paul Miller. 2002. Repeat Rape and Multiple Offending Among Undetected Rapists. *Violence and Victims* 17, 1: 73–84.

Lovejoy, Meg. 2015. Hooking Up as an Individualistic Practice: A Double-Edged Sword for College Women. *Sexuality and Culture* 19, 3: 464–92.

Lovett, Joseph. 2005. *Gay Sex in the '70s*. DVD. New York: Lovett Productions.

Lustig, Kara. 2012. Objectification Theory and Sexual Health among Women. PhD dissertation, Department of Clinical Psychology, University of Massachusetts, Boston, MA.

MacKinnon, Catharine. 1989. *Toward a Feminist Theory of the State*. Cambridge, MA: Harvard University Press.

Mainardi, Nicole. 2014. 6 Reasons Why the College Hookup Culture Isn't All It's Cracked Up To Be. *Uloop*, October 23.

Manzone, Charlotte. 2015. The Inevitable Hookup Culture. *Odyssey*, October 26.

Massey, Alana. 2015. Against Chill. *Medium*, April 1.

McMahon, Sarah. 2010. Rape Myth Beliefs and Bystander Attitudes among Incoming College Students. *Journal of American College Health* 59, 1: 3–11.

McWhorter, Stephanie, Valerie Stander, Lex Merrill, Cynthia Thomsen, and Joel Milner. 2009. Reports of Rape Reperpetration by Newly Enlisted Male Navy Personnel. *Violence and Victims* 24, 2: 204–18.

Media Education Foundation. 2013. Understanding Hookup Culture: What's Really Happening on College Campuses. Youtube website. Retrieved February 14, 2016 (https://www.youtube.com/watch?v=L3Q2L7YQ2Hk).

Mintz, Casey. 2014. Hooking Up Is Hard To Do. *Daily Free Press*, October 28.

Mir, Shabana. 2014. *Muslim American Women on Campus: Undergraduate Social Life and Identity*. Chapel Hill: University of North Carolina Press.

Moffett, Michael. 1989. *Coming of Age in New Jersey: College and American Culture*. New Brunswick and London: Rutgers University Press.

Mohler-Kuo, Meichun, George Dowdall, Mary Koss, and Henry Wechsler.

2004. Correlates of Rape While Intoxicated in a National Sample of College Women. *Journal of Studies on Alcohol and Drugs* 65, 1: 37–45.

Monto, Martin, and Anna Carey. 2014. A New Standard of Sexual Behavior? Are Claims Associated with the "Hookup Culture" Supported by General Social Survey Data? *Journal of Sex Research* 51, 6: 605–15.

Morgan, Richard. 2014. My Own Rape Shows How Much We Get Wrong About These Attacks. *Washington Post*, July 1.

Morris, Alex. 2014. Tales from the Millennials' Sexual Revolution. *Rolling Stone*, March 31.

Moskovitz, Simon. 2015. Mediocre Advice: Sex, Misogyny and Dating (In That Order). *Alligator*, October 28.

Murnen, Sarah, and Marla Kohlman. 2007. Athletic Participation, Fraternity Membership, and Sexual Aggression among College Men: A Meta-Analytic Review. *Sex Roles* 57, 1–2: 145–57.

Najmabadi, Shannon. 2012. Hookup: The Search for Satisfaction. *Daily Californian*, June 11.

National Center for Education Statistics. n.d. *Total Fall Enrollment in Degree-Granting Post-Secondary Institutions, by Attendance Status, Sex of Student, and Control of Institution: Selected Years, 1947 through 2023.* Digest of Education Statistics. Retrieved February 27, 2016 (http://nces.ed.gov/programs/digest/d13/tables/dt13_303.10.asp).

National Panhellenic Council. 2015. Manual of Information: Policies and Best Practices. Retrieved February 10 (timedotcom.files.wordpress.com/2014/09/college_panhellenic_policies_and_best_practices.pdf).

Neufeld, Jacob, Fred Klingbeil, Diane Bryen, Brett Silverman, and Anila Thomas. 2002. Adolescent Sexuality and Disability. *Physical Medicine and Rehabilitation Clinics of North America* 13: 857–73.

New, Jake. 2016. Student Writes Online Essay Accusing U of Richmond of Mishandling Her Sexual Assault. *Inside Higher Ed*, September 9.

Nieves, Alyssa. 2013. "Banging with Friends" Mobile App Assists in Hookup Process. *Alligator*, February 12.

North, Anna. 2010. Student Commits Suicide After Alleged Sexual Assault by Notre Dame Football Player. *Jezebel*, November 22.

———. 2012. Two Assault Charges Make BU's Hockey Team Look Pretty Bad. *Jezebel*, February 20.

Nosal, Meghan. 2015. A Letter to My Random Hookup. *Odyssey*, November 30.

Office of Juvenile Justice and Delinquency Prevention, 2012. Law Enforcement and Juvenile Crime. Retrieved February 24, 2016 (http://www.ojjdp.gov/ojstatbb/crime/JAR_Display.asp?ID=qa05274).

Oliver, Mary Beth, and Janet Hyde. 1993. Gender Differences in Sexuality: A Meta-Analysis. *Psychological Bulletin* 114, 1: 29–51.

Orenstein, Peggy. 2016. *Girls and Sex: Navigating the Complicated New Landscape*. New York: Harper.

O'Sullivan, Lucia, Wadiya Udell, Vernique Montrose, Patricia Antoniollo, and Susie Hoffman. 2010. A Cognitive Analysis of College Students' Explanations for Engaging in Unprotected Sexual Intercourse. *Archives of Sexual Behavior* 39, 5: 1121–31.

Owen, Jesse, Frank Fincham, and Jon Moore. 2011. Short-term Prospective Study of Hooking Up among College Students. *Archives of Sexual Behavior* 40: 331–41.

———, Galena Rhoades, Scott Stanley, and Frank Fincham. 2010. "Hooking Up" Among College Students: Demographic and Psychosocial Correlates. *Archives of Sexual Behavior* 39, 3: 653–63.

Page, Emily. 2011. "When We Graduate, This Is Over": Young Women's Experiences with Hooking Up and Relationships. Senior thesis, Department of Sociology, University of Kansas, Lawrence, KS.

Palmer, Tod. 2014. Sasha Menu Courey's Parents Hope Mizzou Learns from Investigation. *Kansas City Star*, April 14.

Pardes, Arielle. 2013. What It's Really Like to Have Sex at Penn. *Cosmopolitan*, July 15.

Parks, Kathleen, and Brenda Miller. 1997. Bar Victimization of Women. *Psychology of Women Quarterly* 21, 4: 509–25.

Parts, Spencer. 2015. At Princeton, Women Make Strides at Clubs Once Barred to Them. *New York Times*, February 20.

Patrick, Megan, Patrick Wightman, Robert Schoeni, and John Schulenberg. 2012. Socioeconomic Status and Substance Use Among Young Adults: A Comparison Across Constructs and Drugs. *Journal of Studies on Alcohol and Drugs* 73, 5: 772–82.

Paul, Elizabeth, and Kristen Hayes. 2002. The Casualties of "Casual" Sex: A Qualitative Exploration of the Phenomenology of College Students' Hookups. *Journal of Social and Personal Relationships* 19, 5: 639–61.

———, Brian McManus, and Allison Hayes. 2000. "Hookups": Characteristics and Correlates of College Students' Spontaneous and Anonymous Sexual Experiences. *Journal of Sex Research* 37, 1: 7–88.

———, Amy Wenzel, and John Harvey. 2008. Hookups: A Facilitator or a Barrier to Relationship Initiation and Intimacy Development. In S. Sprecher, A. Wenzel and J. Harvey (eds.), *Handbook of Relationship Initiation*. New York: Psychology Press.

Penhollow, Tina, Michael Young, and William Bailey. 2007. Relationship between Religiosity and "Hooking Up" Behavior. *American Journal of Health Education* 38, 6: 338–45.

Peril, Lynn. 2006. *College Girls: Bluestockings, Sex Kittens, and Coeds, Then and Now.* New York: W. W. Norton.

Perrone, Michael, and Amelia Harnish. 2010. Grads Look Back on Sex, Relationships and Dating Scene. *Alligator,* April 15.

Piess, Katherine. 2011. *Hope in a Jar: The Making of America's Beauty Culture.* Philadelphia: University of Pennsylvania Press.

Pitzulo, Carrie. 2011. *Bachelors and Bunnies: The Sexual Politics of Playboy.* Chicago: University of Chicago Press.

Prohaska, Thomas. 2016. Dean Cleared of Rape Coverup, Will Step Down Anyway. *Athletic Business,* February 17.

Pugh, Allison. 2009. *Longing and Belonging: Parents, Children, and Consumer Culture.* Berkeley: University of California Press.

Pusch, Rob. 2003. The Bathroom and Beyond: Transgendered College Students' Perspectives of Transition. PhD dissertation, Department of Instructional Design, Development and Evaluation, Syracuse University, Syracuse, NY.

Qian, Zhenchao, and Daniel Lichter. 2007. Social Boundaries and Marital Assimilation: Interpreting Trends in Racial and Ethnic Intermarriage. *American Sociological Review* 72, 1: 68–94.

———. 2011. Changing Patterns of Interracial Marriage in a Multiracial Society. *Journal of Marriage and Family* 73, 5: 1065–84.

Ranker, Luke. 2016. Lawsuit: KU Was Indifferent to Sexual Assault. *Athletic Business,* March 22.

Rankin, Susan. 2003. *Campus Climate for Gay, Lesbian, Bisexual, and Transgender People: A National Perspective.* New York: National Gay and Lesbian Task Force Policy Institute.

Ray, Rashawn, and Jason Rosow. 2010. Getting Off and Getting Intimate: How Normative Institutional Arrangements Structure Black and White Fraternity Men's Approaches Toward Women. *Men and Masculinities* 12, 5: 523–46.

Reay, Barry. 2014. Promiscuous Intimacies: Rethinking the History of American Casual Sex. *Journal of Historical Sociology* 27, 1: 1–24.

Reed, Lillie. 2013. The Best Four Years, Study Shows. *Chronicle,* August 28.

Reiman, Jeffrey. 2012. *The Rich Get Richer and the Poor Get Prison: Ideology, Class, and Criminal Justice.* 10th edition. New York: Routledge.

Reitman, Janet. 2006. Sex and Scandal at Duke. *Rolling Stone,* June 16.

Renner, Britta, Ralf Schmälzle, and Harald T. Schupp. 2012. First Impressions of HIV Risk: It Takes Only Milliseconds to Scan a Stranger. *PLOS One* 7, 1: e30460.

Reynolds, Pauline. 2014. Representing "U": Popular Culture, Media, and Higher Education. *ASHE Higher Education Report* 41, 4: 1–145.

Rhoades, Galena, and Scott Stanley. 2014. Before "I Do": What Do Premarital Experiences Have to Do with Marital Quality Among Today's Young Adults? The National Marriage Project at the University of Virginia. Retrieved February 16, 2016 (http://nationalmarriageproject.org/wp-content/uploads/2014/08/NMP-BeforeIDoReport-Final.pdf).

Roberts, Kennedy. 2006. Why Are Young College Women Not Using Condoms? Their Perceived Risk, Drug Use, and Developmental Vulnerability May Provide Important Clues to Sexual Risk. *Archives of Psychiatric Nursing* 20, 1: 32–40.

Robillard, Kristen, and Catherine Fichten. 1983. Attributions about Sexuality and Romantic Involvement of Physically Disabled College Students: An Empirical Study. *Sexuality and Disability* 6, 3/4: 197–212.

Ronen, Shelly. 2010. Grinding on the Dance Floor: Gendered Scripts and Sexualized Dancing at College Parties. *Gender and Society* 24, 3: 355–77.

Rosenfeld, Michael, and Reuben Thomas. 2012. Searching for a Mate: The Rise of the Internet as Social Intermediary. *American Sociological Review* 77, 4: 523–47.

Rosin, Hanna. 2012. *The End of Men: And the Rise of Women.* New York: Riverhead.

Rowens, Alissa. 2014. Running Into an Ex-Hookup. *Odyssey*, October 6.

Rudder, Christian. 2009. How Your Race Affects the Messages You Get. *OK Trends*, October 5.

Rudolph, Frederick. 1962 [1990]. *The American College and University: A History.* Athens, GA: University of Georgia Press.

Rupp, Leila, and Verta Taylor. 2010. Straight Girls Kissing. *Contexts* 9, 3: 28–32.

———. 2013. Queer Girls on Campus: New Intimacies and Sexual Identities. In Alan Frank, Patricia Clough, and Steven Seidman (eds.), *Intimacies: A New World of Relational Life*, 82–97. New York: Routledge.

———, Shiri Regev-Messalem, Alison C. K. Fogarty, and Paula England. 2014. Queer Women in the Hookup Scene: Beyond the Closet? *Gender and Society* 28, 2: 212–35.

Russett, Jill. 2008. Women's Perceptions of High-Risk Drinking: Understanding Binge Drinking in a Gender Biased Setting. PhD dissertation, Department of Education, The College of William and Mary in Virginia, Williamsburg, VA.

Ryan, Erin Gloria. 2014. The Story Behind American University's Rapey, Violent "Secret" Frat. *Jezebel*, April 25.

Saad, Lydia. 2014. The "40-Hour" Workweek is Actually Longer—by Seven Hours. Gallup, August 29.

Sales, Nancy Jo. 2015. Tinder and the Dawn of the "Dating Apocalypse." *Vanity Fair*, March.

Sampson, Rana. 2002. Acquaintance Rape of College Students. Problem-Oriented Guides for Police series, no. 17. Washington, DC: U.S. Department of Justice, Office of Community Oriented Policing Services.

Sanchez, Diana, and Amy Kiefer. 2007. Body Concerns In and Out of the Bedroom: Implications for Sexual Pleasure and Problems. *Archives of Sexual Behavior* 36, 6: 808–20.

Sanger, Margaret. 1926. *Happiness in Marriage*. New York: Brentano's.

Schafler, Kelly. 2015. Virginity Lies in the Eye of the Beholder. *Cougar*, February 11.

Schippers, Mimi. n.d. Mononormativity and Gender Inequality in Hookup Culture. Unpublished manuscript.

Schwartz, Martin, and Carol Nogrady. 1996. Fraternity Membership, Rape Myths, and Sexual Aggression on a College Campus. *Violence Against Women* 2, 2: 148–62.

Schwartz, Robert. 2010. *Deans of Men and the Shaping of Modern College Culture*. New York: Palgrave MacMillan.

Sciortino, Karley. 2015. Breathless: In Defense of Hookup Culture. *Vogue*, September 9.

Seidman, Steven. 1990. The Power of Desire and the Danger of Pleasure: Victorian Sexuality Reconsidered. *Journal of Social History* 24, 1: 47-67.

Sinozich, Sofi, and Lynn Langton. 2014. Rape and Sexual Assault Victimization Among College-Age Females, 1995–2013. U.S. Department of Justice. Retrieved February 15, 2016 (http://www.bjs.gov/content/pub/pdf/rsavcaf9513.pdf).

Smith, Christian, with Kari Kristofferson, Hillary Davidson, and Patricia Snell Herzog. 2011. *Lost in Transition: The Dark Side of Emerging Adulthood*. New York: Oxford University Press.

Smith, Howard. 1969. View from Inside. *Village Voice*, July 2.

Smith, William. 1872. *A Complete Etymology of the English Language*. New York and Chicago: A. S. Barnes and Company.

Sopher, Philip. 2014. Still White, Still Male: The Anachronism of Harvard's Final Clubs. *Atlantic*, August 7.

Sperber, Murray. 2000. *Beer and Circus: How Big-Time College Sport is Crippling Undergraduate Education*. New York: Henry Holt.

Spiller, Laura, Beverly Stiles, David Carlston, and Laura Hise. 2012. Perceived Vulnerability to HIV Infection, Anti-Gay Prejudice, and College Student Sexual Behavior. *Psi Chi Journal of Psychological Research* 17, 2: 73–79.

Stearns, Peter. 2002. *Fat History: Bodies and Beauty in the Modern West*. New York: New York University Press.

Stombler, Mindy, and Patricia Yancey Martin. 1994. Bringing Women In,

Keeping Women Down: Fraternity "Little Sister" Organizations. *Journal of Contemporary Ethnography* 23: 150–84.

———, and Irene Padavic. 1997. Sister Acts: Resisting Men's Domination in Black and White Fraternity Little Sister Programs. *Social Problems* 44: 257–75.

Suslovic, Brianna, and Jordan Weiers. 2015. Dismantle Final Clubs Now. *Harvard Crimson*, April 1.

Swartout, Kevin, Mary Koss, Jacquelyn White, Martie Thompson, Antonia Abbey, and Alexandra Bellis. 2015. Trajectory Analysis of the Campus Serial Rapist Assumption. *JAMA Pediatrics* 169, 12: 1148–54.

Sweeney, Brian. 2014a. Masculine Status, Sexual Performance, and the Sexual Stigmatization of Women. *Symbolic Interaction* 37, 3: 369–90.

———. 2014b. To Sexually Perform or Protect: Masculine Identity Construction and Perceptions of Women's Sexuality on a University Campus in the Midwestern USA. *Gender, Place and Culture* 21, 9: 1108-1124.

Syrett, Nicholas. 2009. *The Company He Keeps: A History of White College Fraternities*. Chapel Hill: University of North Carolina Press.

Taylor, Kate. 2013. Sex on Campus: She Can Play That Game, Too. *New York Times*, July 12.

Taylor, Paul. 2014. *The Next America: Boomers, Millennials, and the Looming Generational Showdown*. New York: Public Affairs.

Thelin, John. 2004. *A History of American Higher Education*. Baltimore: Johns Hopkins University Press.

Thompson, Edward, and Elizabeth Cracco. 2008. Sexual Aggression in Bars: What College Men Can Normalize. *Journal of Men's Studies* 16, 1: 82–96.

Thompson, Sharon. 1989. Search for Tomorrow: On Feminism and the Reconstruction of Teen Romance. In C. S. Vance (ed.), *Pleasure and Danger: Exploring Female Sexuality*. London: Pandora.

Tilos, B. J., Misha Wilks, Jenna Alley, Chantal Avakain-Fisher, and David Frederick. 2014. The Orgasm Gaps: Differences in Reported Orgasm Frequency by Gender and Sexual Orientation. Poster presented at the Gender Development Research Conference, San Francisco, CA.

Torres, Kristina. 2013. Georgia Tech Fraternity Suspends Member for "Rape-bait" Email. Retrieved May 19, 2016 (http://www.ajc.com/news/news/georgia-tech-fraternity-under-investigation-for-ra/nbH2q/).

Tracy, Marc. 2016. Florida State Settles Suit Over Jameis Winston Rape Inquiry. *New York Times*, January 25.

Traister, Rebecca. 2016. The Single American Woman. *Cut*, February.

Truscott IV, Lucian. 1969. View from Outside. *Village Voice*, July 2.

Twenge, Jean. 1997. Changes in Masculine and Feminine Traits Over Time: A Meta-Analysis. *Sex Roles* 36, 5/6: 305–25.

———. 2000. The Age of Anxiety? The Birth Cohort Change in Anxiety and Neuroticism, 1952–1993. *Journal of Personality and Social Psychology* 79, 6: 1007–21.

———. 2006. *Generation Me: Why Today's Young Americans are More Confident, Assertive, Entitled—and More Miserable Than Ever Before.* New York: Simon and Schuster.

———, Ryan Sherman, and Brooke Wells. 2015. Changes in American Adults' Sexual Behavior and Attitudes, 1972–2012. *Archives of Sexual Behavior* 44, 8: 2273–85.

Uecker, Jeremy, Lisa Pearce, and Brita Andercheck. 2015. The Four U's: Latent Classes of Hookup Motivations among College Students. *Social Currents* 2, 2: 163–81.

Ulrich, Laurel Thatcher. 1976. Vertuous Women Found: New England Ministerial Literature, 1668–1735. *American Quarterly* 28, 1: 20–40.

United Educators. 2015. Managing Liability Risks at Schools, Colleges, and Universities. *Spectrum*, Spring.

U.S. Census Bureau. 2010. America's Families and Living Arrangements. Table FG-4. Retrieved February 11 (www.census.gov/population/www/socdemo/hh-fam/cps2010.html).

———. 2012. 2010 Census of Population and Housing, Population and Housing Unit Counts, CPH–2–5. Washington, DC: U.S. Census Bureau.

———. n.d. *Estimated Median Age at First Marriage, by Sex: 1890 to the Present.* Retrieved February 20, 2016 (http://www.census.gov/hhes/families/data/marital.html).

Usyk, Paige. 2007. In Defense of the Hookup and My Column. *Alligator*, September 20.

———. 2008. Stop Having Empty, Meaningless Relationships. *Alligator*, April 10.

Vander Ven, Thomas. 2011. *Getting Wasted: Why College Students Drink Too Much and Party Too Hard.* New York: New York University Press.

Vandervilt, Patricia. 2012. The Hook-up Generation. *Huffington Post*, April 28.

Van Syckle, Katie. 2015. Hooking Up Is Easy To Do. *New York*, October 19–November 1.

Vrangalova, Zhana, and Anthony Ong. 2014. Who Benefits from Casual Sex? The Moderating Role of Sociosexuality. *Social Psychological and Personality Science* 5, 8: 883–91.

Wade, Carrie. 2014. Know Me Where It Hurts: Sex, Kink, and Cerebral Palsy. *Autostraddle*, March 11.

Wade, Lisa, and Caroline Heldman. 2012. Hooking Up and Opting Out: Negotiating Sex in the First Year of College. In L. M. Carpenter and

John DeLamater (eds.), *Sex for Life: From Virginity through Viagra, How Sex Changes Throughout Our Lives*. New York: New York University Press.

———, Emily Kremer, and Jessica Brown. 2005. The Incidental Orgasm: The Presence of Clitoral Knowledge and the Absence of Orgasm for Women. *Women and Health* 42, 1: 117–38.

Wadhwani, Anita, and Nate Rau. 2016. Sweeping Sex Assault Suit Filed against University of Tennessee. *Tennessean*, February 14.

Wagoner, Jr., Jennings. 1986. Honor and Dishonor at Mr. Jefferson's University: The Antebellum Years. *History of Education Quarterly* 26, 2: 155–79.

Wasylikiw, Louise, and Michael Currie. 2012. The Animal House Effect: How University-Themed Comedy Films Affect Students' Attitudes. *Social Psychology of Education* 15: 25–40.

Wechsler, Henry, and Meichun Kuo. 2003. Watering Down the Drinks: The Moderating Effect of College Demographics on Alcohol Use of High-Risk Groups. *American Journal of Public Health* 93: 1929–33.

———, and Bernice Wuethrich. 2002. *Dying to Drink: Confronting Binge Drinking on College Campuses*. Emmaus, PA: Rodale Books.

Weitzman, Abigail, and Paula England. 2014. Class and Sex for Young Women. *Contexts*, December 7.

White House Task Force to Protect Students from Sexual Assault. 2014. Not Alone: The First Report of the White House Task Force to Protect Students from Sexual Assault. Retrieved February 15, 2016 (https://www.whitehouse.gov/sites/default/files/docs/report_0.pdf).

Wolf, Naomi. 1991. *The Beauty Myth: How Images of Beauty Are Used Against Women*. New York: William Morrow.

X, Malcolm, and Alex Haley. 1965. *The Autobiography of Malcolm X*. New York: Ballantine Books.

Yacos, Amanda. 2014. The Extinction of Dating: How Hook Up Culture Damages Mental Health. *College Voice*, December 2.

Yoo, Min. 2014. Asian Americans: Why They Participate in and How They Negotiate Rave Culture. Senior thesis, Department of Sociology, Occidental College, Los Angeles, CA.

Yost, Megan, and Genea Thomas. 2012. Gender and Binegativity: Men's and Women's Attitudes Toward Male and Female Bisexuals. *Archives of Sexual Behavior* 41: 691–702.

Zukin, Cliff, and Mark Szeltner. 2012. Talent Report: What Workers Want in 2012. Net Impact. Retrieved February 13, 2016 (https://www.netimpact.org/sites/default/files/documents/what-workers-want-2012.pdf).

Index

Note: Names followed by an asterisk (*) are pseudonyms.

men (*continued*)
  white men, *see* Caucasian/white students
  women catering to, 169, 187
  women competing for, 59–60, 178,
    183–84, 188, 189, 191–94, 196,
    201, 242
  women dependent on, 69, 114
  women's bodies judged by, 189–91
  women's bodies used by, 168, 207
  and work, 57
  in World War II, 60, 189, 243
microaggression, 129
Middlebury College, 95
mind-altering substances, 88
mind-fuck, rape as, 228
mind games, 14
Minjun*, 227–28
Miranda*, 27–28, 29, 30, 39, 125
misogynistic talk, 173
monogamous relationships:
  avoiding, 145
  cheating, 38
  going steady, 60–62, 69
  hookups leading to, 46, 145, 146,
    235, 241
  no protection from violence in, 69
  in sophomore year, 230
  synonyms for, 143
Morgan, Richard, 221
Mott, Eliza, 197
Mount Allison University, 75
moving on, 224–40
  by abstainers, 225
  after first kiss, 227–28
  after freshman year, 224–25, 229–32
  after graduation, 231–32, 233–36
  by dabblers, 225–26
  to dating culture, 234–40
  and focusing on education, 230, 246
  hooking up as learning experience,
    37, 226–28, 232

  by hookup enthusiasts, 225
  to marriage, 235
  to reality, 229
"Murphy make-outs," 84, 186
music, deafening, 208–9

Naomi*, 71–73, 76, 83, 110, 125
Natalie*, 202–4, 211
National Health and Social Life Survey, 166
National Panhellenic Conference, 83
negging (insulting women), 185–86,
  190–91, 200
Netta*, 141–42
New York, 16, 97
New York Times, 16, 60, 136, 189
New York University (NYU), 97, 174
"No," as challenge, 211, 214
nonwhite students, 93–95
norepinephrine, 134
Northwestern University, 68
Nott, Eliphalet, 78
nudity, as foreplay, 40
numbness, 152

Occidental College, 94, 130
Ohio State University, 95
Old School (movie), 75
Omar*, 118, 123–24, 133, 230, 235
Online College Social Life Survey
  (OCSLS), 24, 40
  on alcohol, 43–45
  on committed partnerships, 145
  on frequency of hookups, 46
  on gender gap, 158–60, 177
  on opting out, 92
  on race, 94
  on sexual assault, 204–5
  on sexual satisfaction, 178
opting in, 113–33
  by "dabblers," 121–25